"*The Power of Perception* is the first book to bring together information focused specifically on leadership and emotional intelligence from a gendered perspective. Dr. Shawn Andrews examines barriers to leadership and global diversity trends that impact today's workplace—and offers practical strategies for individuals and organizations. A fascinating and comprehensive must-read."

— **Marshall Goldsmith, international best-selling author or editor of 35 books including *What Got You Here Won't Get You There* and *Triggers***

"If ever there was a time in history that cried out for women's leadership that time is now—and this book underscores why. Thoroughly researched and readable, Dr. Andrews masterfully weaves together an understanding of leadership from the perspectives of the past, present and future. A great read."

— **Lois P. Frankel, Ph.D., best-selling author of *See Jane Lead* and *Nice Girls Don't Get the Corner Office***

"*The Power of Perception* is comprehensive, full of actionable insights and profoundly inspiring. Dr. Andrews has done a superb job of showing how organizations can reap enormous benefits by harnessing the power of women's emotional intelligence. This book is a must-read."

— **Sally Helgesen, best-selling author of *The Female Vision, The Web of Inclusion, The Female Advantage,* and *Thriving in 24/7***

"*The Power of Perception* is a powerful and compelling look at the subtle barriers women face every day, and beautifully describes how women's leadership styles and emotional intelligence traits are naturally suited for today's organizations."

— **Gail Evans, best-selling author of *Play Like a Man, Win Like a Woman* and *She Wins, You Win***

"It's long past time to change the biases and eliminate the barriers that women face. This book offers useful insights on how to do that."
— **Adam Grant, Ph.D.,** *New York Times* **best-selling author of** *Originals* **and** *Give and Take*

"At a time when there's renewed interest in finally solving the gender parity problem, *The Power of Perception* offers fresh insights based on considerable research. Read this book to enhance the power of your perception."
— **Carol Frohlinger, President, Negotiating Women, Inc., author of** *Her Place at the Table* **and** *Nice Girls Just Don't Get It*

"Anyone who wants to understand gender in the workplace should read this book. Dr. Shawn Andrews helps explain current realities, break down misconceptions, and illuminates a path forward that can lead to greater opportunity for individual professionals and better bottom-line results for companies."
— **Dorie Clark, adjunct professor at Duke University's Fuqua School of Business, author of** *Reinventing You* **and** *Stand Out*

"At last! A departure from fix-the-women strategies to a big picture overview of how to adapt twenty-first century business to the consequences of the gender revolution. Essential reading for leaders who want to boost sustainable performance by understanding the multiple perceptions at play."
— **Avivah Wittenberg-Cox, CEO, 20-first, author of** *How Women Mean Business*

"A practical guide for any leader who is a woman who works to further her career."
— **Frances R. Hesselbein, President & CEO, The Frances Hesselbein Leadership Institute**

"Dr. Shawn Andrews does a great job of shining a light on how the same emotional intelligence skills are seen differently in male and female leaders in *The Power of Perception*. She uses rich examples and provides her own original research with women leaders. She goes on to present strategies that all leaders should be aware of."
— **Steven Stein, Ph.D., CEO, Multi-Health Systems, author of *The EQ Leader* and co-author of *The EQ Edge***

"Dr. Shawn Andrews has done a stellar job in invalidating the misconception that men make better leaders than women, by presenting compelling findings demonstrating that there are no gender differences among highly effective leaders in the corporate world. She confirms research findings that my colleagues and I have obtained, which have also shown that businesses led by women are often more profitable than those led by men."
— **Reuven Bar-On, Ph.D., author of the EQ-i emotional intelligence assessment**

"*The Power of Perception* gives both power and discernment to deepen our understanding of transactive management vs. transformative leadership. It is no surprise that women leaders may have a decided developmental edge when it comes to transformative leadership. Get this book to understand why; it's a critical leadership book for both men and women leaders today!"
— **Kevin Cashman, Senior Partner, CEO & Executive Development, Korn Ferry, best-selling author of *Leadership from the Inside Out* and *The Pause Principle***

"*The Power of Perception* tackles the gender divide head on and offers tangible solutions that empower versus blame. A must-read for the individual and those advancing their organization's gender agenda."

— **Laurie Cooke, CEO, Healthcare Businesswomen's Association**

"Dr. Shawn Andrews is committed to developing talent and contributing new research to the study of leadership and emotional intelligence. We know that diversity in the workplace matters, and this book provides fresh insights about the power of perception, which is beneficial to all of us."

— **Tony Bingham, President and CEO, Association for Talent Development, co-author of *The New Social Learning* and *Presenting Learning***

THE POWER OF PERCEPTION

the
POWER
of perception

Leadership,
Emotional Intelligence,
and the
Gender Divide

SHAWN ANDREWS
Ed.D., M.B.A.

NEW YORK

NASHVILLE • MELBOURNE • VANCOUVER

The Power of Perception

Leadership, Emotional Intelligence, and the Gender Divide

Published in New York, New York, by Morgan James Publishing. Morgan James is a trademark of Morgan James, LLC. www.MorganJamesPublishing.com

The Morgan James Speakers Group can bring authors to your live event. For more information or to book an event visit The Morgan James Speakers Group at www.TheMorganJamesSpeakersGroup.com.

ISBN 9781683505792 paperback
ISBN 9781683505808 eBook
Library of Congress Control Number: 2017907415

Cover Design by:
Megan Whitney
megan@creativeninjadesigns.com

Interior Design by:
Chris Treccani
www.3dogcreative.net

In an effort to support local communities, raise awareness and funds, Morgan James Publishing donates a percentage of all book sales for the life of each book to Habitat for Humanity Peninsula and Greater Williamsburg.

Get involved today! Visit
www.MorganJamesBuilds.com

For my mother, Betty Andrews, with love

CONTENTS

INTRODUCTION

The Missing Gender

E quality is not a zero-sum game. A woman's advancement in her career does not mean a man has to step down a rung in his career. In fact, the more women who advance, the greater the diversity, which is in turn better for men and their organizations. More profit means more rewards, jobs, and promotions for everyone. Abundant evidence exists now to show companies that are gender-balanced and diverse outperform those that are not on a variety of measures.

Let's look back to understand where we are today. Women have been in the U.S. workforce for seventy-five years. Since their right to vote was granted in 1920, women have made significant gains on social, political, economic, legal, and cultural fronts, but the path has been winding—pushing to define and redefine their roles inside and outside the home.

The Roaring '20s were characterized by the flappers—women who wore short skirts and bobbed hair, listened to jazz, and represented liberal ideals. These women were active socially and culturally and flaunted their disdain for what was considered acceptable behavior at time. Today, they'd be considered feminists.

Taking a drastic turn, the Great Depression gripped the 1930s and set the country and women on a different course. Devastating poverty and joblessness created a rallying cry to "put people to work." Women become a vital part of the labor movement during this era, while men faced major unemployment. With the disruption of typical breadwinner roles, women maintained employment or even took on new paid labor to support their families.

Changing direction again, the 1940s and World War II brought Rosie the Riveter to the forefront as record numbers of women entered the workforce. But by the end of the war, Rosie and most of the other women retreated from work, as society encouraged women to return to the idyllic homemaker role that characterized them during much of the 1950s.

The 1960s was the start of the early women's movement, with the founding of the National Organization for Women (NOW) and Affirmative Action policies. The Equal Pay Act was signed into law in 1963, and Gloria Steinem became nationally recognized as a leader and spokeswoman for the feminist movement in the late 1960s and early 1970s. Although a few women ventured into the workplace, most were still in the home, as depicted by television shows such as *Leave it to Beaver* and *I Love Lucy*.

The 1970s saw the Equal Rights Amendment, Title IX, and Roe v. Wade laws passed, with more women in the workforce. But, in the 1980s, we saw the most dramatic shift when a flood of women joined the workforce—as represented in the iconic hit movie *9 to 5* starring Dolly Parton, Jane Fonda and Lily Tomlin. The idea of breaking through the glass ceiling became prevalent in the 1980s as more women found employment in professional and management roles.

The 1990s brought more workplace laws and protections, and women at work were commonplace. The "Take Our Daughters to Work" program made its debut, and the Family and Medical Leave Act became law. The first decade of the 2000s saw President Obama signing the Lily Ledbetter Fair Pay Restoration Act, which allows women to file a complaint for wage discrimination.

In 2013, Defense Secretary Leon Panetta announced that the ban on women serving in combat roles would be lifted. In 2015, *Time Magazine* named Angela Merkel, German Chancellor and de facto leader of the European Union as "Person of the Year," and *Sports Illustrated* named tennis great Serena Williams as "Sportsperson of the Year."

In 2016, for the first time in U.S. history, Hillary Clinton became the first female presidential nominee from a major political party vying for the highest office. Although she fell short in her bid for President of the United States, this milestone would have been unthinkable in 1920.

Despite the progress and large numbers of women in the workforce today, very few women have made it to senior leadership levels in any sector or industry worldwide. Per Barber Conable, former President of World Bank, "Women are half the world's population, yet they do two-thirds of the world's work, earn one-tenth of the world's income, and own less than 1 percent of the world's property. They are among the poorest of the world's poor."[1]

How could this be? Women contribute significantly to our societies, organizations, communities, and families. Part of the reason is that in many countries, women start out on unequal footing. Gender inequality starts early and keeps women at a disadvantage throughout their lives. In some countries, infant girls are less likely to survive than infant boys because their parents favor the boys and neglect the girls. Girls often receive less food than boys do, and they are more likely to drop out of school and receive less education than boys.

Historically, women have been seen as less important than men socially, economically, politically, and culturally, and have a smaller gender footprint than men. Simply put, this is the environmental, economic, social, and political impact men and women have purely because they are male or female. In most cultures, men have a much larger footprint than women. This gives men much greater power. This power is often used over women and leaves them disempowered. When women have a larger and stronger gender footprint, families, communities and societies at large benefit.[2]

Men still run the world because men are in decision making positions of power. Thus, women's voices are not heard equally, and women's interests are minimized or omitted altogether. I have been observing these trends with interest for the past twenty years. I graduated from college in 1991 and from graduate school in 1996. I entered the pharmaceutical industry as a sales representative out of college and enjoyed a balanced mix of male and female colleagues. Most of the physicians I called on were male, as were most of the senior leaders at my company, which I attributed to historical differences of fewer women in the workforce.

In 2010, I began my doctoral studies in organizational leadership. I knew from the beginning that I wanted to research and study the topics of leadership and gender. I was both concerned and intrigued when the statistics on the leadership gender gap, pay wage gap, and other inequities hit mainstream media in early 2000s, and I wanted to find out why.

I had also been fascinated by emotional intelligence since it was popularized in the mid-1990s. I learned that emotional intelligence is a key driver both in life and work success, particularly in leadership effectiveness. I wanted to somehow combine all these topics for my dissertation, but wasn't quite sure how to put it together.

Since youth, I've tried to make meaning and connections from different occurrences, and have always been a proponent of meta-integration, which is combining the findings and theories from different disciplines. As I combed through the literature, conducted my interviews, and analyzed the research, I began to see trends.

I realized the topics of leadership, gender, and emotional intelligence were not only related, they overlapped into one single unifying theme—it's all about *perception*—not skills, competencies, personality, or anything else. The blunt truth is that this perception has had, and is still having, a significant impact on promotion. And for many women, perception has become reality.

In searching for solutions to address these issues, I tried to fit everything into a neat, little bento box—like Brené Brown alluded to in her popular TED talk, *The Power of Vulnerability.* Unfortunately, there is no silver bullet. There are a multitude of factors and barriers that keep women from rising to the upper echelons of leadership. These include both overt and subtle sexism, discrimination, and sexual harassment that we often see because of bias, particularly unconscious or hidden biases. Lack of access to informal networks, such as the old boy's network is alive and well, and women still find difficulty getting male sponsors. Women are continually challenged with balancing work and home, and addressing breadwinner and caregiver issues with their partners. In addition, women hold themselves back or self-select out of the workforce for a myriad of reasons.

If these barriers weren't enough to limit advancement, other factors layer in—such as differences in gender culture and emotional intelligence attributes. Gender culture differences between men and women play out every day in the workplace, and most people are completely unaware of these behaviors. Men and women approach virtually every aspect of business differently, and it's these subtle differences that cause misperceptions about women at work.

When I give keynote presentations, one of the questions I ask audiences is, "Which gender is more emotionally intelligent?" Without fail, most hands go up in favor of female, and one or two hands rise in favor of male. From assessments of over a million people worldwide, we know that overall, men and women are equally emotionally intelligent. However, we are strong in different areas considered gender-specific, and these differences can often lead to bias and misperceptions.

These topics are timely because there's a diversity shift occurring worldwide, and both individuals and businesses need help to advance and compete in our fast-paced, global environment. Discussions on the leadership gender gap and barriers are now more common, thanks in part to research from McKinsey and Catalyst, as well as books like *Lean In* by Sheryl Sandberg. Today, there are large numbers of women in the workforce who are educated, experienced, and empowered—and both men and women are actively seeking solutions.

In addition, there's mounting pressure on organizations to appoint women to positions of senior leadership. In March 2015, EBay Inc. agreed to nominate one additional woman to its board of directors in response to mounting public pressure for diversity, and in 2013, Twitter appointed its first female board member after it became a target of intense criticism for its all-male board.

This book is intended for a broad audience. In writing it, I hope to help educate women, men, and businesses on the strengths that women bring to organizations, the barriers that keep women from fully contributing, and the knowledge that perception impacts promotion. The overall objective is to create not only dialog, but action by helping individuals and organizations implement the recommendations and strategies toward full gender equality. To support this, I've included practical strategies, summary points, and reflection questions at the end of every chapter.

For women to fully contribute and succeed in work, home, and society, and for organizations to fully diversify and leverage their talent, we must take responsibility for women's development, and actively address the barriers and misperceptions that hold women back. Equality is not a zero-sum game—we can all be winners. This book will show you how.

PART I

Leadership and Emotional Intelligence

ONE

Startling Statistics

You don't get harmony when everyone sings the same note.
Doug Floyd

In music, harmony is the use of simultaneous pitches or chords. In other words, it is multiple voices singing different tones and notes at the same time that creates an overall harmony. If everyone sang the same note, we would not hear the beautiful sounds and blending of different voices in unison. In global business, the same is true. When we hear only one voice or one type of voice, we miss the nuances and variety of perspectives that multiple people can offer. Yet, that has been the reality in business since its origin.

From a political perspective, of the 195 independent countries in the world, fifteen are led by women.[1] Although these numbers have increased in recent years, it represents only 8 percent of world leaders. In looking at global parliaments, including both lower and upper houses of government, women hold only 23 percent of seats.[2] So, for the vast majority of our world, when it comes to decisions that shape our laws and policies, a woman's voice—any woman's voice—is simply not being heard.

◇◇◇◇◇◇◇◇◇◇◇◇◇◇◇◇◇

When we hear only one voice or one type of voice, we miss the nuances and variety of perspectives that multiple people can offer.

◇◇◇◇◇◇◇◇◇◇◇◇◇◇◇◇◇

From a legal perspective, women experience inequities and some countries still deny women basic civil rights. In 103 economies, there is at least one legal differentiation between men and women that can prevent women from getting a job, owning property, or starting their own businesses. A report from the World Bank in 2012 measured twenty-one differentiations for unmarried women and twenty-four differentiations for married women, for a total of forty-five gender-based differences in the law, across five topics.[3] Because of this disparity in legal rights, women end up legally and economically dependent upon their husbands or other male relatives, despite commitments that some of their governments have made to ensure they are on an equal footing with men.

From an economic and social perspective, the plight of women is even more disheartening. Of the 1.3 billion people living in poverty around the world, 70 percent are women. This equates to 910 million women who struggle to care for themselves and their families. Regarding education, there are 130 million primary school age children who do not attend school, and 60 percent of these are girls. If they are lucky enough to attend school, by age eighteen, girls have received an average of 4.4 years less education than boys.[4]

Pregnancies and childbirth-related health problems also take their toll on women in many countries. These complications take the lives of around 500,000 women each year—that's one woman every minute! In sub-Saharan

Africa, a woman faces a one in thirteen chance of dying in childbirth. In Western Europe, the risk is one in 3,200.

When it comes to violence, women are disproportionately affected. Worldwide, approximately 4.4 million women are victims of forced sexual exploitation.[5] At least one in three girls and women has been beaten or abused in her lifetime, and of every ten people killed or wounded during armed conflict, eight are women or children.[6] It is no surprise then, if women have less power politically, legally, economically, and socially, why progress toward global gender equality has been so painstakingly slow.

Red, White and Blue

In the United States, we pledge allegiance to liberty and justice for all, yet the disparity in leadership roles and gender equality is not much better inside our borders. Women now comprise 57 percent of the total job market and a full 60 percent of bachelor's degrees at U.S. universities.[7] Women also outpace men in the total number of master and doctorate degrees.[8] In government, women hold 104 (19 percent) of the 535 seats in the 115th U.S. Congress, which comprises twenty-one (21 percent) of the one hundred seats in the Senate and eighty-three (19 percent) of the 435 seats in the House of Representatives. In addition, seven women hold federal executive positions, which are presidential cabinet or cabinet-level, and three women are Supreme Court justices. In addition, of the one hundred largest U.S. cities, there are twenty women mayors.[9]

According to the U.S. Labor Department, the *top three most common occupations for women* in 2014 were secretaries and/or administrative assistants, followed by elementary and/or middle school teachers, and then registered nurses.[10] Despite an increasing presence in the workforce and greater education, women are still pursuing or adhering to stereotypical female roles. These traditional female jobs make up not only the top three most common occupations, they comprise half of the top twenty-five occupations for women.

◇◇◇◇◇◇◇◇◇◇◇◇◇◇

In none of the top twenty-five most common occupations for women, do women earn more than men. Not one.

◇◇◇◇◇◇◇◇◇◇◇◇◇◇

Even within those top traditionally female jobs, a pay wage gap exists. Female secretaries and administrative assistants earn 85 percent of men's salary, female elementary and middle school teachers earn 87 percent of men's salary, and female registered nurses earn 90 percent of men's salary.[11] In fact, in none of the top twenty-five most common occupations for women, do women earn more than men. Not one.

Looking at the overall earnings ratio and wage gap for *all* occupations, the median annual earnings of full-time, year-round workers in 2014 were $50,383 for men, and $39,621 for women.[12] This represents a gap of 21 percent, which means that women earn seventy-nine cents for every dollar that men earn.[13] This number has climbed from fifty-nine cents per dollar in 1960, and in the past five years, has only increased one cent. Once again, progress toward gender equality has been painstakingly slow.

What's important about the pay wage gap is the message it sends. Companies all over the globe are consistently telling women the same message—you are valued less than men. That's the bottom line. Despite how much a woman may contribute to her company, her years of experience, her skills and competencies, or her title, the message is the same and it comes across loud and clear. It's no wonder many women are so passionate about this issue. How would you feel if you found out that you were paid $20,000 less per year than a peer you work with every day? It'd be even worse if that colleague was your direct report.

Teri is vice president of business development at a major commercial construction company, and has worked in this role for ten years. This is on top of twenty-seven years in other construction industry roles, which makes her a seasoned veteran with thirty-seven years' experience. As a VP, she sits on the executive team, make decisions that affect the company, and is privy to financial and employee information. A year ago, Teri was part of a team evaluating candidates for a director role that would eventually report to her. The candidate was hired and assigned to Teri's team. It was then she realized that he made $30,000 more than she, was fifteen years younger, and had less experience!

After discussions with her boss and other executives on the issue, human resources examined the pay of all women across the company. They found that women in the same positions as men made, on average, $10,000 less than their male counterparts—without exception. The company now monitors all salaries to try and level pay inequities. Granted, Teri works in a male-dominated industry made up of 9 percent women.[14] However, this is not an isolated or unique situation. Stories like this occur across all industries and all types of positions.

<><><><><><><><><><><><>

Men control the pace at which women will be allowed into leadership positions.

<><><><><><><><><><><><>

During the past three decades, women have achieved parity with men in both number of employees in the workforce and positions in middle management. Given these statistics, a natural shift to a more gender-balanced senior management should be a reasonable, expected outcome. Despite this fact, female leaders are few and far between, especially in key executive leadership positions. Although women have made some strides in the past decades, men still occupy far more positions that confer decision-making authority and the ability to influence other's pay or promotions. In fact, men control the pace at which women will be allowed into leadership positions.

The Fortune 500

Women occupy 52 percent of all management and professional occupations, such as physician and attorney.[15] Yet, at *Fortune* 500 companies, they hold only 19 percent of board seats, 15 percent of executive officer positions, and the number of female CEOs at these companies is a paltry 4 percent.[16] Women of color—Asian, black, and Latina—are absent on most *Fortune* 500 boards, with their share of seats at only 3 percent.[17]

For those of you who are quick at calculations, 4 percent of 500 companies equals twenty female CEOs. However, it also means there are 480 male CEOs running the remaining 500 companies—from this perspective, women have a long way to go. Note that the number of *Fortune* 500 female CEOs has become a barometer for measuring the amount of progress towards gender parity, more than any other statistic. This number changes throughout the year and has fluctuated from 3 percent to about 6 percent in the past several years, with an average of 4.5 percent.

The below table lists these twenty pioneering women ranked in terms of their companies' revenue and *Fortune* rank as of December 2016—note that some of these companies are outside the top 500. I've also included the ratio and percentage of female to male executives and board members at these companies. Since 1998, *Fortune* magazine has published it's "50 Most Powerful Women" list, and 2015 had a record nineteen women leading *Fortune* 500 companies—a vast improvement since 1998 when they first launched the list with only two *Fortune* 500 female CEOs among the fifty.

F500 Rank	F500 Company	CEO	Executive Team Women/ Men	Percent	Board Members Women/ Men	Percent
6	General Motors Co.	Mary Barra	6/24	25%	5/12	42%
19	Hewlett-Packard Enterprise	Meg Whitman	1/11	9%	4/13	31%
24	IBM Corp.	Virginia Rometty	5/19	26%	3/14	21%
44	PepsiCo, Inc.	Indra Nooyi	3/11	27%	4/14	29%
64	Lockheed Martin Corp.	Marillyn Hewson	2/7	29%	4/12	33%
81	Oracle Corp.	Safra Catz (co-CEO)	6/31	19%	3/13	23%

91	Mondelez International Inc.	Irene Rosenfeld	2/13	15%	4/13	31%
100	General Dynamics Corp.	Phebe Novakovic	2/13	15%	3/12	25%
116	Duke Energy Corp.	Lynn Good	6/24	25%	3/15	20%
143	Xerox Corp.	Ursula Burns	7/29	24%	3/8	38%
269	Ross Stores Inc.	Barbara Rentler	1/5	20%	2/11	18%
270	Sempra Energy Corp.	Debra Reed	5/16	31%	3/12	25%
337	Reynolds American Inc.	Susan Cameron	4/11	36%	2/13	15%
342	Campbell Soup Co.	Denise Morrison	1/10	10%	3/12	25%
441	TEGNA	Gracia Martore	2/7	29%	5/10	50%
561	Yahoo Inc.	Marissa Mayer	2/12	17%	3/8	38%
592	KeyCorp	Beth E. Mooney	3/11	27%	5/14	36%
740	Ventas Inc.	Debra A. Cafaro	1/12	8%	2/10	20%
932	HCP Inc.	Lauralee E. Martin	1/8	13%	2/8	25%
-	Mylan Inc.	Heather Bresch	1/5	20%	4/13	31%

As you can see from these numbers, even at these female-run large cap corporations, the percentage of executive-level women and officers ranges from near zero to 36 percent, with Reynolds American having the highest number of female executives, and Hewlett-Packard, Campbell Soup, and Ventas having the lowest number of females. The average percentage of women executives across all twenty companies is 21 percent.

When looking at the board of directors for each company, it's clear the numbers are better for women on the boards than on the senior management teams within each company. The number ranges from 15 percent to a whopping 50 percent, with an average of 29 percent women board members. The company on this list with the highest percentage of women on their board is TEGNA, led by Gracia Martore, which is a digital marketing, online and media company.

◇◇◇◇◇◇◇◇◇◇◇◇◇◇◇◇◇

Few women in senior management means no pipeline to CEO positions, which means fewer opportunities for board service.

◇◇◇◇◇◇◇◇◇◇◇◇◇◇◇◇◇

The board average of 29 percent women at these twenty women-led companies is far above the average for all S&P 500 companies, which stands at 19 percent. It shouldn't come as a surprise that companies with a female CEO attracts more women from other companies to serve as board members. What is surprising, however, is that the average number of women on internal management teams within each company is relatively low. Few women in senior management means no pipeline to CEO positions, which also means fewer opportunities for board service, since most current boards want members with at least six years of board experience.[18]

European countries have taken it a step further. In 2015, Germany passed a law that requires companies to give 30 percent of board positions to women. The quota will apply to the country's one hundred biggest companies where women currently hold just 19 percent of board seats. With less than 20 percent women on their boards, Germany is surpassed by many of its European peers. Norway tops the list with 36 percent female boards, followed by Finland, France, and Sweden, which all have just under 30 percent female representation. Belgium, the United Kingdom, Denmark, and the Netherlands are all above 20 percent. Interestingly, Australia's women's share of board seats is exactly equal to the U.S. at 19 percent.[19]

What makes these countries stand out is the policies they already have in place for board diversity. Norway was the first to pass a gender quota in 2008, while France, Finland, Belgium, the Netherlands, Denmark, Spain, Italy and Iceland have all followed suit. Sweden and the United Kingdom don't have binding laws, but Sweden has threatened to institute one if companies don't increase diversity, while the U.K. set a goal of 25 percent women on boards that spurred rapid diversification.[20]

The *one rule* the U.S. has for gender diversity on boards lies with the Securities and Exchange Commission, which requires them to disclose how they consider diversity when choosing board members. But, it's so vaguely written that few companies take it to mean gender or racial diversity, instead focusing on diversity in experience or background. Some also comply with the rule by simply saying they don't take diversity into account. Another reason the U.S. is behind other countries in terms of diversity is due to the cultural barriers and gender biases that still exist in many parts of the U.S.

Quotas, on the other hand, appear to work, at least when it comes to increasing women's representation on boards. Norway's quota hasn't just significantly increased the number of women on boards, but has also increased the quality of female candidates. Other research has found that since it's been in place, corporate directors now value women's contributions and have come to support it. However, there has been some resistance to this quota law with some Norwegian companies opting to go private rather than comply with the directive.

Companies stand to benefit from better board diversity. One Catalyst report showed that companies with women board directors had higher return on equity, higher return on sales, and higher return on invested capital compared to companies with no women board members.[21] Gender diversity also leads companies to make decisions that protect company value and performance and away from those that lead to fraud, corruption, or other scandals—an all too common (and unnecessary) part of business.

◇◇◇◇◇◇◇◇◇◇◇◇◇◇◇◇◇◇◇◇

The key question we should be asking is whether a company is keeping pace with the labor market and taking strides to make cultural and diversity changes.

◇◇◇◇◇◇◇◇◇◇◇◇◇◇◇◇◇◇◇◇

Despite diversity benefits, these statistics confirm that there are few women in senior leadership positions in *any* corporation. The key question we should be asking is whether a company is keeping pace with the labor market, and taking strides to make cultural and diversity changes. We need to keep asking why there are so few women at senior levels and what the company is doing to attract, develop and promote women.

100+ Years to Gender Parity

I often tell my audiences that it will take a generation or more before we see true gender equality in the C-suite. A recent report by McKinsey & Company and *LeanIn.org* has confirmed this statement. Based on the change observed at each level between the 2012 and 2015 studies, there was a 0.9 percent increase in female representation in the C-suite over three years.[22] With this slow rate of progress, it will take twenty-five years to reach gender parity at the senior-VP level, and more than one hundred years to reach parity in the C-suite.

The World Economic Forum predicts a more dismal picture. Since the pace of change has slowed over the last few years, based on the current trajectory and with all else remaining equal, it will take 170 years for the world to close the gender gap completely.[23] It's difficult to wrap our minds around this. Here's a sobering thought—*nobody reading this book will be alive.*

The annual study measures the relative gaps between women and men in education, health, economic opportunity, and political power in 144 countries. Even as more women are obtaining education and outpacing men, progress toward gender parity in other areas has slowed. Nordic nations—Iceland, Finland, Norway, and Sweden—claim the top four spots on the global ranking for gender equity, and the African nation of Rwanda ranks fifth. The U.S. failed to crack the top twenty-five, ranking a dismal forty-fifth place, a seventeen-spot slide from last year. Ironically, the U.S. earns a number one ranking for educational equality, but seventy-third in political empowerment, sixty-second in health and survival, and twenty-sixth in economic participation and opportunity.[24] As we've seen, women are severely underrepresented on the boards of publicly traded companies, which are 81 percent male.

We are well into the twenty-first century; we are long past women's suffrage and liberation movements; we are more enlightened and diverse than ever, with women making-up the majority of professional occupations, and getting degrees at higher rates than men. By all accounts, women *should* be equal to men in the workplace. Not only has the leadership needle barely budged in the last three decades, women are still significantly underrepresented at *every* corporate and pipeline level (entry-level, manager, director, vice president, senior vice president, and the C-suite). And, men outpace women in leadership roles across every sector in the world—corporate, not-for-profit, government, education, medicine, military, and religion.

◇◇◇◇◇◇◇◇◇◇◇◇◇◇◇

Women are not learning essential skills such as the business, strategic, and financial acumen needed to be a corporate leader.

◇◇◇◇◇◇◇◇◇◇◇◇◇◇◇

How could this be happening? Well, the answer is not a simple one. Women face significant barriers in the workplace that men do not have to face (which will be explored in subsequent chapters). The data shows that women are less likely and slower to advance than men at *all* levels, and fewer women hold roles that lead to the C-suite. Recall that the top three most common occupations for women in 2014 were secretaries and administrative assistants, elementary and middle school teachers, and registered nurses, in that order. These are staff roles, not line roles. A staff role provides support for an organization, such as legal, human resources, and information technology, whereas a line role has profit and loss responsibility and is focused on core operations. More men hold line roles at every corporate level, which prepare them for top roles. Women are simply not getting this experience nor are they learning essential skills such as the business, strategic, and financial acumen needed to be a corporate leader.

Another interesting point is that women see and experience a workplace that favors men, but men don't see it that way. Women are almost four times more likely than men to think they have fewer opportunities to advance because of their gender, and twice as likely to think their gender will make it harder to advance in the future. In fact, women are three times more likely than men to say they have personally missed out on an assignment, promotion, or raise because of their gender, and women also report that they are consulted less often on important decisions.[25] This shows a clear disconnect between men and women about the perceived impact of gender at work. One explanation is that men do not experience bias to the same degree themselves, so men don't notice bias against women. Women not only observe a workplace biased against them, they believe they are disadvantaged by it.

Despite a growing consensus among top executives that gender diversity is both an ethical and a business imperative, there appears to be a disconnect between CEOs and employees on the priority of gender diversity. Seventy-four percent of companies report that gender diversity is a top CEO priority, but less than half of workers believe it.[26] This is a big problem. Organizations need to demonstrate that gender diversity is a top priority, and commit to a comprehensive and sustained investment in programs and processes that change company practices and culture. If they don't, employees will see diversity initiatives as lip service that carries little weight.

Even McKinsey & Company, a global management consulting firm which has been on the forefront of researching and publishing statistics about women at work for several years, acknowledges their own struggles with gender equality—and that they are not yet where they want to be. Women now represent about 39 percent of McKinsey's entry-level hires, but occupy just 11 percent of the senior-leadership roles within the firm. There are currently four women on their thirty-member Shareholders Council. These numbers are certainly up from a decade ago, but less than they would like.[27] Like all firms, McKinsey's ability to help their clients with their toughest problems depends on attracting and retaining the world's best people who can offer the diverse perspectives that enhance creative problem solving.

One hundred years is too long to wait for any hard-working individual trying to advance in their career. Female leadership is an imperative for organizations that want to perform at the highest levels. As the quote at the beginning of the chapter reads, "You don't get harmony when everyone sings the same note." Let's be open to hearing the blending of different voices and perspectives. We need to rethink work, rethink leadership, and rethink gender.

Summary Points

- Globally, women have less power politically, legally, economically, and socially—which explains why progress toward global gender equality has been slow.
- In the United States, women comprise most the labor force and bachelor degrees, but are still a minority in the business world.
- A pay wage gap exists between men and women, even among the top three most common female occupations.
- At *Fortune* 500 companies, women occupy only 19 percent of board seats, 15 percent of executive officer positions, and 4 percent of CEO positions.
- Twenty female CEOs currently lead *Fortune* 500 companies.
- European companies have the highest female board representation.
- There's a disconnect between men and women about the perceived impact of gender at work.
- There's a disconnect between CEOs and employees on the priority of gender diversity.
- With the current rate of progress, it will take more than one hundred years to reach gender parity in the C-suite.

Reflection Questions

- ✓ Have you experienced any political, legal, economic, or social inequities in your life? If so, what were they? How have they impacted your life and career?
- ✓ What types of roles have you had in your organization? Do you gravitate more toward staff or line roles?

✓ Do you aspire to be in a different type of role? If so, can you create a path for yourself at your company?

✓ In your role, are you learning about the business, strategic, and financial aspects of your company? Can you comfortably discuss these topics in conversation or at a meeting?

✓ Is your company committed to gender diversity? Do they communicate about initiatives that are in place or being developed? Do you participate in any gender or diversity programs at work?

TWO

Leadership is Leadership, or is It?

Most people fail in life not because they aim too high and miss, but
because they aim too low and hit.
Les Brown

I've always loved this quote, and I think it's emblematic of leadership. Whether we are organizational leaders or not, we are all leaders in our own lives, and we influence others by our actions. The broad topic of leadership is the most extensively discussed and published aspect of business. Bookshelves are filled with best-selling books about leaders and offering advice on how to be a leader. There are over thirty different leadership models that have been extensively studied, tested, and practiced the past several decades.

Transformational leadership, transactional leadership, situational leadership, servant leadership, trait theory, skills approach, path-goal theory, psychodynamic approach, contingency theory, authentic leadership, leader-member exchange theory, style approach—and the list goes on. These models and theories are accompanied by their own leadership instrument, assessment or questionnaire, and each has its own strengths and criticisms. Emotional intelligence, which will be explored in the next chapter, is a type of trait theory.

It is assumed that with proper training, development and practice, anyone can enhance their leadership skills, which is generally true. What varies, however, is the style in which we lead and our degree of effectiveness. First, let's discuss an essential distinction. Although there are some commonalities between leaders and managers—both involve influence, working with people, and goal accomplishment—there are many ways in which the two differ.

Leadership is the ability to influence a group toward the achievement of a vision or set of goals. It includes establishing direction, aligning people, motivating, and inspiring. The source of this influence can be formal, such as managerial ranks within an organization, or informal, such as influence that arises outside the formal structure. This type of influence without authority is often as important or more important than formal influence—and will be discussed in more detail later in this chapter. In contrast to leadership, management is the process of dealing with or controlling things or people. It's a set of functions that include planning, budgeting, organizing, staffing, and problem solving.

◇◇◇◇◇◇◇◇◇◇◇◇◇◇

Management is about seeking order and consistency, and leadership is about seeking change and movement.

◇◇◇◇◇◇◇◇◇◇◇◇◇◇

Peter Northouse, professor of communication at Western Michigan University, explains that leadership can be traced back to Aristotle, and management emerged around the turn of the twentieth century with the advent of our industrialized society. Management was created to reduce chaos in organizations and make them run more effectively and efficiently.[1] In other words, management is about seeking order and consistency, and leadership is about seeking change and movement. It's important to note that not all leaders are managers, nor are all managers leaders. There are many times when people perform both roles at the same time and may display a combination of behaviors.

Leaders have followers and managers have subordinates. Leaders do not have subordinates, at least not when they are leading. Many organizational leaders do have subordinates, but only because they are also managers. When a person assumes the role of a leader, they give up formal authoritarian control because to lead is to have followers, and following is always a voluntary activity.

The biggest difference between leaders and managers is the way they motivate the people who work with or follow them. The table below outlines the differences between the two, on a wide range of subjects.

SUBJECT	LEADER	MANAGER
Style	Transformational	Transactional
Essence	Change	Stability
Focus	Leading people	Managing work
Have	Followers	Subordinates
Seeks	Vision	Objectives
Decision	Facilitates	Makes
Power	Personal charisma	Formal authority
Appeal to	Heart	Head
Energy	Passion	Control
Exchange	Excitement for work	Money for work

Wants	Achievement	Results
Risks	Takes	Minimizes

Management style is generally transactional, in that the manager tells the subordinate what to do, and the subordinate does it because they have been promised a reward (such as their salary) for doing so. On the other hand, a leader with a strong personal charisma attracts people to their cause with the promise of transformational benefits, such that their followers will not just receive extrinsic rewards, but will somehow become better people as a result. Now, let's look at some of the most popular and contemporary leadership styles.

Transactional Leadership

Simon is a component engineer at a technology firm with an accomplished work history. He has a good relationship with his boss, Doug, whom he's worked with for three years. Doug recently told him that if he completes the microchip project on time and within budget, he would offer him a promotion to the project lead position. By offering Simon this promotion, Doug has exhibited an example of transactional leadership, which focuses on the exchanges that occur between leaders and their followers. In this example, the positive outcome is a win-win situation for both Simon and Doug.

Let's look at another example. In politics, this type of leadership style is widespread. Party leaders will often horse-trade for political delegates. They may offer tickets to state dinners at the white house, tickets to sporting events, meet-and-greets with celebrities, pay travel expenses for lavish trips, or offer a delegate the possibility of a high-level post in the administration.

A teacher who gives a student a grade for work completed, a politician who promises no new taxes to win votes, a parent who tells a child he can stay up later if he eats his vegetables—these are all examples of transactional leadership. This exchange dimension is very common and can be observed at many levels throughout all types of organizations.

This style is generally based on positive and constructive transactions and contingent rewards (I do this for you; you do this for me), but can also be negative. It can lead to corrective criticism, negative feedback, and negative reinforcement. For example, a manager gives an employee a poor performance evaluation without ever talking with the employee about his or her prior work performance. Another example is a manager who watches closely for mistakes or rule violations and then takes corrective action.

◇◇◇◇◇◇◇◇◇◇◇◇◇◇◇◇◇

Transactional leadership is more commonly associated with male leaders.

◇◇◇◇◇◇◇◇◇◇◇◇◇◇◇◇◇

Transactional leadership is more commonly associated with male leaders. Research has aligned transactional leadership style with strong masculine characteristics and qualities of competitiveness, hierarchical authority, high control, and analytical problem solving.[2] This type of leadership style certainly has its place in organizations, and can be effective in motivating employees. However, as organizations become increasingly complex and diverse, the emphasis has shifted from exchange-based to relationship-based leadership.

Transformational Leadership

As the name implies, transformational leadership is a process that changes and transforms people. It focuses on emotions, values, ethics, standards, and long-term goals. It involves assessing follower's motives, satisfying their needs and treating them as full human beings.[3] The transformational leader motivates and inspires the follower to transcend their own self-interests for the good of the organization. Transactional and transformational leadership complement each other; they aren't opposing approaches to getting things done. Transformational leadership *builds* on transactional leadership and produces levels of follower effort and performance beyond what transactional leadership alone can do.

Mahatma Gandhi is a classic example of transformational leadership—he raised the hopes and demands of millions of his people, and in the process, was changed himself. Richard Branson of the Virgin Group is another example. He pays attention to the concerns and needs of individual followers, changes their awareness of issues by helping them look at old problems in new ways, and excites and inspires followers to put forth extra effort to achieve group goals.

Transformational leadership refers to a relationship between leader and follower that is built around cooperation, collaboration, lower levels of control, and collective problem solving and decision making, which are based on intuition and rationality.[4] It involves an exceptional form of influence that moves followers to accomplish more than what is usually expected of them, and is a process that often incorporates charismatic and visionary leadership. It means displaying signs of wisdom and expertise and being a role model. It allows people to influence others even in the absence of formal authority or power—which is often the case for women. Transformational leaders enjoy being respected and admired, but they aren't as interested in having power or always getting their way as are more dominant leadership styles. Indeed, relationship-oriented leaders often allow others to set the course, while subtly directing people from behind.

Transformational leaders provide essential contributions to idea-generating and decision-making processes, but at the same time, they listen to and incorporate input from others. Listening is as important as talking for transformational leaders. This creates a safe environment where team members feel respected and free to innovate and generate creative solutions. This style works well in organizational cultures marked by relatively egalitarian relationships among coworkers, in which people at all levels of the organization are used to having their viewpoints heard and respected. Now, let's take a brief look at the data on gender and transformational leadership.

In the late 1990s, researchers found that women leaders provided a working environment that "encourages considerate, warm, participative, and interpersonal relationships," thus facilitating stronger dyadic bonds that fostered productivity, effectiveness, satisfaction, and commitment. As such, the data provided support that transformational leadership positively relates to follower empowerment and significantly correlates with female leadership.[5]

◇◇◇◇◇◇◇◇◇◇◇◇◇◇◇

Individuals who are effective transformational leaders score high in emotional intelligence.

◇◇◇◇◇◇◇◇◇◇◇◇◇◇◇

Later studies showed similar findings in that transformational leadership to a large extent characterizes a feminine model and is generally associated with female leaders.[6] In today's organizations, which are flatter and less hierarchical in structure, these are precisely the characteristics and qualities that are required of effective leadership. Interestingly, these studies also found a significant predictive relationship between transformational leadership style and emotional intelligence, in that those individuals who are effective transformational leaders also score high in emotional intelligence.

Alice Eagly and Linda Carli, authors of the bestselling book *Through the Labyrinth,* found that women rated higher than men on all transformational factors. Thus, they linked the effectiveness of transformational leadership to women and concluded that, "All of the aspects of leadership style on which women exceeded men relate positively to leaders' effectiveness, whereas all of the aspects on which men exceeded women have negative or null relations to effectiveness".[7]

Internationally acclaimed writer, speaker, and consultant, Sally Helgesen, further supports the findings that women offer a unique style of leadership, apart from men, for today's organizations. Her bestselling classic *The Female Advantage* was the first book to focus on what women have to contribute instead of how they need to change and adapt. Continuing to focus on opportunity, the author highlights the reasons that women's gifts are particularly suited to the demands of today's workplace. These skills include building and managing relationships, having a bias for direct communication, leading from the center rather than the top, comfort (as opposed to tolerance) with diversity, and the ability to integrate work and life and draw information broadly.

◇◇◇◇◇◇◇◇◇◇◇◇◇◇◇◇

Women are more likely to possess leadership characteristics that are predominately effective in contemporary organizations.

◇◇◇◇◇◇◇◇◇◇◇◇◇◇◇◇

Her research further shows how marketplace trends of the last two decades have supported women's skills and brought them into the mainstream. For example, organizations today seek to connect directly with customers and clients—which is evident in the explosion of businesses who use social media, such as Facebook, Twitter and even Instagram and Pinterest to connect with customers. New architectures of technology now support webs instead of hierarchies, the global economy continually expands the pool of diverse talent and markets, and 24/7 intensity requires greater work-life integration. As as result of this increased organizational complexity and diversity, teams and partnerships have become the dominant unit of work.[8]

Data has shown that both female and male workers perform best with leaders whose styles provided a connection or bond with workers, and that female leaders were rated significantly stronger in this style of leadership. The results of the research suggest that developing leadership styles that support workers' needs to connect, while simultaneously providing structure and task-orientation, is important to successful leadership.[9] Together, all these findings confirm that women are more likely to possess leadership characteristics and attributes that are predominately effective in contemporary organizations as compared with their male counterparts.

It is no wonder transformational leadership has garnered so much attention in the business world. Its popularity is due, in part, to its emphasis on intrinsic motivation and follower development. This type of leadership engenders trust and loyalty, improves engagement and productivity, leads to higher retention rates, and ultimately maximizes shareholder value by generating as much profit as possible—the holy grail for most publicly-held companies. Transformational leadership fits the needs of today's work groups who want to be inspired and empowered to succeed in times of uncertainty.

So, given the natural transformational characteristics women possess, and the need of today's organizations, why don't we see more women leading? Let's explore further.

Leadership and Gender

Early scholars and researchers studying leadership defined the field of leadership in a strictly male context. Not surprisingly, these scholars and researchers were men—men practiced leadership and men wrote about it. This male dominance in leadership history is perceived, even today, as a major reason for the *perception* of women not being viewed as an appropriate fit in a management or leadership role.

◇◇◇◇◇◇◇◇◇◇◇◇◇◇◇◇

Research questions have shifted from whether women can lead, to the style and effectiveness of women compared to men.

◇◇◇◇◇◇◇◇◇◇◇◇◇◇◇◇

The topic of gender and leadership has become increasingly popular during the past three decades. This roughly corresponds to the rise of the women's movement and the influx of college-educated, career-focused women into the work force and academia, which have fueled scholarly interest in the study of female leaders. Thus, research questions have shifted from whether women *can* lead, to the style and effectiveness of women compared to men, and the biases associated with women ascending the corporate ladder.

Today, we can point to highly effective female leaders in a variety of domains. These women include U.K. Prime Minister Margaret Thatcher, German Chancellor Angela Merkel, Prime Minister Indira Gandhi, Chair of the Federal Reserve Janet Yellen, Founder of Huffington Post Arianna Huffington, media mogul Oprah Winfrey, General Motors' CEO Mary Barra, PepsiCo's CEO Indra Nooyi, Facebook's COO Sheryl Sandberg, four-star General Ann E. Dunwoody, former Speaker of the House Nancy Pelosi, and former U.S. presidential candidate Hillary Clinton.

What all these women have in common is that they were able to rise to positions of power within their given fields. The concept of power is related to leadership because it is part of the influence process. Power is the capacity or potential to influence and is defined as the ability to affect others' beliefs, attitudes, and courses of action. Doctors, teachers, ministers, and coaches are just some examples of people who have the potential to influence us.

In organizations, there are two major kinds of power: *position power* and *personal power*. Position power is the power a person derives from an office or rank in a formal organizational system, and includes legitimate, reward and coercive power. In contrast, personal power is the influence capacity a leader derives from being seen by followers as likable and knowledgeable, and includes referent and expert power.[10]

◇◇◇◇◇◇◇◇◇◇◇◇◇◇◇

Influence without authority comes naturally for most women, and is part of being a transformational leader.

◇◇◇◇◇◇◇◇◇◇◇◇◇◇◇

Why is the type of power important? Based on statistics discussed in the last chapter, the clear majority of decision-making leadership positions globally are held by men. As a result, men are automatically granted position power that they can exert over others. In contrast, for women to influence others in their organizations, it is necessary to leverage personal power or lead by natural influence. If you've ever attended a women's event or webinar, or participated in a women's affinity group, a common topic discussed is how to "influence without authority." I've attended and taught these courses myself, and believe it is an important skill set for women to possess and develop. Fortunately, this skill comes naturally for most women, and is part of being a transformational leader. Even though you may not have a formal leadership position, it's important to know that influencing without authority *is* leadership.

One of the women I interviewed for this book is Dorie Clark, marketing strategy consultant, author, professional speaker, adjunct professor, and frequent contributor to the *Harvard Business Review*, *TIME*, *Entrepreneur*, and the World Economic Forum blog. Dorie is enjoying her tenth year as a successful entrepreneur. She has been able to amass thousands of followers and clients through the power of influence, not formal authority. As an entrepreneur, no one *has* to listen to her, yet they have. She has accomplished this through sharing her ideas and helping others with their ideas, communicating clearly and frequently, providing reason and careful explanation, connecting people to one another, and building a network and community. These types of activities engender trust, build relationships, and create followers.

Transactional and transformational leadership illustrate differences in leadership style. Although these styles predict effectiveness, in several studies, overall, men and women were found to be equally effective leaders. However, there were gender differences such that women and men were more effective in leadership roles that were congruent with their gender.[11] Thus, women were less effective to the extent that the leader role was masculinized and men were less effective when the leader role was feminized.

For example, women were less effective than men were in military positions, but were somewhat more effective than men in education, government, and social service organizations, and substantially more effective than men in middle management positions, where communal interpersonal skills are highly valued. In addition, women were less effective than men were when they supervised a higher proportion of male subordinates or when a greater proportion of male raters assessed female performance.[12]

Let's look at two real-life examples. John recently enlisted in the army and was assigned to a platoon with a female leader. What assumptions might he make? "She won't be able to give commands." "She won't take necessary risks." "She won't be tough enough to handle the male recruits." As a result of these assumptions, John didn't support or respect her as leader, became disengaged in his role, and lax in his duties—putting the rest of his platoon in jeopardy.

Last June, Betty was admitted to the hospital for respiratory issues, and Sherwin, a male nurse, was in charge of her care. Betty assumed that Sherwin would not give her the same level of attention as female nurses, wouldn't notice critical details, nor give her the gentle and nurturing care that she desired. As a result of her concerns, Betty asked to be assigned a female nurse and refused to be cared for by Sherwin. In both examples, none of the assumptions were correct. A female leader in the military can be very effective, but she may not be supported because she's in a role considered to be incongruent with a female. Similary, a man can be an excellent nurse, but he may not be met positively by those he cares for because he's in a role incongruent with his gender.

The take-home message here is that if you are currently in a role, or interested in a role, that is considered to be incongruent with your gender, you may have to work harder to prove yourself. It doesn't mean that you won't be successful or effective, or that it's good or bad. Remember, society's assumptions about what types of roles people have are based on age-old gender stereotypes, and with time, stereotypes can change. If you are passionate about a specific type of role or industry, then you should go for it—regardless of the stereotype that surrounds it.

◇◇◇◇◇◇◇◇◇◇◇◇◇◇◇◇◇

Both men and women make assumptions about women as leaders.

◇◇◇◇◇◇◇◇◇◇◇◇◇◇◇◇◇

Just as assumptions were made in the examples of role congruity, both men *and* women make assumptions about women as leaders. "She won't take an additional assignment because her family responsibilities prevent her from traveling." "She won't be able to handle the stress of an executive position." "She's not strategic or decisive enough." "She can't be the leader; it must be the male." Again, these generalized assumptions are unfounded, and not only limit a woman's opportunity, but can prevent opportunities from occurring altogether. All too often, women are not even asked if they want to take on a stretch assignment, want to travel, want to advance, or want to lead. We need to stop making assumptions about women as leaders and start asking.

Denise owns a financial investment advisory firm, and has worked in the financial industry for more than twenty years, with experience ranging from banking to large investment firms. When she answers the phone at her own investment company and the callers hear her voice, they inevitably ask to speak with the broker, which frustrates her. People assume that because she's female, she must be the secretary. The same assumptions are made in meetings. Who usually gets asked to get the coffee? The assumption is that the female can't possibly be leading the meeting, she must be some type of support staff.

Let's look at another example. A car accident occurred in which the father was killed, and the son was brought to the emergency room in critical condition. The surgeon working on the case saw the boy and said, "I can't operate because he's my son." Some people assume the surgeon is a gay parent, some assume he's the boy's father-in-law, others assume he is an adoptive father or a godfather. The surgeon is the boy's mother, but people do all these mental gymnastics because they can't see beyond their bias, and they try to simplify things. We have not come as far as we would like to think in our perceptions of women as leaders, and we need to question all of our knee-jerk responses, assumptions, and biases.

Another phenomenon related to roles and gender, is viewing men in authority as father figures—and many women view men as leaders regardless of their position. This can happen to women at all levels and all industries. A woman who is smart, assertive, and confident with most people, can act like a little girl in the presence of a male boss, attempting to obey all rules and not do anything to displease him. This usually occurs if she had a father who was critical and hard to please. When we hear or observe similar behavior that our fathers exhibited, we revert back to our childhood tendencies, instead of building independent, objective relationships with our bosses. If you find yourself reponding in this way to male authority figures, ask yourself whom does he remind you of, how do you act when you're around him, how do you act when you're around other people, and why do you give up so much power to him? These questions can help you see the situation more objectively and respond appropriately.

In sum, women are just as qualified to lead as men, and possess characteristics essential to today's organizations. A recent analysis of ninty-five studies on gender differences showed that when it comes to leadership skills, although men are generally more confident, women are more competent.[13] Women experience slight effectiveness disadvantages in masculine leader roles, whereas roles that are more feminine offer them some advantages. In addition, we make assumptions about women as leaders, and viewing men as father figures can affect how we're perceived and subsequently treated at work. These are some of the reasons that women are largely absent from leadership roles. Other reasons will be explored in following chapters.

Leadership Strategies

So, how can you maximize your natural transformational characteristics and become more of who you are? There are four basic principles of transformational leadership: individualized consideration, intellectual stimulation, inspirational motivation, and idealized influence.[14]

Individualized consideration is giving your followers or team personal attention, listening, empathizing, treating each employee individually, coaching, mentoring, and advising. Intellectual stimulation means encouraging careful problem solving, decision making, creativity, and independence. In other words, its empowering individual followers to develop their skills, enhance their abilities, and increase self-efficacy.

Inspirational motivation is communicating high expectations for your team clearly and directly, using words, symbols, ideas, and behaviors to help focus efforts, helping them to look at old problems in new ways, and expressing important goals in simple terms. This type of motivation instills a positive "can do" spirit in the team. Idealized influence means providing a clear vision and sense of mission, instilling pride, and building mutual respect and trust. It is also important to emphasize group goals, shared values and beliefs, and unified efforts to gain buy-in and commitment.

◇◇◇◇◇◇◇◇◇◇◇◇◇◇

Women possess characteristics that favor authentic, ethical and servant leadership styles.

◇◇◇◇◇◇◇◇◇◇◇◇◇◇

These efforts are most effective when responsibility is decentralized, when leaders can directly interact with the workforce and make decisions independently, when there's a propensity to take risks, and when compensation plans are geared toward long-term results—all of which facilitate corporate entrepreneurship, and help followers to transcend their own self-interests for the good of the organization.

Women also possess characteristics that favor authentic, ethical, and servant leadership styles. Authentic leadership is based primarily on trust, and focuses on the moral aspects of being a leader. These leaders know who they are, know what they believe in and value, and acts on those values and beliefs openly and candidly. Authentic leaders readily share information, enourage open communication, and stick to their ideals. Campbell Soup's CEO Denise Morrison decided to lower sodium in the company's soup products simply because it was the right thing to do.[15]

Transformational leadership has ethical implications since these leaders change the way followers think. Ethical leadership is a core value for many women who place a premium on trust and integrity above all else. Ethical shortcomings or bad leader behavior is a turn off for most women—scandals, deception, cheating, lying, fraud, egotism—all fall into this category. Leaders who treat their followers with fairness, and provide honest, frequent, and accurate information are seen as more effective. Humbleness is another characteristic that ethical leaders often exhibit as part of being authentic. Rarely do you see a female leader who is more concerned with her own needs or pleasures over her team's.

Servant leadership has garnered much attention in the past few years. Servant leaders go beyond their self-interest and focus on opportunities to help followers grow and develop. They don't use power to achieve ends; they emphasize persuasion. Characteristic behaviors include listening, empathizing, persuading, accepting stewardship, and actively developing followers' potential. These are all characteristics ideally suited for women. A recent study of 126 CEOs found that servant leadership is negatively correlated with the trait of narcissism.[16] In other words, the more that a leader focused on himself the less he served his team. Mother Teresa is an example of someone who epitomized servant leadership.

◇◇◇◇◇◇◇◇◇◇◇◇◇◇◇◇

To fully maximize the benefits of diverse perspectives, ideas and methods, we need balanced leadership.

◇◇◇◇◇◇◇◇◇◇◇◇◇◇◇◇

Like transformational leadership, authentic, ethical, and servant leadership are also tied to postive outcomes. Higher levels of organizational commitment, team performance, creativity, trust, perceptions of justice, and a sense of unity are all results from these contemporary leadership styles. Studies show that approximately 70 percent of people are disengaged and don't feel appreciated at work—female leadership skills affect morale and culture and make people feel valued.

The key takeaway here, is that women need not try to fit in and "be like a man." Women are different, and women need to lead differently. To fully maximize the benefits of diverse perspectves, ideas, and methods, we need balanced leadership in our global organizations, institutions, and governments. As shown in this chapter, women possess characteristics that are effective in today's organizations, and we need an open and honest dialogue about gender and leadership. By honing the leadership skills that come naturally for most women, and giving women the opportunity to lead, both individuals and organizations stand to benefit greatly from enhanced relationships and performance. Consistent with the quote at the chapter's beginnning, in the spirit of leadership…aim high.

Summary Points

- Management is about seeking order and consistency, and leadership is about seeking change and movement.
- Transactional leadership focuses on the exchanges that occur between leaders and their followers—and is generally associated with male leaders.
- Transformational leadership is a process that changes and transforms both leaders and followers—and is generally associated with female leaders.
- Transformational leadership fits the needs of today's work groups who want to be inspired and empowered to succeed in times of uncertainty.
- Research questions have shifted from whether women can lead, to the style and effectiveness of women compared to men.
- Two types of power in organizations: position power (formal authority) and personal power (natural influence).
- Women and men were more effective in leadership roles that were congruent with their gender.
- Four basic principles of transformational leadership—individualized consideration, intellectual stimulation, inspirational motivation, and idealized influence.
- Women possess characteristics that favor authentic, ethical and servant leadership styles.
- There are strategies to help you maximize your natural transformational characteristics and leadership strengths.

Reflection Questions

- ✓ Do you tend to motivate others based on leader or manager characteristics?
- ✓ Have you experienced transactional or transformational leadership styles in your organization as a follower? Can you think of examples?
- ✓ How would you characterize the leadership styles in your organization?

✓ As a leader, do you gravitate more toward a transactional or transformational style? When have you demonstrated these styles? What did it look like?

✓ Are you more comfortable leading by formal authority, or influencing without authority? What are some examples of each?

✓ At your organization, would your role be perceived as feminine, masculine, or neutral? What effect has the type of role had on your performance and leadership effectiveness, if any?

✓ How do you respond to male authority figures? Is it different from how you respond to everyone else?

✓ Do you consider yourself to have an authentic, ethical, or servant leadership style? What does it look like? How have you used it?

THREE

Why You Should Care About EQ

People will forget what you said, people will forget what you did,
but people will never forget how you made them feel.

Maya Angelou

Before reading this chapter, consider the successes and failures of eleven U.S. presidents that were evaluated on six qualities: communication, organization, political skill, vision, cognitive style, and emotional intelligence (EQ). The key quality that differentiated the successful from the unsuccessful was emotional intelligence. Which presidents do you think rated the highest? Without knowing much about emotional intelligence, intuitively, you already know the answer. The most successful presidents, those highest in EQ, were found to be Roosevelt, Kennedy, and Reagan, and the unsuccessful, those lowest in EQ, were found to be Johnson, Carter, and Nixon.[1] This study was conducted at Princeton in 2001. If we were to consider presidents in recent history based on their display of emotional intelligence, we could add Clinton and Obama to the successful list, and G. W. Bush, Trump, and vice president Gore to the unsuccessful list.

This example is not meant to be partisan, but to illustrate the power of emotional intelligence in both work and life success. What made certain U.S. presidents successful or unsuccessful? It was their ability to connect with, motivate, inspire, and influence others. They were able to engage their followers, communicate their ideas effectively, and get them to buy into their vision. Emotional intelligence is defined as a form of social intelligence that involves the ability to monitor one's own and others' feelings and emotions, to discriminate among them, and to use the information to guide one's thinking and action.[2]

◇◇◇◇◇◇◇◇◇◇◇◇◇◇◇

The key quality that differentiated successful from unsuccessful U.S. presidents was emotional intelligence.

◇◇◇◇◇◇◇◇◇◇◇◇◇◇◇

Research on emotional intelligence goes back as far as the late 1920s, with reference to social intelligence as the ability to get along with other people. However, in the past thirty years the concept has been studied extensively. Here's a brief history.

In 1985, Reuven Bar-On coined the term emotional quotient or EQ when he was a Ph.D. student in South Africa. He was curious about factors that determine one's ability to be effective in life, and observed that people can have very high IQs, but not succeed. In 1990, Peter Salovey and John Mayer expanded Bar-On's work and introduced the term emotional intelligence in several scientific articles. In 1995, Daniel Goleman became aware of Salovey and Mayer's work which eventually led to his groundbreaking book *Emotional Intelligence*. Goleman was a science writer for the *New York Times* whose beat was brain and behavior research. He had been trained as a psychologist at Harvard where he worked with motivation expert David McClelland, among others.[3]

In doing the research for his first book, Goleman became familiar with a wealth of research pointing to the importance of social and emotional abilities for personal success. Some of this research came from personality and social psychology, and some came from the burgeoning field of neuropsychology. What makes Goleman's research relevant is that he applied it within the context of work performance, competencies, and leadership. He was the first to identify an individual's emotional intelligence as a key aspect and driver of leadership effectiveness, and helped simplify the concept for a public audience.

Goleman suggests that emotional intelligence consists of a set of four personal and social competencies—self-awareness, self-management, social awareness, and social management. *Self-awareness* is how well you understand your own emotions in the moment, and how well you understand your tendencies toward people and situations you interact with. *Self-management* is what you do with your emotions once you're aware of them. *Social awareness* is how well you understand the emotions and experience of other people. *Social management* requires that you use self-awareness, self-management, and social awareness in concert to better your relationships with other people.

Bar-On's work is based on similar competencies with somewhat different terms. His work suggests a set of five emotional and social competencies—self-perception, self-expression, interpersonal skills, decision making, and stress tolerance. *Self-perception* is understanding your own emotions. *Self-expression* is the ability to express your emotions effectively. *Interpersonal skills* are needed to develop and maintain healthy relationships. *Decision making* is using emotions to make better decisions. And finally, *stress tolerance* is coping with challenges. This model is most widely used in academia and consulting practices.

In my research, teaching, speaking, and consulting, I reference both models. I have taken the liberty of overlaying these two models in the table below so you can get a complete picture of what specific EQ competencies look like. Words in italics indicate overlapping competencies between the models, or competencies specific to the Bar-On model only.

	WHAT I SEE	WHAT I DO
	SELF-AWARENESS	SELF-MANAGEMENT
PERSONAL COMPETENCE	Accurate Self-Assessment *Emotional Self-Awareness* *Self-Confidence/Self-Regard* *Self-Actualization*	Self-Regulation Accountability Motivation Initiative Achievement Trustworthiness/Transparency Persistence/Commitment *Adaptability/Flexibility* *Optimism* *Emotional Expression* *Assertiveness* *Independence* *Stress Tolerance*
	SOCIAL AWARENESS	SOCIAL MANAGEMENT
SOCIAL COMPETENCE	Leveraging Diversity Service Orientation Organizational Awareness *Empathy* *Social Responsibility*	Influence Communication Conflict Management Leadership Teamwork/Collaboration Developing Others Change Catalyst *Problem Solving* *Reality Testing* *Impulse Control* *Interpersonal Relationships*

These EQ competencies are important because they're how we define and identify specific work and leader behaviors. In the following sections, we will explore how EQ affects the brain, gender, and leadership, as well as the impact that these competencies can have on perception.

EQ and the Brain

Who we are and how we express ourselves results from the combination of our personality, IQ, and EQ. Personality is our inherited traits, preferences, and tendencies; IQ refers to our level of intellectual intelligence; and EQ is our level of social intelligence. Our brain is made up of three parts—reptilian brain, limbic brain, and neocortex. The reptilian brain is responsible for survival instincts such as food, aggression, and fight or flight responses. The limbic brain is responsible for our emotions, and the neocortex is responsible for reasoning, creativity, planning, and intellect.

Emotional intelligence is born largely in the neurotransmitters of the brain's limbic system, which governs feelings, impulses, and drives. Research from numerous studies indicates that the limbic system learns best through motivation, extended practice, and feedback. In contrast, the neocortex, which governs analytical and technical ability, grasps concepts and logic. Emotional intelligence entails not only being aware of one's own emotions, but also using these emotions in cognitive processes, such as decision making and planning. So, what does this mean? It means that EQ brings the limbic (emotional) and neocortex (rational) brains together. If we work on developing and practicing our EQ skills, it increases the flow of information between these two brains because it's building neural pathways—also referred to as neural plasticity.

◇◇◇◇◇◇◇◇◇◇◇◇◇◇

EQ brings the emotional and rational brains together.

◇◇◇◇◇◇◇◇◇◇◇◇◇◇

It is now clear that emotions are critical to rational thinking. An example of this can be found with Phineas Gage, a railroad worker in Vermont. One September day in 1848, a three-foot and seven-inch iron bar flew into his lower-left jaw and out through the top of his skull from an explosive charge. Remarkably, Gage survived his injury, could read and speak, and performed well above average on cognitive ability tests. However, he completely lost his ability to experience emotion. Gage's inability to express emotion eventually took away his ability to reason. As a result, he often behaved erratically and against his own self-interests. Gage drifted from job to job, eventually joining a circus.[4] The example of Phineas Gage and many other brain injury studies show we must have the ability to experience emotions to be rational.

Why? Because our emotions provide important information about how we understand the world around us.

When it comes to business, how many times have you heard the phrase, "Leave your emotions out of it"? The truth is that it's impossible to "leave our emotions out of it" or "check our emotions at the door." We are emotional creatures, not robots, and we need our emotions to guide our behavior and help us make decisions. Thus, emotional intelligence is not the touchy-feely soft skill as some have alluded to—and the science proves it.

EQ and Gender

I'd like to pose a question. *Which gender do you think is more emotionally intelligent? Men or women?* If you answered men, you are incorrect. If you answered women, you are also incorrect. The answer is that EQ assessments have found men and women to be equally emotionally intelligent, but strong in different areas considered gender-specific. For example, overall, men tend to score higher than women in areas of self-confidence, assertiveness, and stress tolerance. Overall, women outperform men in areas of empathy, social responsibility, and interpersonal relationships.[5] There were also small but statistically significant differences that gave men an advantage in independence and problem solving, and women an advantage in emotional self-awareness and emotional expression.[6] There are many EQ competencies that are considered gender-neutral where men and women perform equally well, examples include self-actualization, flexibility, motivation, reality testing, impulse control, and optimism.

◇◇◇◇◇◇◇◇◇◇◇◇◇◇◇◇◇

Men and women are equally emotionally intelligent, but strong in different areas considered gender-specific.

◇◇◇◇◇◇◇◇◇◇◇◇◇◇◇◇◇

It's worth pointing out that not all men and women fall into gender-specific patterns. Some women are higher in male-specific competencies, and some men are higher in female-specific competencies. But when looking at EQ assessments in over 1.5 million people worldwide, the gender-specific patterns listed above are not uncommon.

When I took my first EQ assessment back in 2009, I was surprised to find that I scored highest in assertiveness, independence, self-confidence—which are generally associated with males, and lowest in empathy—which is associated with females. I also scored high in emotional self-awareness and optimism, which are gender-neutral. Conversely, I've had men approach me after a presentation or workshop and tell me that they score higher in female-specific competencies. This is all perfectly natural.

What's important is that these attributes or competencies play a significant role in how we perceive men and women as leaders in the workplace. The importance of one gender-specific emotional intelligence attribute compared to another are valued differently. Further, these attributes, or lack thereof, could have a negative effect on a woman's advancement into leadership positions within her organization. In my dissertation research, I administered EQ assessments and conducted interviews with women at various levels of a *Fortune* 500 company. Here are some real-life stories specific to emotional intelligence.

◇◇◇◇◇◇◇◇◇◇◇◇◇◇◇◇

EQ attributes play a significant role in how we perceive men and women as leaders in the workplace.

◇◇◇◇◇◇◇◇◇◇◇◇◇◇◇◇

Lisa was vice president of a sales division at a pharmaceutical company. She'd been with the company for nearly twenty years in a variety of leadership roles, both in the U.S. and abroad, and was an accomplished and experienced executive. In her EQ assessment, she scored highest on assertiveness and emotional expression. Even though she was high in some male-specific competencies, she was told by men that she was too direct and honest, and that she needed to tone down her assertiveness, be more of a team player, and be more social.

The comments she received about her assertiveness are consistent with role congruity and social expectations of women—meaning that the way she expressed herself was not viewed as congruent with female behavior, and that women are expected to display communal traits (such as being social and being good teammates). Lisa is a confident, assertive leader, but because she freely and directly expresses herself, she is *perceived* as aggressive by others. In contrast, a confident, assertive male leader who directly expresses himself is viewed as decisive and competent. This double standard has existed for decades, and as a result, women have to walk a fine line of being too nice and too forceful.

Lisa's emotional expression strength also caused problems for her. She shared with me that during an annual performance review with her male boss, she started crying. They talked through the difficult situation together, then everything proceeded as normal. She didn't realize it at the time, but because she cried, her boss perceived her as too reactive, unstable, and unable to handle stress. As a result, she no longer received the special projects, opportunities, or resources she requested or needed. In effect, it damaged her credibility.

Her boss's reaction to her emotional expression was completely unfounded, yet it became reality for Lisa. This is an example of how gender-specific EQ competencies can be biased against women. Let's look at another example.

◇◇◇◇◇◇◇◇◇◇◇◇◇

Empathy is the one EQ competency where women significantly outperform men.

◇◇◇◇◇◇◇◇◇◇◇◇◇

Shari was a director-level leader who managed a team of field-based employees. Among her peers, Shari was the most popular director and her team loved working for her. In her EQ assessment, Shari scored highest on empathy—this is the one EQ competency in which women significantly outperform men. As an empathetic leader, she listened to her team, recognized and acknowledged their feelings, and valued and appreciated their efforts. The team was also highest in productivity.

Despite Shari's successes leading her team, her male boss perceived her as lacking substance and intelligence simply because she was outwardly empathetic. This view was shared by other leaders and colleagues as well. Shari told me that somehow people view being empathetic and analytical as mutually exclusive, and that if a woman is empathetic, she can't be a strong, decisive leader. Given that industrial culture has traditionally viewed toughness as an essential element of leadership, and that leadership is seen as synonymous with vision, it makes sense that those perceived as proficient in what's often described as soft skills or people skills might routinely be under-assessed when it comes to vision and leadership.[7]

◇◇◇◇◇◇◇◇◇◇◇◇◇◇◇◇

As organizations grow more dependent upon relationships, the ability to see decisions in a human context becomes an essential, and profoundly strategic, advantage.

◇◇◇◇◇◇◇◇◇◇◇◇◇◇◇◇

On the flip side, there are positive EQ examples as well. Recall that women score higher than men in empathy, interpersonal skills, and social responsibility. Women who hold positions as middle managers tend to do very well. Why? Because as a middle manager, you get work done through others. To accomplish this successfully, women need to leverage their interpersonal skills by developing and maintaining good relationships—communicating, listening, being empathetic, working as teams, being collaborative, following-though on commitments, developing others, showing optimism about future goals, and exercising a great deal of influence and persuasion— all without having positional power. As organizations grow more dependent upon relationships and the nurturance of talent, the ability to see decisions in a larger human context becomes an essential, and profoundly strategic, advantage.

A study of 105 managers in a financial services institution showed a strong pattern of significant differences between male and female leaders. The profile of successful female leaders included a broad range of emotional intelligence competencies, and indicated that for female leaders to be successful, they were required to demonstrate a combination of gender congruent and incongruent ways of behaving. Nevertheless, while successful male leaders also had a broad range of emotional intelligence competencies, those who exercised male-expected behaviors were rewarded, and were not successful if they exhibited leadership styles incongruent with their expected gender role.[8] This supports the role congruity discussion in chapter two.

EQ and Leadership

Emotional intelligence is strongly tied to both leadership and job performance. EQ is responsible for 58 percent of performance in all types of jobs, and 90 percent of top performers are high in EQ. In addition, people with high EQ scores make, on average, $29,000 more per year than their lower EQ counterparts. These findings hold true for people in all industries, at all levels, in every region of the world.[9]

◇◇◇◇◇◇◇◇◇◇◇◇◇◇◇◇

Emotional intelligence is strongly tied to both leadership and job performance.

◇◇◇◇◇◇◇◇◇◇◇◇◇◇◇◇

Based on the evidence to date, more employers are starting to use EQ measures to hire people. A study of U.S. Air Force recruiters showed that top-performing recruiters exhibited high levels of EQ. Using these findings, the Air Force revamped its selection criteria. A follow-up investigation found future hires who had high EQ scores were 2.6 times more successful than those who didn't. At French cosmetics company, L'Oréal, salespersons selected on EQ scores outsold those hired using the company's old selection procedure—hiring based solely on experience and education. On an annual basis, salespeople selected for their emotional competence sold $91,370 more than other salespeople did, for a net revenue increase of over $2.5 million.[10]

In 2003, the Center for Creative Leadership conducted a study to assess whether specific elements of emotional intelligence were linked to specific behaviors associated with leadership effectiveness. They examined 236 executives working in a variety of leadership positions in various industries across North America. Each executive was subjected to 360-degree ratings from their superiors, peers, and direct reports, across sixteen components of leadership skills and five derailment scales. They found that the top 25 percent (the most successful leaders) outscored the bottom 25 percent (the least successful leaders) across all EQ subscales or competencies—many of the differences between the groups were statistically significant.[11] Their conclusion was that higher emotional intelligence results in better leadership.

◇◇◇◇◇◇◇◇◇◇◇◇◇◇◇◇

The expression of emotion in speeches is often the critical element that makes us accept or reject a leader's message.

◇◇◇◇◇◇◇◇◇◇◇◇◇◇◇◇

Effective leaders rely on emotional appeals to help convey their messages. In fact, the expression of emotion in speeches is often the critical element that makes us accept or reject a leader's message. Think Martin Luther King, Jr.'s "I Have a Dream" speech, Abraham Lincoln's Gettysburg Address, FDR's Pearl Harbor Address, and British suffragette Emmeline Pankhurst's "Freedom or Death" speech. As discussed in chapter two, transformational leaders realize the effect emotion has on their followers and often freely share emotions—a strength for female leaders.

Corporate executives know emotional content is critical if employees are to buy into their vision of the company's future and accept change. When executives share new visions with vague or distant goals, it is often difficult for employees to accept the changes they'll bring. By arousing emotions and linking them to an appealing vision, leaders increase the likelihood that managers and employees alike will accept change. Leaders who focus on inspirational goals also generate greater optimism and enthusiasm in employees, leading to more positive social interactions with co-workers and customers. Howard Schultz, CEO of Starbucks, is a leader high in emotional intelligence. His optimism, excitement, and enthusiasm energize employees and motivate them to accept his vision of the company's future.

In 2000, Goleman and colleagues found six distinct leadership styles, each springing from different components of emotional intelligence. These styles are 1) Coercive—to deal with disasters, 2) Authoritative—to engineer a turnaround, 3) Affiliative—to build team harmony and morale, 4) Democratic—to give employees a voice in decisions, 5) Pacesetting—to define and exemplify high performance standards, and 6) Coaching—to support others' development.[12]

These styles, taken individually, appear to have a direct and unique impact on the working atmosphere of a company, division, or team, and in turn, on its financial performance. Perhaps most important, the research indicates that leaders with the best results do not rely on only one leadership style; they use most of them in a given week, seamlessly and in different measure, depending on the situation.

◇◇◇◇◇◇◇◇◇◇◇◇◇◇◇◇◇

The affiliative and democratic EQ leadership styles are deemed feminine styles.

◇◇◇◇◇◇◇◇◇◇◇◇◇◇◇◇◇

According to Goleman, the authoritative, coercive, and pacesetting leadership styles are generally considered male styles; whereas, affiliative and democratic styles are deemed feminine leadership styles. The coaching leadership style is typically viewed as being gender-neutral. Goleman states that the most effective leaders have mastered four or more of the six leadership styles. Additionally, they are keenly sensitive to the impact they are having on others, and switch flexibly and fluidly among the leadership styles as needed.[13] Let's look at affiliate, democratic and coaching styles more in depth.

The affiliative leader creates harmony and builds emotional bonds, believing that "People come first". With its focus on people, this leadership style has an overall positive impact on organizational climate and works best to heal rifts in a team or to motivate people during stressful circumstances. Underlying emotional intelligence competencies of the affiliative leader are empathy, building relationships, and communication.

The democratic style, which is positive overall, forges consensus through participation and engages people through asking, "What do you think?" to obtain buy-in, gain consensus, or get input from valuable employees. The democratic leader possesses emotional intelligence competencies in collaboration, team leadership, and communication.

Finally, the coaching style develops people for the future and has an overall positive impact on the organizational climate. This style works best to help an employee improve performance or to develop long-term strengths by saying "Try this". Coaching leaders possess underlying emotional intelligence competencies in developing others, empathy, and self-awareness.

◇◇◇◇◇◇◇◇◇◇◇◇◇◇◇◇

The natural leadership strengths that women possess have a positive impact on organizational culture.

◇◇◇◇◇◇◇◇◇◇◇◇◇◇◇◇

Once again, this data is consistent with data discussed earlier about female leadership characteristics. The affiliative, democratic, and coaching styles have much in common with transformational, authentic, and servant leadership—empathy, self-awareness, relationship building, communication, collaboration, team focus, and developing others—all are traits that today's companies are looking for. Further proof of the natural leadership strengths that women possess, which have a positive impact on organizational culture.

As a leadership ability or trait, emotional intelligence appears to be a very important construct. The underlying premise is that people who are more sensitive to their own and other's emotions, and can understand and regulate the impact of their emotions on others, will be the most effective leaders.

EQ Strategies

In this section, I have outlined specific and practical strategies you can apply to improve your emotional intelligence. These strategies align with the Bar-On model of five emotional and social composites—which are self-perception, self-expression, interpersonal skills, decision making, and stress tolerance. There are three competencies that make up each of the five major composites, for a total of fifteen EQ competencies.

◇◇◇◇◇◇◇◇◇◇◇◇◇◇

Don't eliminate certain dreams because you lack the skills or experience.

◇◇◇◇◇◇◇◇◇◇◇◇◇◇

Self-perception is understanding your own emotions, and includes *self-regard*—respecting oneself or confidence, *self-actualization*—pursuit of meaning or self-improvement, and *emotional self-awareness*—understanding own emotions.

To improve your *self-regard*, try to let go of negative self-talk and reinforce positive beliefs about yourself. This is especially important for women because women engage in negative self-talk much more often than men. Another suggestion is to have conversations with people you respect and are close to—ask them what they see as your strengths and weaknesses and why. This will give you objective data to confirm whether your self-beliefs are in line with what others see.[14] Finally, get physically stronger. Yoga, Pilates, weights, and fitness training can all give a boost of confidence.

To improve *self-actualization*, don't eliminate certain dreams because you lack the skills or experience. Be open to possibilities because you can learn new skills if you have the passion. Recall that the brain can build new neural pathways giving us a vast capacity to learn. Another idea is to find a mentor either within or outside your organization. Mentorship is a proven way to get exposed to new areas, develop new skills, build relationships, and see new opportunities which can all lead you down the path toward your dreams.

To improve *emotional self-awareness*, think about what signals you are sending other people, both verbally and non-verbally. Does your behavior really match your feelings? Have you heard the saying, "Do as I say, not as I do"? Often, our behavior does not reflect how we truly feel, and is sometimes contradictory. It takes lots of time and reflection for our internal self to be aligned with our external self. Another suggestion is to try and pick up on the emotional cues of others. What do their facial expressions, tone of voice, choice of words, and body language tell you about their mood?[15] By practicing picking up on the smallest cues from others, it will improve your own emotional self-awareness.

<><><><><><><><><><><><>

Obstacles to independent behavior may be rooted in low self-regard, and dependent people are driven by fear.

<><><><><><><><><><><><>

Self-expression is the ability to express your emotions effectively, and includes *emotional expression*—constructive expression of emotions, *assertiveness*—non-offensive communication of feelings and beliefs, and *independence*—self-directed and free from emotional dependency.

To improve *emotional expression*, count to ten. Seems simple, but really works because it shifts the focus from your emotions to counting and breathing, which causes you to relax and pause before speaking. This allows time for your neocortex or rational brain to develop a clearer perspective of the situation and keep your emotions from taking over.[16] Also, when expressing emotions at work, try to back up your emotions with business rationale to explain the source of your emotions. Remember when Lisa cried during a performance review? If she would have said something along the lines of, "Jim, I'm nervous about this because the last time we restructured the division, people were upset and we lost several top performers. I'm worried we may lose good talent again." This statement tells him the source of what made her cry, and knowing this information, he may not have viewed her as unstable, unable to handle stress, or too emotional.

To improve *assertiveness*, be aware of situations in which you hold back, not saying what is on your mind. Over the next two weeks, write down situations in which you behave assertively, passively, or aggressively. List your self-talk that accompanies each situation. What are the reasons you were unable to be assertive? Do you see a pattern? If you are high on assertiveness, one thing you can do is be mindful of times when you interrupt others. For example, interrupting others in a meeting is a sign that you are no longer being respectful, and have crossed the line between passive and aggressive. If this occurs, openly apologize to the interrupted person and be silent until it is your time to speak.

To improve *independence*, examine your level of self-regard and self-esteem. Obstacles to independent behavior may be rooted in low self-regard, and dependent people are driven by fear.[17] Write down what you are fearful of and actions you can take to overcome these fears. Another idea is to reframe the way you look at problems. Treat mistakes and failures as opportunities to learn. Standing alone involves pushing the envelope, taking chances, and suggesting bold initiatives. Challenge yourself—you may be pleasantly surprised.

◇◇◇◇◇◇◇◇◇◇◇◇◇◇◇

Take the time to really listen to what others are saying and reflect their statements and feelings.

◇◇◇◇◇◇◇◇◇◇◇◇◇◇◇

The Interpersonal EQ composite is needed to develop and maintain healthy relationships. It includes *interpersonal relationships*—mutually satisfying relationships, *empathy*—understanding and appreciating how others feel, and *social responsibility*—social consciousness and being helpful.

To improve *interpersonal relationships*, there are lots of things we can do. For example, greet people by name and make a concerted effort to learn and remember names. This helps make a personal connection and shows that you care. Examine your method for giving feedback and recognition to others. Do you provide constructive feedback? How often do you meet with them? Do you celebrate birthdays, promotions, or a job well done? Do you know what type of recognition they prefer—public or private? Another suggestion is to identify someone whose relationship with you is ineffective. What have you done to earn this person's trust and willingness to help you? Meet and arrive at action play to support one another's mutual needs.

To improve *empathy*, practice your listening skills. Are you truly listening or waiting to speak? Often, we are just waiting for a pause in the conversation so we can jump in with our opinion. Take the time to really listen to what others are saying and reflect their statements and feelings so they know you're with them. To practice empathy and put yourself in the shoes of others, regularly ask yourself, "If I were this person, how would I respond or feel?" There's no better way to build a trusting relationship than with empathy. Finally, with some of your lesser known colleagues, take the time to connect with them on topics outside of their field of work, such as children, sports, current events, or travel. People generally enjoy talking about themselves, and it makes us all feel good when people know us personally.

To improve *social responsibility*, write down one thing per week you could do to help others—at work, home, or in your community. It could be helping your department set up a fundraising activity, mentoring a new employee, donating blood, volunteering for a committee, or participating in a charitable event. How often do you do these things? What was your role? What was the effect on you? What was the effect on others? Look for areas where you have gaps in your active roles. Are you more socially responsible at work than in your community, or vice versa? Create for yourself a new role with a group of people or with a cause you have not previously engaged in.

◇◇◇◇◇◇◇◇◇◇◇◇◇◇◇

Practice holding back your first response long enough to think of your second, and then your third response, before you act.

◇◇◇◇◇◇◇◇◇◇◇◇◇◇◇

Decision making is using emotions to make better decisions, and includes *problem solving*—finding solutions when emotions are involved, *reality testing*—being objective and seeing things as they really are, and *impulse control*—resisting or delaying the impulse to act.

To improve *problem solving*, write down a problem you have experienced this week. Was it a technical problem or interpersonal difficulty? How did you attempt to solve it? Was there anyone else involved? Was the outcome positive or negative? To ensure you fully understand a problem, create more opportunities at work to solve problems together, such as organizing teams that deal with problems as they arise. Emotions play different roles in the decision-making process. Another suggestion is to identify ways to generate a positive mood to help you stay open to ideas and brainstorm creative solutions, such as listening to music, exercising or talking with a friend.

To improve *reality testing*, try framing situations from many different perspectives—think about the stakeholders, your employees, your manager, and the organization when weighing decisions. To determine whether you see things as they really are, do others indicate that you tend to overlook problems or minimize difficulties? Do you sweat the small stuff and think everything is a catastrophe? If so, consider talking to others and getting feedback. Search for objective evidence to support what you are feeling and thinking when assessing a situation, and try to develop a pragmatic, show-me-the-evidence approach.

To improve *impulse control*, know that people often say or do the first thing that occurs to them. Practice holding back your first response long enough to think of your second, and then your third, before you act. This technique is also very effective in minimizing bias, because it causes your brain to pause long enough for your unconscious biases to become conscious biases. More about bias will be discussed in upcoming chapters. Other questions to consider—are you a perfectionist? Are you impatient? If you tend to be a perfectionist, lack of control and outbursts occurs when things don't go as you planned. Try to put some slack in your plans, list worst-case scenarios, and don't be so hard on yourself. If you tend to be impatient, then impulse control issues surface because you can't accept delay of what you want. Try to be more patient of others and make a habit of listening more and talking less.

◇◇◇◇◇◇◇◇◇◇◇◇◇◇◇

Do someone a favor. This allows you to shift from being a problem sufferer to a problem solver, and put problems in perspective.

◇◇◇◇◇◇◇◇◇◇◇◇◇◇◇

Stress management is coping with challenges, and includes *flexibility*—adapting your emotions, thoughts and behaviors, *stress tolerance*—coping with stressful situations, and *optimism*—having a positive attitude and outlook on life.

To improve *flexibility*, know that low self-awareness and negative self-talk are key to flexibility. Anytime you see yourself as being inflexible, push yourself to be more open to new ideas and new ways of doing things. Write down three small things you'd ordinarily be afraid to try. Pick one and commit to doing it this week; once you've done that, work your way down the list. Try using a "what if" mindset. If you tend to be resistant to change (as many people are), solicit the opinions of trusted colleagues and embrace their views on a specific problem or issue. In a team environment, it is very important to make sure your colleagues are aware of any changes you are thinking about and embracing, then try to document your reasons for the change. This will go a long way in instilling trust and gaining buy-in from your colleagues.[18]

To improve *stress tolerance*, when the going gets tough, go elsewhere. Don't be afraid to physically remove yourself from a situation that feels stressful. Recuse yourself from a meeting, talk a walk outside, talk to your colleagues. It is not only okay to do this in a stressful situation, but encouraged. Be vigilant that you are not taking on too much—this is especially true for women who are trying to balance work and life responsibilities. Subtle changes in your emotions may signal that you are close to exhaustion, so it's important to pay attention to little cues. Finally, one of my favorite suggestions I often give to audiences is to do someone a favor. This allows you to shift the focus from being a problem sufferer to a problem solver, and helps put problems in perspective.

To improve *optimism,* write down typical scenarios in which your pessimism seems to emerge, then shift gears to look for positive ways out of these situations. Also, think about someone who is eternally optimistic. What can you learn from them? What do you observe in your interactions with them? Another simple but effective suggestion is to smile and laugh more. When you do, your face sends signals to your brain that you are happy. Your brain literally responds to the nerves and muscles in your face to determine your emotional state.[19] So, how can this help your optimism? When you're stuck in a frustrating thought or situation and are feeling pessimistic, forcing yourself to smile or laugh counteracts the negative emotional state. Another benefit is that other people will likely respond to you positively, which will lift your mood, and in turn, makes you see the situation more optimistically.

◇◇◇◇◇◇◇◇◇◇◇◇◇◇◇◇

Power poses increase testosterone levels and decrease cortisol levels, which are correlated with leadership.

◇◇◇◇◇◇◇◇◇◇◇◇◇◇◇◇

Finally, I have one last suggestion for those who want to improve their EQ competencies of self-regard and assertiveness. Amy Cuddy, social psychologist at Harvard Business School, has done extensive work on "power posing." She showed that by standing in an open, powerful, space-occupying position for two minutes—such as Wonder Woman with legs spread and hands on hips, or the Starfish with legs spread and arms high in the air—can give us a feeling of power, even if we don't feel powerful at the time.

These power poses increase testosterone levels and decrease cortisol levels, which are correlated with leadership. Testosterone is associated with confidence, assertiveness, competition, and risk tolerance. Cortisol, which is our stress hormone, is associated with stress, anxiety, insecurity, fear, less confidence, and risk avoidance. Her data shows that our bodies change our minds, our minds change our behavior, and our behavior changes our outcomes. Her mantra is "Fake it until you become it."

I was fortunate to meet Dr. Cuddy at a conference two years ago, and we discussed my research on emotional intelligence, women, and leadership. Since her data shows that testosterone is associated with confidence, assertiveness, and risk-taking, I asked her if it meant that men were more effective leaders because they have higher levels of testosterone than women. I was pleased with her response. She said that it's not about the amount of basal or circulating testosterone initially; it's about the change in testosterone *relative* to cortisol—and both genders can change testosterone and cortisol levels. So, it's not about what you start with, it's about the amount of change. Thus, women can be equally effective leaders as men. She has a great TED talk on the subject that you might want to check out.

Summary Points

- Goleman suggests EQ consists of four personal and social competencies—self-awareness, self-management, social awareness, and social management.
- Bar-On suggests EQ consists of five emotional and social competencies—self-perception, self-expression, interpersonal skills, decision making, and stress tolerance.
- Who we are and how we express ourselves results from the combination of our personality, IQ and EQ.
- EQ brings the limbic (emotional) and neocortex (rational) brains together, and emotions are critical to rational thinking.

- Men and women are equally emotionally intelligent, but strong in different areas considered gender-specific.
- EQ attributes or competencies play a significant role in how we perceive men and women as leaders in the workplace.
- Empathy is the one EQ competency where women markedly outperform men.
- Emotional intelligence is strongly tied to both leadership and job performance.
- Authoritative, coercive, and pacesetting leadership styles are considered male styles; whereas, affiliative and democratic styles are deemed feminine leadership styles.
- The natural leadership strengths that women possess have a positive impact on organizational culture.
- Several specific and practical strategies can be applied to improve your emotional intelligence.

Reflection Questions

✓ Have you ever had an emotional intelligence assessment? If so, do you know which model it was?

✓ If you haven't had an assessment, in which EQ competencies do you think you would score the highest? In which would you score the lowest?

✓ What have you done to improve your EQ competencies?

✓ At your organization, are your EQ competencies valued or not? Can you think of an example?

✓ How are you perceived as a leader? Has your EQ helped or hindered your career advancement? Your interpersonal relationships? Your job performance?

✓ Do you express emotions openly when you give speeches? Do you include emotional content to inspire followers?

✓ What is your preferred type of EQ leadership style? Has it been effective for you? How do others respond to this style? Can you think of an example?

✓ What specific EQ strategies will you use to improve your EQ competencies?

FOUR

A Bit of Research Goes a Long Way

A mind is stretched by a new idea or sensation, and never shrinks back to its former dimensions.
Oliver Wendell Holmes

For more than twenty years, I worked in the biopharmaceutical industry in various roles, including sales, marketing, medical affairs, research and development, and training and development. In these roles, I could both observe and experience gender differences across many aspects of work and life—such as attitudes, ambitions, preferences, behaviors, styles, and leadership.

I was lucky to have had many supportive and collaborative peers, but I've also seen the other side of the coin—peers who were focused solely on self-interests. I've seen colleagues who were 100 percent committed to their jobs, and others who were 100 percent disengaged. I've had both great bosses and terrible bosses, and have watched talented, high performers leave companies they loved because of their bosses. I've seen hardworking, ambitious men and women advance, and I've seen others promoted who were less deserving. But in most cases, I've watched men climb the ladder and witnessed years of struggle and frustration for many women who both wanted and tried to advance. It doesn't have to be this way, nor should it.

◇◇◇◇◇◇◇◇◇◇◇◇◇◇

Only 4 percent of CEOs at Fortune 500 companies are women.

◇◇◇◇◇◇◇◇◇◇◇◇◇◇

As mentioned in the introduction, when I began my doctoral studies in organizational leadership, I knew from the beginning I wanted to research the topics of leadership and gender. I was both concerned and intrigued when I first saw the leadership gap statistics in early 2000s, and I wanted to find out what was driving those numbers. How could women comprise more than half of all management and professional occupations, obtain most educational degrees, and makeup less than 5 percent of female CEOs? The math just doesn't add up and highlights an enormously wide and disturbing leadership gender gap.

As we learned in the last chapter, the concept of EQ, rather than IQ, is a key driver in life success, work success, and leadership effectiveness. Men and women are equal in overall scores, but strong in different areas considered gender-specific. Most companies that promote and sell EQ assessments tend to minimize gender differences, if addressed at all, because it doesn't impact the overall EQ scores, which is valid. However, I sensed that these gender differences might have more of an impact in the workplace than what was being discussed. Thus, I combined the topics of leadership, emotional intelligence and gender for my dissertation research.

Nuts and Bolts

So, what's the problem? The problem is that women enter professional and managerial ranks in equal or greater numbers than men, yet very few hold senior leadership positions. Although women have made some strides in the past decades, men still occupy far more positions that confer decision-making authority and the ability to influence other's pay or promotions.[1] Even though overall EQ scores are the same, the different strengths that men and women possess has not proven to be an asset for women's career advancement across any industry, government, or organization.

I administered EQ assessments and conducted in-depth interviews with numerous women at various levels of a *Fortune* 500 pharmaceutical company to yield both quantitative and qualitative data. The levels were vice president, director, manager, and administrative assistant. The women varied widely in years of experience, level of leadership, breadth and depth of knowledge, age, race, formal education, marital status, and whether they had children. There were also wide ranges observed in both their total EQ scores and in specific EQ competencies.

◇◇◇◇◇◇◇◇◇◇◇◇◇◇◇◇

A natural shift to a more gender-balanced senior management should be a reasonable, expected outcome.

◇◇◇◇◇◇◇◇◇◇◇◇◇◇◇◇

The overall purpose was to understand each participant lived experiences with leadership, career advancement, emotional intelligence, and gender bias or barriers. I also wanted to see if any differences emerged with respect to different generations—Veterans, Baby Boomers, Generation X, and Millennials.

Why is this important? The study relates to the ability of corporations to leverage the enormous pool of talent inherent in their employees. Given that women account for more than half of professional workforces, a natural shift to a more gender-balanced senior management *should* be a reasonable, expected outcome. At 4 percent of CEOs, and 15 percent of executive officers, women's talents are not being utilized at our biggest and most powerful companies.

When corporations seek to develop new leaders, the female employee population is clearly underrepresented. If companies tap their female employees, it would have a positive impact on diversity both in middle management and the board of directors. In addition, stakeholders of a corporation expect that the company will appropriately manage and maximize their resources, including human capital. If companies poorly manage resources, they stand to lose investors.

Quotes and Results

When analyzing each participant's assessment results and interview responses, and crossing it with the literature, I began to see themes, and a clear difference emerged between the groups when looking at gender-specific EQ attributes. I found that women at the highest leadership level in the study, vice presidents, had group mean EQ scores that were higher in male-specific competencies—such as confidence, assertiveness, and stress tolerance. I also found that women at the middle manager level had group mean EQ scores that were higher in female-specific competencies—such as interpersonal relationships, empathy, and social responsibility. The data suggests that women adapt and exhibit more male EQ attributes as they rise to ranks of leadership. Let's look more in depth.

The vice presidents were higher in the decision making and self-expression composites than the director, manager, or administrative assistant groups of women. The decision-making composite includes problem solving, reality testing, and impulse control, and the self-expression composite includes emotional expression, assertiveness, and independence. These are consistent with stereotypically viewed leader traits that are associated with males. The first few questions in the interview centered on specific EQ attributes, their effect on each participant's career advancement, and whether these traits were innately born or if they've worked to develop them over the span of their careers.

◇◇◇◇◇◇◇◇◇◇◇◇◇◇◇◇◇

Women adapt and exhibit more male EQ attributes as they rise to ranks of leadership.

◇◇◇◇◇◇◇◇◇◇◇◇◇◇◇◇◇

When asked, "Which EQ attributes do you believe have contributed most to your career advancement?", the most frequent responses cited by all participants were *self-regard, assertiveness, interpersonal relationships, problem solving*, and *stress tolerance*. These are typically male-specific with the exception of interpersonal relationships, which is considered female–specific. Women at all levels agreed that these attributes helped get them to where they are in their career.

Interestingly, some participants noted that the one EQ attribute that had a *negative* effect on their career advancement was emotional expression. Remember the example of Lisa, the VP, that was discussed in the last chapter? Half of the participants gave examples of negative responses from their managers when they expressed emotions at work, such as crying or having emotional reactions to situations. They noted that women are both *perceived* and *expected* to be more emotional than men, but when emotions were expressed, it led to negative impressions from their bosses. A classic catch-22 situation.

Regarding nature versus nurture, some of the women felt that these traits were innate, but others had to work to develop them in order to obtain leadership positions or be perceived as a leader by their superiors, peers, and direct reports. Our level of emotional intelligence is not fixed genetically, nor does it develop only in early childhood. Unlike IQ, which changes little after our teen years, emotional intelligence seems to be largely learned, and continues to develop as we journey through life and learn from our experiences.[2] Thus, our EQ competence keeps growing.

◇◇◇◇◇◇◇◇◇◇◇◇◇◇◇◇

Middle managers scored significantly higher in interpersonal relationships than women in top leadership positions.

◇◇◇◇◇◇◇◇◇◇◇◇◇◇◇◇

In contrast to women at both the vice president and director levels, women at the middle manager level scored significantly higher in the interpersonal composite, which includes empathy, interpersonal relationships, and social responsibility—and exceeded the women who were in top leadership positions. Remember that successful middle managers must use a broad range of emotional intelligence competencies to get things done, and exercise a great deal of influence and persuasion, all without having positional power. Women are exceptionally strong in this area and these traits occur naturally for many women.

The next interview questions pertained to whether women want to be promoted to leadership, how being a woman has impacted their career aspirations, and what EQ attributes are most valued in leaders at their organization. I deliberately asked the question about desires to be promoted because the assumption should not be made that all women want to advance and be promoted, and that is exactly what the data showed. One-third of the women in the study had no desire to move up, and the distribution broke evenly across all four groups—vice president, director, manager, and administrative assistant.

The reasons given for not wanting to advance were, "This job matches my skill sets," "I don't want to lead," "My work-life balance is more important," "I'm as high as I want to go," and "I don't want the stress and politics at the next level." I've heard these comments repeated by women at various organizations, conferences, professional associations, social media, and in the classroom—and it reflects differences in what men and women want, value, perceive, and experience.

◇◇◇◇◇◇◇◇◇◇◇◇◇◇

Men care more about attaining the next level, women care more about being fulfilled in their work.

◇◇◇◇◇◇◇◇◇◇◇◇◇◇

I asked the participants how being a woman has influenced their career aspirations, and the responses varied widely. Among the VP and director groups, only two women felt that being a woman has not affected their career choices at all, while others have sacrificed marriage, children, or both for their careers. Many women felt that stereotypes have held them back, such as Shari's comment in chapter three that, "Men assume a woman can't be empathetic and analytical at same time." The administrative assistants agreed, citing stereotypes of female roles as primary reasons for their lack of career advancement. One woman has only been in traditionally female roles, another woman passed up promotions because her husband was breadwinner, and another cited her upbringing by saying she was taught, "Women were supposed to either get married, or be a secretary, nurse, or flight attendant".

Interestingly, Diane, who was VP of global learning and organizational development, sees women as having an advantage at work *because* of stereotypes. In society, more pressure is put on men to continually advance in their career, and most men's identities and sense of self-worth are closely tied to their jobs. In general, men care more about attaining the next level, and women care more about being fulfilled in their work regardless of the level. Even today, many men are validated by their careers. As a VP, Diane had no desire to advance to the next step, executive VP, which would require interfacing with the board of directors and being at their beck and call—with little to no work-life balance. As a woman, she felt no pressure to move on, unlike her male colleagues who were constantly pushed and expected to advance. Thus, she feels that women have more choices at work and men are more limited because of gender stereotypes.

◇◇◇◇◇◇◇◇◇◇◇◇◇◇◇◇◇

Work-life choices can make women more focused and productive than men at work.

◇◇◇◇◇◇◇◇◇◇◇◇◇◇◇◇◇

Kayla, a systems manager in the medical affairs division, also feels that females have an advantage at work *because* of work-life balance priorities. Kayla has two daughters, one is six years old and the other is six months old. Because of her parenting demands, she works more efficiently when she's at work, so that she's not forced to take work home with her. She's learned that if she's focused and productive, she can control her work output, which is important, because as much as she tries, she can't control parenthood. Thus, she is super-efficient during the allotted work hours, and can shift attention to her family when she goes home. Kayla also stated that pursuit of goals and dreams, called self-actualization in EQ terms, can be more difficult for women because of the work-life choices they must make. However, it can make women more efficient than men at work, and more balanced long-term.

When asked, "What EQ attributes are most valued in leaders at your organization?", the top three attributes cited were assertiveness, problem solving, and interpersonal relationships, in that order. Other attributes valued in leaders were stress tolerance, reality testing, independence, and self-regard. Note that this is similar to the responses given when asked, "Which EQ attributes do you believe have contributed most to your career advancement?" The good news is that what helps women most in their careers—self-regard, assertiveness, and interpersonal relationships—is also what is most valued at their organization. Think about your organization. What attributes are truly valued in your leaders? Do they align with your strengths?

Further interview questions focused on understanding gender bias and discrimination because of their specific EQ attributes. Most women in all four groups experienced some type of gender discrimination—which can come from men and women. One VP who is strong in male attributes stated that "People have a difficult time accepting me as a leader because they *expect* an empathetic woman". This is the exact opposite from Shari's experience, who is strong in empathy, but *not* viewed as a leader. What this illustrates is that it doesn't matter if a woman is high in male or high in female-specific EQ attributes, she is still subject to bias and discrimination.

◇◇◇◇◇◇◇◇◇◇◇◇◇◇◇◇

When it comes to assertiveness, women are viewed as either bulldogs or puppy dogs.

◇◇◇◇◇◇◇◇◇◇◇◇◇◇◇◇

One of the director-level women who is strong in male attributes—she's independent and assertive—has encountered challenges with other women. Laura was director of project team communication and training within the project management division. She found that other women were threatened by her independence and viewed her as a non-team player, which insulted them personally. In contrast, men liked her independence because in her words, "Men don't want hassles." When it comes to assertiveness, women are viewed as extremes—either a bulldog or puppy dog. Since Laura is strongly assertive, she's seen as a bulldog most of the time, which intimidates or turns off other women. As a result, she finds it difficult to work with her female colleagues.

So, how does gender bias and discrimination because of EQ contribute to the leadership gap? First, our interpersonal relationships play a strong role. Men hire men similar to themselves—those high in confidence, assertiveness, and independence—*not* those high in empathy and social responsibility. Also, men network more with other men, which keeps the number of men in leadership at a high level.

Second, women who are high in empathy are not generally viewed as strong leaders, which is based on nothing more than bias. Third, there's a double standard in our expression of assertiveness. When men are assertive, they are viewed as confident go-getters. When women are assertive, they are viewed as aggressive or bossy. Fourth, there's a double standard in our perception of independence. Independent men are viewed as strong and taking initiative, whereas independent women are seen as non-social or poor team players.

◇◇◇◇◇◇◇◇◇◇◇◇◇◇◇◇

The double standards need to stop and we need to change our antiquated, old-fashioned ways of perceiving men and women at work.

◇◇◇◇◇◇◇◇◇◇◇◇◇◇◇◇

Fifth, our emotional self-expression falls victim to bias and discrimination. When men display emotions at work—even anger—they are viewed as either assertive or bold. When women display emotions, like anger or crying, they are viewed as unstable or unable to handle stress. All these aspects of EQ contribute to the leadership gender gap. These double standards need to stop and we need to change our antiquated, old-fashioned ways of *perceiving* men and women at work.

Finally, my data showed that the two oldest women, an administrative assistant who was sixty-six years old, and a vice president who was sixty-two years old, had the highest overall emotional intelligence scores of 133 and 128, respectively—well above the average EQ-i 2.0 assessment score of one hundred.[3] This is consistent with the literature that EQ increases as we age, and increases with every generation—from Millennials having the lowest EQ on average to veterans having the highest. I expected that the oldest participants would have higher total EQ scores, but I did not expect that some of the women with the highest scores would be in the lowest level positions. Therefore, high total EQ scores are *not* correlated with the leadership position we are in.

In the last set of interview questions, I asked the participants which attribute they felt has improved the most as they have aged. Their answer? Stress tolerance. As women and men age, they cope much better to the stresses of work and life compared to their younger counterparts. We are more relaxed, focused, and able to put things in perspective and context. Other attributes that were reported as improved with age are problem solving, empathy, self-regard, interpersonal relationships, and impulse control.

What Does It Mean?

My expected outcome was that the participants in both the vice president and director groups would have higher total EQ scores than participants in either the manager or administrative assistant groups because of the professional level they had reached. The data; however, showed the opposite. Women in the middle manager group had the highest overall group scores. It is interesting that even though those in formal leadership positions were higher in male-specific EQ attributes, the manager group was highest in both overall EQ scores, *and* highest in female-specific EQ attributes.

Thus, EQ peaks at the middle manager level, then drops steadily downward. This is consistent with other studies which show that CEOs, on average, have the lowest EQ scores in the workplace.[4] Why would this be? You might think that the higher the position, the better the people skills. Unfortunately, too many leaders are promoted because of what they know, who they know, or how long they've worked, rather than their skill of managing others. As I found in my research, once a man *or* woman reaches the top, they spend less time cultivating relationships and interacting with staff. Yet, among executives, those with the highest EQ scores are the best performers, and the same holds true for every other job title—those with the highest EQ scores within any position outperform their peers.

◇◇◇◇◇◇◇◇◇◇◇◇◇◇◇

EQ peaks at the middle manager level then drops steadily downward.

◇◇◇◇◇◇◇◇◇◇◇◇◇◇◇

Given that women score higher in interpersonal relationships than men, why would executive women spend less time leveraging this skill? I have two hypotheses for you to consider. First, as women climb the corporate ladder, many adapt and exhibit more male—and less female—EQ skills because that's what's expected of them as leaders. Second, interpersonal relationships are one of the five EQ competencies cited by the participants as having the most impact on their career advancement. Women managers had the highest levels of this skill, while women VPs were low. This suggests that even though this skill is considered valuable for a woman's success, it is not valued in leaders as much as the other EQ attributes.

Emotional intelligence and leadership are closely related concepts. The findings of my study confirm this, but the data also illustrate that the reasons for the leadership gender gap is multi-factorial, and goes much deeper than emotional intelligence or leadership alone. As a researcher, I had to ask the question, "Does having a high EQ always lead to success?" The answer is no. However, most experts conclude that intellectual ability or IQ accounts for only 10 to 20 percent of work and life success, and most of the rest of the factors involve emotional intelligence. A growing body of research also supports a significant association between diverse measures of EQ and job performance, particularly in positions requiring social and interpersonal competence.[5] The bottom line is that, with all other things being equal, EQ can drastically improve individual, leadership, and group job performance.

EQ Advice

As noted earlier, five EQ competencies came up repeatedly as having the most impact on career success, and the ones to focus on to advance. These were *self-regard, assertiveness, interpersonal relationships, problem solving,* and *stress tolerance.* In other words, you have to have confidence in your abilities, you have to speak up for what you want and care about, you have to build strong relationships, you have to be able to address issues, and you have to manage your temperment. In chapter three, I outlined specific action steps you can take to help improve these five EQ competencies. Remember that EQ improves as we age, so with focus and effort, you can turn these attributes into bona fide strengths to boost your career advancement.

The final interview question asked was, "What advice would you give other women seeking leadership levels in terms of emotional intelligence?"

They also added other comments regarding their journey, leadership, and gender. The responses are both insightful and encouraging.

Regarding EQ, all advice focused on the seven attributes below.

- Improve self-regard – "Be confident and don't be so hard on yourself."
- Improve assertiveness – "Don't be afraid to ask for what you want."
- Improve problem solving – "Bring more value to your organization."
- Improve self-actualization – "Do what you really want to do."
- Improve stress tolerance – "Talk to others and think things through."
- Control emotional expression – "Don't overly express emotions."
- Don't lose empathy – "It's important and people appreciate it."

Here is their advice about their journey, leadership and gender.

- "Be an authentic woman and don't be afraid to be feminine."
- "Seek both male and female mentors and ask for advice often."
- "Look for opportunities to serve as mentor to other women."
- "Reach out and cultivate a strong network, and put the effort in to maintain it."
- "Know your brand and be clear about your strengths and what you have to offer."
- "If you're not confident in something, go figure it out and acquire the skills needed."
- "Do things that are valued in your organization and talk about them more."
- "Remember that everything is a learning opportunity, so be patient and observe."
- "Don't get stuck in your generation (e.g., Baby Boomer or Generation X), branch out, learn new things, and connect with younger generations."

These suggestions stem from a cross-functional, multi-generational population of women, and reflect not only the collective lived experiences of the study group, but the shared experiences of millions of career-minded women across the globe. They serve as powerful advice to help women who are seeking to advance in their careers in terms of leadership, emotional intelligence, and gender.

◇◇◇◇◇◇◇◇◇◇◇◇◇◇◇

Men and women have different perceptions of the issues, different perceptions of each other, and different perceptions of themselves.

◇◇◇◇◇◇◇◇◇◇◇◇◇◇◇

This chapter summarized my research on these topics We discussed the nuts, bolts, quotes, and results, what they mean, how they contribute to the leadership gap, and discussed participant advice. We are well into the twenty-first century, and *still* looking at stats that show less than 5 percent women at the helm of the biggest companies. Why is it that the data on diversity and the benefits of women leaders are falling on deaf ears? Why has the number of women in leadership barely budged in the last thirty years? The answer is because men and women have different *perceptions* of the issues, different *perceptions* of each other, and different *perceptions* of themselves. Now, let's explore the barriers that keep women from advancing into leadership positions.

Summary Points

- The problem is that women enter professional and managerial ranks in equal or greater numbers than men, yet very few hold senior leadership positions.
- Women and men are equally emotionally intelligent, but this has not proven to be an asset for women's career advancement across *any* industry, government, or organization.

- Dissertation participants included women at four levels of a *Fortune 500* company—vice president, director, manager, and administrative assistant.
- Participants were given EQ assessments followed by in-depth interviews to yield both quantitative and qualitative data.
- Women at the vice president level had group mean EQ scores that were higher in male-specific competencies—confidence, assertiveness and stress tolerance.
- Women at the middle manager level scored significantly higher in female-specific competencies—empathy, interpersonal relationships, and social responsibility.
- Five EQ attributes were cited by all participants as having the most impact on career advancement—self-regard, assertiveness, interpersonal relationships, problem solving, and stress tolerance.
- EQ peaks at the middle manager level, but for titles of director and above, it drops steadily downward.
- Men and women have different perceptions of the issues, different perceptions of each other, and different perceptions of themselves.
- Study participants share advice on a woman's journey, leadership, gender, and emotional intelligence.

Reflection Questions

✓ What has been your career advancement experience? What have you observed with your peers? Your bosses? Your direct reports?

✓ Have you ever adapted or changed your behaviors as you've climbed the corporate ladder? Can you think of an example or two?

✓ Have you ever cried in front of your boss? Was his/her reaction positive or negative? What was the outcome? Did anything change in your relationship with your boss?

✓ How has being a woman positively or negatively impacted your career aspirations, if at all?

✓ Have you ever self-selected out of a leadership or potential leadership role? If so, what were the reasons? If you could do it again, would you accept that leadership role?

✓ Do you feel that women have an advantage at work, due to stereotypes, work-life priorities, or other factors? If so, how can you leverage this?

✓ What EQ attributes are truly valued in leaders at your organization? Do they align with your strengths?

✓ Have you ever experienced gender bias or discrimination because of your EQ attributes? What was the outcome?

✓ How strong are you in the five EQ competencies that were cited as having the most impact on career success—self-regard, assertiveness, interpersonal relationships, problem solving, and stress tolerance? Which of the actionable strategies in chapter three will you implement to improve these competencies?

PART II

Barriers and Perceptions

FIVE

The Power of Bias

Be who you are and say what you feel, because those who mind don't
matter and those who matter don't mind.
Dr. Seuss

J anet is in a meeting with twelve of her colleagues. The goal is to come
up with solutions for a problem that has arisen on the team project. Janet
suggests a solution that has not been tried before, but her suggestion
goes unacknowledged and is largely disregarded by the group. Ten minutes
later, John suggests the same solution as Janet, using slightly different words.
Several people comment on and praise John's suggestion as something that
should be explored further.

So, what happened here? The technical name for it is *unintentional
invisible bias*. It's when female voices simply are not heard. This occurs
frequently in meetings, and for many women—from front line worker to

CEO—this is a shared global experience. As the name implies, this type of bias is unintentional, and most people are unaware of it when it happens. In most cases, it's men who do not hear women's voices, and in some cases, men experience this bias as well. Because of this dynamic, women often don't speak up or limit their comments in meetings. The danger is that this type of bias deprives organizations of valuable ideas.

First, let's define bias. Bias is a prejudice in favor of or against a person, thing, or group compared with another, usually in a way considered to be unfair. It can also be defined as a deep-seated resistance to the different—any kind of different. Can be gender, race, ethnicity, age, height, weight, religion, culture, sexual orientation, gender identity, personality type, disability, pregnancy/children, socio-economic status, and even introverts.

◇◇◇◇◇◇◇◇◇◇◇◇◇◇

Numerous studies point to gender bias as the fundamental issue concerning women's advancement.

◇◇◇◇◇◇◇◇◇◇◇◇◇◇

Gender bias represents one of the major barriers that women have faced for decades, including the concepts of gender stereotyping, role congruity theory, agentic leader behaviors, and the impact of social expectations about how women and men are supposed to behave. Numerous studies point to gender bias as the fundamental issue concerning women's advancement.[1] Bias significantly impacts the perception of women in general, of women leaders, and of gender-specific emotional intelligence competencies. To overcome these societal barriers, both individuals and organizations must take steps to eliminate biases; otherwise, women leaders will continue to be undermined and misjudged regardless of their abilities.

Unconscious Bias

Bias used to be blatant. Cindy, a colleague of mine who runs a networking group in southern California, shared with me that when she worked in aerospace in the 1980s, men would have Playboy pinup calendars in their offices and cubicles. Can you imagine walking down the hall at your company and seeing pictures of naked women openly displayed? Seems absurd now, but back then, overt sexism and racism were common. Fortunately, society has evolved and we've made progress in that area.

Today, however, bias is still prevalent, but is more hidden and subtle. And, it often comes in the form of almost imperceptible differences in opportunity. For example, an introduction not made, key information not shared, or an event invitation not given. If you are on the receiving end, these subtleties can have a tremendous impact on your ability to network with key stakeholders, acquire more customers, keep current on market opportunities, and succeed in your job.

◇◇◇◇◇◇◇◇◇◇◇◇◇◇◇◇

Today, bias is still prevalent, but is more hidden and subtle.

◇◇◇◇◇◇◇◇◇◇◇◇◇◇◇◇

You may have heard the term *unconscious bias*. It's a recent and emerging field of social psychology, cognitive sciences, and neurosciences. Our brain has two types of processes, conscious and unconscious—and most our day we operate through unconscious or habitual processes. Research has found that it's not as much the conscious, explicit, or overt bias that causes barriers, misunderstandings, and limits potential, but the unconscious, implicit, or hidden biases that are really problematic.

These hidden, reflexive preferences shape our world views and can profoundly affect how welcoming and open a workplace is to different people and ideas. Further, these unconscious predispositions shape the decisions we make by affecting the way we interpret information and how we evaluate and interact with others. Part of what drives these hidden biases lies in neuroscience. Our brain is wired to make lightning-fast decisions that draw on a variety of assumptions and experiences. This is great for survival and fight-or-flight instincts—the next time you are running from a bear you'll be thankful for this system!

Nonetheless, this system often results in misguided generalizations while dismissing subtle, more important distinctions. In addition, our brain empathizes with those who are like us. For instance, when we meet someone from another race, we quickly make assumptions about their beliefs, preferences, and behaviors—and base our decisions on these assumptions. By doing this, we've overlooked individual differences based on life experiences, background, upbringing, education, knowledge, skills, and abilities. Putting people in boxes by stereotyping limits both individual potential and diversity.

◇◇◇◇◇◇◇◇◇◇◇◇◇◇◇◇◇◇

Putting people in boxes by stereotyping limits both individual potential and diversity.

◇◇◇◇◇◇◇◇◇◇◇◇◇◇◇◇◇◇

In today's organizations, there is overwhelming evidence of a strong business case for diversity and inclusion. Diversity has emerged as a business-critical factor in the ability to innovate, attract clients, and retain and cultivate the best talent amidst a changing population and often unpredictable business conditions—and bias is the key issue that undermines diversity. More on diversity and inclusion in chapter ten.

Last year, I was fortunate to meet Mahzarin Banaji, social psychologist at Harvard University and author of *Blind Spot: Hidden Biases of Good People.* Dr. Banaji talks about the widespread prevalence of unconscious bias. Did you know that female-named hurricanes take more lives than male-named hurricanes? Why? Because people take the female-named hurricanes less serious than the male-named hurricanes. In her words, this points to nothing more than our stupidity. If we are biased about the names given to weather systems, imagine the biases that we hold against each other. Another type of illogical bias can be found in the faces of infants. Since female faces are softer and closer to baby faces, women are seen as more trustworthy, but less competent than men. Men are the opposite. Men are viewed as less trustworthy, but more competent than women.

One type of unconscious bias that is particularly powerful is called *affinity bias*. This bias favor family, community, or people with whom we're connected based on shared characteristics or experiences. It can include our neighbors, members of our church, people who attended our school, people who grew up in our neighborhood, or fellow fans of our favorite sports teams. Do you have children? If so, do you feel that your children are the absolute best children in the entire world? Of course, they are! Being biased toward our loved ones is a type of affinity bias.

◇◇◇◇◇◇◇◇◇◇◇◇◇◇◇◇

Affinity bias fosters unequal opportunities that promote the status quo and limit diversity.

◇◇◇◇◇◇◇◇◇◇◇◇◇◇◇◇

Affinity bias is an urge to help someone with whom we have a bond. We may offer to get our neighbor's son an interview at our company. We may choose to mentor a new hire with a shared alma mater. We may give a scholarship to our niece. How are these things negative? A little nudge of opportunity, leads to another nudge of opportunity, which leads to another nudge of opportunity—this eventually leads to a real, tangible advantage. These behaviors foster unequal opportunities that promote the status quo and limit diversity.

For example, let's take the neighbor's son. Let's assume that you have a great relationship with your neighbor. You want to maintain this relationship, so you agree to help get his son that interview. You know of someone in another department who is hiring, and you pass along his resume to the hiring manager—bypassing the standard candidate selection process. With this one, innocent gesture, you've unwittingly given the son an advantage over other candidates. To take it further, let's assume he gets the job over more qualified candidates. In a year, he gets promoted, gets a raise, and is given more responsibility. In two years, he gets another opportunity and is promoted into a leadership position. By that one simple act of passing along his resume, he was given an advantage and is further along in his career than others who were equally or even more qualified for his position.

Now, let's apply this to gender. We hire, promote, support, and help people who are like us—not based on skills or competencies. Since the majority of leadership positions worldwide are held by men, who are men hiring, promoting, supporting, and helping? Other men. Thus, male leadership perpetuates itself and affinity bias is a big part of it. I would challenge all of you to do your best to resist the power of these natural affinities. It's one way to help break the cycle and promote more women and diversity within organizations.

So, what's the impact of unconscious bias at work? It leads to decision making that's neither optimal nor informed. It affects recruiting and hiring, promotion and succession planning, performance evaluations and compensation, team and project assignments, budget decisions, client or customer service, and openness to new sources of ideas and innovation. If unconscious bias is left unchecked, the stakes are high—talent languishes and leaves, worthwhile ideas go unheeded, the organization loses out on market opportunities, loss in revenue and productivity, client service suffers, and innovation and creativity stalls.

Bias and Gender

Let's look at the technology industry. Women who work in this industry love technology, but frequently hate the technology companies they work for—that's the conclusion of multiple research surveys recently published in the *Harvard Business Review* and *Fortune*.[2] Companies like Intel, Google, Apple, and Facebook can't seem to raise the percentage of women in their technical force above 20 percent. The overall percentage of male employees at Intel is 75 percent, Google 69 percent, Apple 68 percent, and Facebook 68 percent. Part of the reason for these numbers is the flood of women leaving after ten to fifteen years of fighting gender bias, unfriendly policies, lack of leadership opportunities, and women-hostile cultures.

New research from McKinsey, Accenture, and MIT confirm that women's thinking, versatility, and social intelligence or EQ, gives them leadership advantages desperately needed in complex, collaborative working environments. This isn't just a theory—a woman's thinking patterns improve customer-valued innovations (growth) and lean execution (profit). MIT's research is based on 156 trials of teams working to solve complex problems and the teams with the most women got the best results. The numbers are clear, and bias severely impacts both the human and financial elements of organizations.

◇◇◇◇◇◇◇◇◇◇◇◇◇◇◇◇

The problem with stereotypes is that they are incomplete and don't account for individual differences and nuances.

◇◇◇◇◇◇◇◇◇◇◇◇◇◇◇◇

Let's look at some common gender stereotypes. Men—confident leaders, competitive, inadequate communicators, driven by sex, love sports, beer, and action movies, must control TV remote, and won't ask for directions when lost. Women—caring and supportive, communal, extensive communicators, love shopping, chocolate and musicals, moody, gossip, and fixated on weddings. Of course, this is just a partial list of our assumptions about men and women. The problem with stereotypes is that they are *incomplete* and don't account for individual differences and nuances. Personally speaking, I agree with the love of chocolate and musicals, but I hate shopping. And, I know many men who are not confident leaders, and could care less about sports.

Now, let's look at how these stereotypes play out. Denise, who owns a financial advisory firm and has worked in the industry for twenty years, has many female clients. One of the reasons for this is that men assume that because she's a woman, she can't be smart or competent in finance. She shared with me that when couples seek her advice, the men find it very difficult to take direction from a woman, and as a result, switch to male financial advisors.

However, when husbands pass away, the wives often return to Denise because she listens to them, unlike many of the male advisors they had experienced.

Leena is senior director of business development at a technology company. She's worked at her company for eight years and leading comes naturally for her. She had opportunities to manage people very early in her career, and earned a reputation for her integrity, creativity, hard work, and consistency. When she delivered her first child, her boss and others assumed that she would cease to take on challenges, and her male colleagues were given opportunities to shine. Leena wanted challenges and additional responsibility, but these assumptions and stereotypes took away her opportunities.

<><><><><><><><><><><><>

The best solution is to ask your employees what they want, and make no assumptions of men or women.

<><><><><><><><><><><><>

Allison, a senior manager at a major telecommunications firm, had a similar experience. She has been with the firm for six years, and has two young children at home. She applied for a leadership role that requires more travel than her current position. She didn't get the job and was told that another candidate was more qualified. She later found out the real reason she was not given the opportunity is because her boss incorrectly assumed that because she has young children, she wouldn't want to travel and wouldn't be committed to the assignment. It is true that some women do not want additional responsibility or travel when they have children, and that is perfectly understandable. In Allison's case, she would have welcomed the travel, but was passed over because of gender stereotypes. The best solution is to ask your employees what they want, and make no assumptions of men or women.

In chapter two, we discussed role congruity theory and the examples of female military leaders and male nurses. As a society, we have specific expectations about how men and women should dress, act, and interact with others. Women are viewed positively when they meet or align themselves with the typical expectations of the female role. The same can be said for men. While gender expectations have changed throughout the years, from the Victorians to the present day, there is still a set of traits that women are expected to embody and personify. Prejudice toward female leaders occurs because inconsistencies exist between the characteristics associated with the female gender stereotype and those associated with the typical leader. In fact, one of the main causes of prejudice preventing women from achievement of high-status positions is the *perception* of women when placed in leadership roles.

◇◇◇◇◇◇◇◇◇◇◇◇◇◇◇◇

One of the main causes of prejudice is the perception of women when placed in leadership roles.

◇◇◇◇◇◇◇◇◇◇◇◇◇◇◇◇

In addition, the gender make-up of a team changes leadership dominance. In a 2004 study, women and men, based on their levels of dominance, were placed in groups consisting of either (man, man), (woman, man), or (woman, woman) and then assigned tasks randomly. Participants with higher dominance ratings emerged as leaders in all groups except for (woman, man) pairs. When tasks were of a masculine or gender-neutral nature, males emerged as leaders more often than females. These findings suggest that even when women possess dominant characteristics, masculinized tasks as well as gender stereotypes prohibit the emergence of women into leadership positions.[3]

In other words, gender differences in leader emergence persist even for dominant women. In mixed gender settings, women take a back seat to men based on assumed gender roles. These social roles contain all the direct and indirect messages a child receives growing up in their respective gender culture. Leaders, whether male or female, carry those messages around with them and those messages are part of *who* that leader is and *how* he or she performs as a leader.

Can you think of a time when you've observed this behavior, or perhaps done it yourself? I see this in the classroom every week. As a professor in Pepperdine University's MBA program, I'm privy to gender dynamics, especially in the millennial population. In classes with more females, women are more outspoken and talkative. In classes with more males, women hold back and let the men dominate conversations. Why would this be? If you're a woman who normally contributes and speaks your mind at work, home or the classroom, why would you suppress your opinions just because there are men in the room? This illustrates the power of role congruity and social expectations on women.

Negotiations are another area in which we see gender stereotypes. A popular stereotype is that women are more cooperative and pleasant in negotiations than are men. Though this is controversial, there is some truth to it. Men tend to place higher value on status, power, and recognition, whereas women tend to place higher value on compassion and altruism. Also, women tend to value relationship outcomes more than men, and men value economic outcomes more than women. These differences affect both negotiation behavior and outcomes. Compared to men, women tend to behave in a less assertive, less self-interested, and more accommodating manner. One review showed that women are more reluctant to initiate negotiations, and when they do, they ask for less, and are more willing to accept the initial offer. A study of MBA students at Carnegie-Mellon University found that male MBA students took the step of negotiating their first offer 57 percent of the time, compared to four percent for female MBA students. The net result? A $4,000 difference in starting salaries.[4]

◇◇◇◇◇◇◇◇◇◇◇◇◇◇◇◇◇◇

Men negotiate competitively; women negotiate cooperatively.

◇◇◇◇◇◇◇◇◇◇◇◇◇◇◇◇◇◇

The disparity goes even further. Because of the way women approach negotiation, other negotiators seek to exploit females by, for example, making lower salary offers. There is also some evidence that men hold a gender double standard—when women behave stereotypically, men are more likely to take advantage of the cooperative behavior, but when women behave assertively, their behavior is viewed more negatively than if the same behavior were demonstrated by men.

What can be done? As is the case with any stereotype, there is always individual variation. The good news is women can control their own negotiating behavior. For example, if economic outcomes are valued—behave aggressively. If social outcomes are valued—behave cooperatively. In addition, men and women need to know it is acceptable for each to show a full range of negotiating behaviors. Thus, a female negotiator who behaves competitively and a male negotiator who behaves cooperatively need to know they are not violating expectations.

When looking at gender variations among cultures, one of the most widely referenced approaches was done in the late 1970s by Geert Hofstede. Hofstede is a Dutch social psychologist who analyzed thousands of IBM employees in fifty-three countries and found that managers and employees vary on five value dimensions of national culture—one dimension being masculinity versus femininity. Masculinity is the degree to which the culture favors traditional masculine roles such as achievement, power, and control, as opposed to viewing men and women as equals. A high masculinity rating indicates the culture has separate roles for men and women, with men dominating the society. A high feminine rating means the culture sees little differentiation between male and female roles and treats women as equals of men in all respects.[5]

The United States scored relatively high—ranked fifteen out of fifty-three—on masculinity with most people emphasizing traditional gender roles. The country that ranked the highest is Japan, and the countries that had the lowest masculinity (and highest femininity score) were the Scandinavian countries of Denmark, Finland, Norway, and Sweden. What this means is that relative to most global nations, the American culture values male roles more than female roles. It is no wonder then, that such a large gap in leadership gender roles persists.

◇◇◇◇◇◇◇◇◇◇◇◇◇◇◇◇

Relative to most global nations, the American culture values male roles more than female roles.

◇◇◇◇◇◇◇◇◇◇◇◇◇◇◇◇

Finally, researchers at Harvard University have developed a test to help assess personal biases and measure attitudes and beliefs that people may be unwilling or unable to report. It's called the Implicit Association Test (IAT).[6] There are fourteen different tests, and two of them are gender related. One is called the Gender-Career IAT—it measures how strongly we associate males and females with career and home. Out of millions who have taken the test, 76 percent of both men and women associate men with career and women with home. Given that my areas of expertise and research centered on this topic, I was surprised to find that I also showed a "strong association" for males with career, and females with home. What these tests reveal is potential hidden biases that we may hold, as well as how deeply ingrained these beliefs can be. If you're interested, check out the IAT on the Harvard website—the tests are free and they don't take long to complete.

Bias and Leadership

When you think of a leader, what characteristics come to mind? If you're like most people, you'll say strong, competitive, confident, visionary, assertive, independent, or decisive. We rarely hear leadership characteristics like empathy, relationship-oriented, strong communicator, collaborative, compassionate, socially responsible, or supportive.

Both men and women associate leadership traits with behaviors believed to be more common or appropriate in men, such as decisive, assertive and independent—these are called *agentic leader qualities*. By contrast, women are thought to be communal—friendly, unselfish, and care-taking. These beliefs powerfully and unwittingly communicate that women are ill-suited for leadership roles and sets women up for inherent conflicts as they advance in their careers.

◇◇◇◇◇◇◇◇◇◇◇◇◇◇

*The socialization process has produced the
expectation that male qualities also happen to be
leadership qualities.*

◇◇◇◇◇◇◇◇◇◇◇◇◇◇

These gender roles create an inconsistency that exists between communal qualities and the agentic qualities associated with a leader. The problem is that leadership qualities are the same as those used to describe males because the socialization process has produced the expectation that male social qualities also happen to be leadership qualities. Therefore, the belief is that when women are in a leadership position, they should demonstrate agentic qualities, fulfilling the expectation that leaders are assertive, masterful, competent, and dominant. The catch is that agentic behavior is viewed as less desirable in women, creating the classic double standard that favors men.

For example, women may encounter negative reactions when they behave in a clearly agentic manner, especially if that style entails exerting control and dominance over others. When female leaders fail to temper the agentic behaviors required by a leader role with sufficient displays of female-typical communal behaviors, they can incur a backlash and may be passed over for hiring and promotion. Recall the story of Lisa from chapter three; she was VP of a pharmaceutical sales division who was told by her boss to tone down her assertiveness, be more of a team player, and be more social. This is a classic example of opposing gender expectations at play. As a high-ranking leader, Lisa displayed agentic qualities, but when she did, she got pigeon-holed into a stereotypic female role.

The cross-pressure of communal qualities people prefer in *women* and agentic qualities people prefer in *leaders* puts a tremendous burden on female leaders who are trying to find a leadership style that works for them. The consensus of much of the research is that a coach or teacher style, as epitomized by transformational leadership, might approximate a balance because it has culturally feminine aspects, especially in its individualized consideration behaviors, and is considered androgynous.[7] This is good news for women—as discussed in chapter two, women are naturally suited to be transformational leaders.

◇◇◇◇◇◇◇◇◇◇◇◇◇◇◇◇

The cross-pressure of communal qualities people prefer in women and agentic qualities people prefer in leaders puts a tremendous burden on female leaders.

◇◇◇◇◇◇◇◇◇◇◇◇◇◇◇◇

As leaders, women should be aggressive and tough, but as women, they should be feminine and caring. These opposing expectations often result in the *perception* that women are less qualified for elite leadership positions than men. Used to successful executives being and acting like men, leaders expect women to model the same behavior. One CEO told McKinsey, "Women don't knock on my door the way men do or ask for advice. I wish they were more proactive."[8] This exemplifies a typical biased mindset that is pervasive across global corporations.

Another example of bias and leadership is a practice called leader-member exchange (LMX).[9] It's a fancy name for something very simple. Think of a leader you know. Does this leader have favorites? If you answered yes, you're acknowledging the foundation of LMX. The theory argues that, because of time pressures, leaders establish a special relationship with a small group of their followers. These individuals make up the *ingroup*—they are trusted, receive a disproportionate amount of the leader's attention, and are more likely to receive special privileges. Other followers fall into the *outgroup.*

You can probably already imagine the problems with this practice. Leaders induce LMX by rewarding employees with whom they want a closer linkage and punishing those with whom they do not. For the relationship to remain intact, the leaders and follower must invest in the relationship. How does a leader choose who's in the ingroup and who's in the outgroup? You guessed it—it's based on bias. Ingroup members have demographic, attitude, and personality characteristics similar to those of their leader. Leaders and followers of the same gender tend to have closer relationships than those of different genders. Even though the leader does the choosing, the follower's characteristics drive the categorizing decision.

◇◇◇◇◇◇◇◇◇◇◇◇◇◇◇◇

If most leaders are male, and leaders choose ingroup members who are like them, then a large portion of outgroup members will be women.

◇◇◇◇◇◇◇◇◇◇◇◇◇◇◇◇

What's the result? Not surprisingly, ingroup members have higher performance ratings, engage in more helping or citizenship behaviors at work, have greater commitment to the organization, and report greater satisfaction with their superior. Outgroup members feel left out, have more negative work attitudes, and higher levels of withdrawal behavior. As mentioned in the previous section, we hire, promote, support, and help people who are like us—not based on skills or competencies. Therefore, if most leaders are male, and leaders choose ingroup members who are like them, then a large portion of outgroup members will be women.

So, what's the leadership impact of gender bias? Because of gender stereotypes, role congruity, and agentic leader behaviors, as a society, we really aren't satisfied with any leadership situation. We don't always like how men lead, we don't always like how women lead, we don't like when men lead like women, and we don't like when women lead like men—quite a quandary. To develop and sustain healthy organizations, we *must* let go of these outdated beliefs and allow ourselves to think more broadly about leadership and gender. We need to have a blend of the best leadership of both genders.

Bias Strategies

Eliminating, or even minimizing, bias is not an easy task. Bias is deep-seated, ingrained, and has been reinforced in each generation for centuries. Therefore, it's easier to take bias out of processes than to take it out of people—although we can make strides individually. Instead of just pointing out that biases are widespread, we need to clearly communicate that these biases are undesirable and unacceptable, so we don't legitimize prejudice. By reinforcing the idea that people want to conquer their biases and that there are benefits to doing so, we send a more effective message—most people don't want to discriminate and you shouldn't either. I recently created and led a series of workshops on unconscious bias for a client. Listed below are things we can do from both organizational and individual perspectives to mitigate the damaging effects of bias.

From an *organizational* perspective, we need to take the onus off women and put it on organizations to improve their structure and processes. There are a handful of organizations and institutions that have invested millions of dollars and a considerable amount of time developing resources and programs to combat bias—some of these include Google, Facebook, Pfizer, Genentech, Broadcom, and BAE Systems. Listed below are actionable strategies for organizations that have been shown to reduce bias.

- Blind resumes (remove names)
- Diversity goals or quotas
- Joint and structured interviews
- Make decisions collectively
- Competency-based succession planning
- Objective standards for hiring, evaluating performance and assigning opportunities
- Challenge the concept of "fit"—makes it too easy to choose the same
- Cross-functional teams
- Rotating project lead roles
- If-then plans and decision guides
- Measure and collect data at both the individual and group level
- Diverse physical spaces and common meeting places
- Set ground rules and norms for meeting dynamics—establish a no-interruption rule for everyone
- Question decisions and ask if same standards apply to other groups

- Don't make assumptions that women are limited in their commitment, ability to travel, or take on new assignments
- Accountability
  - Hold yourself accountable for self-reflection, learning, and continually analyzing your behaviors and experiences
  - Everyone needs to model desired behaviors
  - Explain decisions on hiring, evaluation and peer reviews
  - Communicate bias differences (e.g., gender promotion rates)
  - Empower everyone to call out bias

From an *individual* perspective, if you improve your emotional intelligence, you can reduce some biases. This is accomplished through increased levels of self-awareness and mindfulness. One solution is to make sure that you proactively and consistently communicate your career desires—whether they are to advance, increase (or decrease) travel, increase (or decrease) responsibility, be developed for a leadership role, take a new assignment domestically or globally, mentor others, or just stay in your current role. This type of communication will help put to rest any assumptions made about you. Listed below are actionable strategies for individuals that have been shown to reduce bias.

- Be honest with yourself about blind spots
- Adopt a mindful approach to your interactions and decision making
- Question your first impression—take a minute to allow unconscious thoughts to become conscious
- Make conscious effort to seek out and learn from others different from you—disrupt your normal process
- Ask yourself if the biases you are experiencing or enacting are consistent with your personal and organizational values
- Listen to all voices equally—speak out if you suspect a colleague's contribution is being ignored or dismissed
- Consult with trusted colleagues (manager, mentor, sponsor) to seek feedback on your behaviors

- Be aware of the words and physical reactions that surface in your interactions with others
- Share your experiences with others and seek common ground
- Be open-minded and willing to learn outside your comfort zone
- Avoid watching movies or television shows that promote negative stereotypes of women or minorities
- Get support, help and guidance from your leadership team and human resources

In addition to these strategies, there are numerous books, articles, YouTube videos, TED videos, and other resources available to help address bias. To overcome these institutional and societal barriers, both individuals and organizations must take steps to eliminate biases. It's important because our minds are not as consistent as we think, our memories are faulty, and our stereotypes are usually outdated. People make assumptions about women at work, and as leaders, based on their roles in society. These biased assumptions limit women's advancement, or worse, prevent them from ever getting the opportunity.

We need to take the onus off women and put it on organizations to improve their structure and processes.

So, why minimize bias? Because it's good business practice for everyone, it makes good legal sense, we need people with different roles and perspectives on our team, and it's in sync with our intentions—none of us want to intentionally offend, hurt or limit someone else. Remember, not all biases are bad. Ask yourself: Is this a bias I want to have? Do I like it? Is it good for my company?

In summary, our brains are wired toward bias, which can lead to quick assumptions about others and ill-informed business decisions. The good news is that we have a fat prefrontal cortex and can learn (or unlearn) new ways of thinking and behaving. It's important to note that we are not bad people because we have biases. We try to simplify things, but by doing so, we put people in boxes and limit potential. Unconscious bias can impact hiring, retention, promotion, performance evaluation, team assignments, budget decisions, and openness to new ideas and innovative solutions. Fortunately, there are many organizational and individual strategies to help minimize bias and create an environment where others can fully contribute.

It's a life-long journey to shift the way our brains allow us to respond, imagine and behave. If we allow ourselves to become aware of biases, and commit to acting, that is inclusive leadership at its best.

Summary Points

- Bias is defined as a deep-seated resistance to the different
- Numerous studies point to gender bias as the fundamental issue concerning women's advancement.
- Institutional and societal barriers include gender bias, gender stereotyping, role congruity theory, and agentic leader behaviors.
- Our brain is wired to make lightning-fast decisions that result in misguided generalizations while dismissing subtle, more important distinctions.
- Affinity bias fosters unequal opportunities that promote the status quo and limit diversity.
- Unconscious bias negatively affects numerous organizational processes, from recruiting and hiring to client or customer service.
- As a society, we have specific expectations about how men and women should dress, act, and interact with others.
- Men negotiate competitively; women negotiate cooperatively.
- The socialization process has produced the expectation that male social qualities also happen to be leadership qualities.
- There are many organizational and individual strategies to mitigate the damaging effects of bias.

Reflection Questions

✓ How often do your ideas get interrupted or disregarded in meetings? Who interrupts you? How have you dealt with this situation?

✓ Have you ever had an experience with bias or discrimination because of your gender? If so, what was your experience? What did you do? What was the outcome?

✓ Reflecting honestly, what types of personal biases or stereotypes do you hold toward others?

✓ Have you helped someone or been helped yourself by affinity bias? What was the result? Would you do it again?

✓ Can you think of a time when you've held your opinion or taken a back seat to men because of gender roles?

✓ Do you consider yourself a good negotiator? When negotiating, do you value economic or relationship outcomes more? How can you be a better negotiator?

✓ Have you ever experienced the cross-pressure of communal qualities people prefer in women and agentic qualities people prefer in leaders? How have you handled this?

✓ When have you been part of your boss's ingroup? When have you been in the outgroup? What impact did it have on you?

SIX

The Glass Golf Club

Life shrinks or expands in proportion to one's courage.
Anais Nin

S usan is vice president of operations for a National Hockey League team. She has worked for the team for three years, and is one of only a few women working in the male-dominated sport. Every year, the team leadership takes an all-expense paid golf outing to Pebble Beach Golf Course. Susan heard about the trip informally from one of her male VP colleagues, so she decided to confront her boss about it. She asked why she had not been invited, and after waffling for a few minutes, he told her that the trip was full and that arrangements had already been made. She pressed further and, flustered, he eventually said, "We assumed being a woman that you wouldn't want to go." He finally told her that she could attend, but she had to provide her own transportation. Susan decided to go and did pay for her own way,

97

knowing this would be a key networking opportunity that could help her fit in better with the team.

Teri is vice president of business development at a major commercial construction company. The COO owns a cabin in Arizona and several times a year, the leadership team schedules weekend golf outings at the cabin. The COO invites four to ten guys primarily at the VP level and above. Sometimes he invites guys they are recruiting or guys identified on succession plans who will eventually be VPs. In ten years as VP at this company, Teri has never been invited to a golf weekend. She does not consistently push the issue to attend because it's socially awkward for her to be at a cabin for the weekend with all men. I asked if any women have ever attended, and she cited one time the COO invited a high-ranking female, then took his wife, so they could hang out for the weekend while the men played golf.

Julie works as a financial advisor for one of the top three financial institutions. One year, the company sponsored a celebrity golf tournament and each of the advisors received tickets to invite their biggest clients to attend with them. Julie had a $10-million-dollar client, larger than many of the male advisors. When she asked for a ticket to the tournament, she was denied. The reason given was that they only had a limited number of tickets and that this event was "more appropriate" for men. Thus, to break the bad news to her client, Julie had to make-up reasons that sounded more legitimate and professional. This incident angered both Julie and her client, and reflected poorly on the institution.

◇◇◇◇◇◇◇◇◇◇◇◇◇◇◇◇

It's only when we question why things are as they are, that we create opportunities for meaningful change.

◇◇◇◇◇◇◇◇◇◇◇◇◇◇◇◇

You might be thinking that these stories are from the 1980s, and the experience that these women had are not reflective of current behaviors and attitudes. I wish I could tell you otherwise, but these stories occurred in recent years, and still happen today. Golf has been the standard means of building client relationships for decades, and in some industries, it's the preferred method. Even though many women now play golf, this practice is still a predominantly male bastion—and it's often a reason that women are left out.

Consistent with the Anais Nin quote at the chapter's start, Susan, Teri, and Julie all displayed tremendous courage by confronting their bosses—and in Susan's case, it took even more grit for her to pay her own way to attend the all-male event. It's only when we push back or question why things are as they are, that we create opportunities for meaningful change.

Structural Barriers

This lack of access to informal networks, such as golf, sporting events, dinner, a club, or just drinks after work, are considered structural barriers for many women—and for some men too. There's another name for these informal networks that you're probably very familiar with, it's the old boys club—and it's alive and well.

This lack of entry to these all-important networks restricts access to essential information and relationship building that's critical to a career. Think of how much business gets done in an informal setting like a golf course, over a nice dinner, or at a game. There's lots of time to chat, you're in a relaxed setting, you get to know others on a personal level, and people let their guards down. Who wouldn't want to be in an environment like this? Often, men assume women don't want to take part in these types of events, so they don't invite them.

◇◇◇◇◇◇◇◇◇◇◇◇◇◇◇◇◇◇

You won't find the club on an organization chart.

◇◇◇◇◇◇◇◇◇◇◇◇◇◇◇◇◇◇

The club exists in the group of individuals who freely share information and value each other's contributions no matter how small those contributions may be. The members who are "in" are exempt from failure—in the sense that its not recognized as such—and in some cases even continue to be rewarded for poor performance.

You won't find the club on an organization chart. It's often described as having a gang or tribal mentality that blocks all ideas that are different from their own, yet because it's a faction within the company's organizational hierarchy, it has power to influence ideas and outcomes, while diluting the club leaders' and members' accountability for results. Simply put, the club is comprised of people in an organization who may or may not have direct power over other individuals, and yet the group shepherds its members to new growth opportunities and career advancement.[1]

So, what's the downside? For women, it's a significant lack of opportunity, but it also affects clients. Consider this: If Julie has the best rapport with a client, and golf is the default method of building client relationships at your organization, what are the implications if the best person for the account doesn't play? It can hinder the client relationship, raise a flag as to why Julie isn't there, and could lose Julie the account.

Let's look at another example. A major healthcare company had its annual conference in New York City last year. They were given a free evening, so a large group of men decided to catch the basketball game at Madison Square Garden. Since the men had left, a group of women decided to go to dinner. The next morning, they were discussing the prior evening's activities. The men asked the women, "Why didn't you invite us to dinner?" Puzzled, the women asked the men, "Why didn't you invite us to the game?" This is a classic example of how assumptions lead to exclusion.

◇◇◇◇◇◇◇◇◇◇◇◇◇◇

Selection for these ingroups are largely based on bias.

◇◇◇◇◇◇◇◇◇◇◇◇◇◇

When we conjure up images of the glass ceiling, we think of an invisible but impenetrable barrier between women and the executive suite, preventing them from reaching the highest levels of the business world, regardless of their accomplishments and merits. Just as golf is an impassable barrier for many women, so is the glass ceiling. Some researchers have identified limitations with the glass ceiling metaphor. They posit an alternative image of a labyrinth conveying the impression of a journey riddled with challenges all along the way (not just near the top), as women navigate indirect, complex and often discontinuous paths toward leadership.[2] The labyrinth is a more accurate description of the barriers that women face in contemporary organizations, as we've discussed with systemic gender biases in both leadership and emotional intelligence.

Recall our discussion about ingroups and outgroups from the last chapter. Selection for these groups are largely based on bias. Leaders choose followers who are like them, and followers of the same gender tend to have closer relationships than those of different genders. The exact same principle drives the old boys club. It's reminiscent of grade school when we anxiously waited to be picked for the kickball team! If you're lucky enough to be invited into one of these informal networks, you're in the ingroup, and will likely have higher performance ratings and report greater satisfaction with both your superior and organization. Outgroup members feel left out, have more negative work attitudes, and higher levels of withdrawal behavior, which leads to higher turnover.[3]

What's interesting is that when women do become part of these ingroups, they don't always help other women gain entry. Leena is senior director of business development at a technology company, which is highly male-dominated. She shared with me that there were very few females in her group and the males were always leaning to promote other males who were willing to go to parties or clubs after hours (not appropriate ones). Thus, she was never considered part of the ingroup, but her female boss was. Since her boss had built trust with the male leaders, she was in a position to "break the nonsense" as Leena put it. But, because she too was joining the boys club, and was brought up by male leaders, she wasn't willing to help Leena or any other woman in the tech company.

Why don't women help other women? Here are some explanations. When there are few females in an organization or few females at the top, the competition for "spots" in these favored ingroups increases, so women are less inclined to bring other women along. Another explanation is that because women battle obstacles all along their career journey, and achieve hard-fought success, their attitude toward other women is, "I figured it out; you should too." In addition, executive women often allow themselves to become overly encumbered with duties and tasks, which cause them to avoid the roles and responsibilities of supporting and mentoring young women.

◇◇◇◇◇◇◇◇◇◇◇◇◇◇

Women cut other women to preserve the dead-even power relationship.

◇◇◇◇◇◇◇◇◇◇◇◇◇◇

Another reason for the lack of women supporting women is the *power dead-even rule*, a term coined by Pat Heim and colleagues in their book, *In the Company of Women*.[4] Through socialization and the games they play, girls learn very early that relationships are the most important thing—and need to be preserved at all costs. The power dead-even rule is an invisible natural law that operates behind the scenes and helps shape our reactions to other women in our lives. It explains the connection among relationships, power, and self-esteem. For a positive relationship to be possible between two women, the self-esteem and power of one must be, in the perception of each woman, similar in weight to the self-esteem and power of the other. These essential elements must be kept "dead even."

What happens when this power balance gets disrupted? When a girl (or woman) rises in status, other girls act quickly to bring her back down. This is accomplished by verbally belittling her, talking behind her back, or ostracizing her from the group. These actions of cutting other women may sound harsh—and sometimes they are—but they are in effort to preserve the dead-even power relationship that women have grown up with their entire lives. Can you think of an example when you've seen this, or perhaps acted this way yourself?

From an emotional intelligence standpoint, as illustrated in chapter three, women at the highest leadership levels tend to display more male-specific EQ competencies—such as self-confidence and assertiveness, and leverage less female-specific EQ competencies—such as empathy and interpersonal relationships. So, if a female leader puts less of a premium on the value of relationships or is less empathetic to other women, she will not extend a helping hand or spend the time necessary to cultivate relationships with junior women.

This is also called Queen Bee Syndrome.[5] It's when a woman deliberately behaves in ways more typical of a man to display toughness and protect herself from men. For women at the very top, part of their success is due to convincing men that they aren't like other women. Denying their status as women becomes a reflex. So, when they get high up enough—far from making a difference for the women who come after them—they're still in the business of proving to the guys that they're *not* one of the girls.

Even though male leaders share similar characteristics as some women, in general, men tend to be much better about reaching out to junior male colleagues, with a symbolic arm around their shoulder, saying, "Come with me, I'll show you how." Women leaders don't generally do this with junior women—and this needs to change.

It's important to note that these informal networks—sporting events, drinks or clubs—aren't always conducive to a woman's style and are often less appealing to women. Many women don't care about attending a game, or having drinks after hours, or going to a club. Women value different things and often prefer to go home to family, have free time to themselves, or not extend the work day further by socializing with colleagues.

◇◇◇◇◇◇◇◇◇◇◇◇◇◇◇

Informal networks aren't always conducive to a woman's style and are often less appealing to women.

◇◇◇◇◇◇◇◇◇◇◇◇◇◇◇

I can relate to both sides of this coin. When I worked in pharmaceutical sales in the 1990s, golf was a staple at every major meeting. We were at a resort in West Palm Beach, Florida, and were given a free day to either golf, go to the spa, or have free time. I signed up for golf for a few reasons—I enjoy it; my boss, Rick, was playing; and I thought it would be good networking with the leadership team. To my surprise, I was the only female who played. All the other women chose the spa. As it turned out, we had a great time, and my relationship with my boss and other leaders improved because of that event.

On the other hand, as I have progressed in my career, I have found that after spending a full day with colleagues at work or at a meeting, the last thing I want to do is spend another three hours at dinner or a social event. This is not a reflection on my colleagues; sometimes I just prefer downtime to unplug and unwind by going home, exercising, calling loved ones, or just relaxing in my hotel room. Women value their time, their families, and their relationships—and don't want to sacrifice these. Men are generally more political than women, and often invest the time and energy needed into these after work activities.

You might be thinking that if these informal networks and events reflect men's style, then why would men invite women to attend? Because these work activities, rituals, and groups are an important part of how work is structured, and women are disadvantaged if they don't participate. Period.

◇◇◇◇◇◇◇◇◇◇◇◇◇◇◇◇◇

If you have a bunch of people who have the same sensibility, it's not going to dawn on anyone that something's missing.

◇◇◇◇◇◇◇◇◇◇◇◇◇◇◇◇◇

By denying access to these informal networks, men hinder women. Most of the time, this hindrance is unintentional. Most men are simply unaware that women are excluded and they just don't think about it. If you have a bunch of people who have the same sensibility, it's not going to dawn on anyone that something's missing. Nonetheless, it creates a significant barrier for women who are trying to build relationships and succeed in their careers.

The bottom line—we simply must be more inclusive with our networks and social events. Men need to invite women, and women need to invite men.

Everyone should be given the opportunity to participate, and chances are, they'll have fun too.

Can You Help Me?

Nobody succeeds without help. It doesn't matter how smart you are, how skilled you are, or how talented you are—no one makes it to the top without help and support. Having role models, mentors and sponsors is critical for career progression. Not having access to these relationships are considered structural barriers for women. First, let's define each.

A role model is a person whose behavior, example, or success can be emulated by others, especially by younger people. Role models are crucial to anyone's success, regardless of the profession or industry. Grandparents, parents, big brothers or sisters, teachers, coaches, athletes, celebrities, musicians, artists, business leaders, religious leaders, political leaders, or even our friends. It's someone to look up to who shows us that it can be done, and that we can do it. We generally identify with role models who are similar to us in gender, background, ethnicity, age, culture, or other characteristics.

A lack of role models discourages ambitions. For women in business, it's particularly important to have visible female role models to be able to see a pathway to success. Because there are few female leaders, many women emulate role models from their own lives or from TV or movies. When there is a strong female presence in an organization, it's often cited as one of the critical success factors for other women. Look at companies that have strong female leaders—GM, PepsiCo, Xerox, Facebook—it's no surprise that these companies attract more women applicants, and have a higher percentage of women on their leadership teams and boards of directors.

◇◇◇◇◇◇◇◇◇◇◇◇◇◇

For women in business, it's particularly important to have visible female role models to be able to see a pathway to success.

◇◇◇◇◇◇◇◇◇◇◇◇◇◇

Mentors and sponsors have both similarities and differences. A mentor is someone providing you guidance and advice as you build your career. Sponsors are your advocates who promote your visibility at the opportune time. Another way to think about it is a mentor helps you in your *current* position, and a sponsor helps you get your *next* position.

Mentors and sponsors are *similar* in that they both rely on individual relationships, which can range from peers to high-level leaders; they include support, advice and feedback; they involve periodic meetings and communication; they are focused on career development; and relationships are generally founded on common interests or shared characteristics.

Mentors and sponsors *differ* in what they focus on. Mentors tend to focus on helping you improve in your current role. Sponsors focus on future positions, help you get to your next role, and include advocacy and not just advice. Another difference is that corporate mentorship programs can be informal or formal, whereas sponsorship usually occurs organically or by informal referral. Finally, mentorship is often a reciprocal relationship. The mentee receives direct assistance and advice, and the mentor learns useful information, receives validation and recognition, and a sense of fulfillment and pride. Although sponsors also get a sense of fulfillment and pride, sponsorship is less reciprocal in that the sponsor champions for the candidate when the time is appropriate.

Just as the informal networks discussed above are forged, mentoring and sponsorship relationships often form between individuals who have common interests or when the junior members remind the senior members of themselves. This means men will often gravitate toward mentoring and sponsoring younger men with whom they connect more naturally. For junior women, it's not possible to get enough support unless senior men jump in too. We need to make male leaders aware of this shortage and encourage them to widen their circle by sponsoring and mentoring women.

◇◇◇◇◇◇◇◇◇◇◇◇◇◇

For junior women, it's not possible to get enough support unless senior men jump in too.

◇◇◇◇◇◇◇◇◇◇◇◇◇◇

It's important for women to have both male and female mentors to help build their careers. This gives a variety of different perspectives based on divergent backgrounds and lived experiences—not to mention the invaluable benefit of building relationships with a diverse group of people. With sponsors, it's a bit different.

Men and women have different networks, which result in different levels of support. Although women and men's networks are similar in size, men predominantly have male networks, and women have mostly female networks. Given that men are more likely to hold leadership positions; women may end up with less access to senior-level sponsorship. In fact, nearly two-thirds of men say that the senior leaders who have helped them advance were other men, compared to just one-third of women who said that men helped them advance.[6] We also know that women with sponsors are more likely to ask for stretch assignments and pay raises than women without sponsors.[7]

◇◇◇◇◇◇◇◇◇◇◇◇◇◇◇

It's the optics of having a male sponsor that gives more creditability to women.

◇◇◇◇◇◇◇◇◇◇◇◇◇◇◇

For women, it's important to have male sponsors because men are in decision-making positions of authority, and it gives more credibility to women. How? Imagine a closed-door meeting with senior leaders at your company discussing succession planning. Carol speaks up and says, "I think Mary should be promoted." The perception may be that Carol is only advocating for Mary because she's a woman. However, if Barry speaks up and says, "I think Mary should be promoted," that often carries more weight because the perception is if a male leader is singing her praises, then it's based on merit and not on any kind of favoritism. Now, neither of these perceptions may be accurate, but it's the optics of having a male sponsor that gives more credibility to women.

Structural Strategies

Lack of access to informal networks—sports, dinner, drinks—are a type of barrier for women. The lack of entry to these all-important networks restricts access to essential information and relationship-building that's critical. We must not underestimate the power that these informal networks have to significantly boost a career.

Unfortunately, when leaders are doing succesion planning and thinking of who's next in line for promotion, it's often the guy they play golf with, or their racquetball buddy, or the guy they've dined with several times and have forged a personal relationship.

Although dinner is nice, it blurs the lines between work and personal time, and professional and personal relationships. Some executives have set their own rules by having only breakfast and lunch meetings (and no dinners) for everybody. This makes all access equal and removes any indications of inappropriate relationships—a fantastic approach that more executive and senior leaders should adopt.

For men, the next time you enjoy a game, dinner, drinks, or golf—invite the women—interactions are often positive when diverse groups can interact, and you never know what the outcome may be. For women, ask to join in. Having men and women equally participating and contributing is the best way to fully leverage talent and remain competitive in any industry.

◇◇◇◇◇◇◇◇◇◇◇◇◇◇◇◇

Although dinner is nice, it blurs the lines between work and personal time, and professional and personal relationships.

◇◇◇◇◇◇◇◇◇◇◇◇◇◇◇◇

When it comes to *role models*, we generally identify with those who are like us in gender, background, ethnicity, age, or culture. If you're a male or female leader in any industry, then you're also a role model. Girls often look to the women in their lives for cues about how to think and act, and boys do the same with men in their lives. As female role models, when we speak confidently, take risks, and own our accomplishments, we set positive examples for girls to follow. As male role models, when we treat everyone equally, care about others, and communicate often, we set positive examples for boys to follow. If you're a male or female leader, you have a tremendous opportunity to make an impact and set an example for young men and women—because there's always someone watching.

In grade school, boys often get more airtime than girls—they are more likely to call out answers and less likely to be interrupted. I see this play out as adults every week in my classes. I teach Organizational Behavior, Leadership and Ethics, and Diversity in Organizations courses to MBA students. The young men blurt out their answers and dominate the conversation. The young women whom are bright and insightful, stay quiet and speak less often than the men. Being a female professor, I am keenly aware of gender dynamics, and do my best to set a strong example. I encourage everyone to share their opinion, but I often must ask the women specifically for their perspectives.

The same dynamics play out in the workplace. Men tend to dominate meetings, resist being influenced in public, speak in a declamatory voice, and interrupt others. Women tend to speak briefly, raise their hands, phrase their points as questions, wait their turn, and smile more. As role models, it's important that we teach both girls and women to speak confidently and speak often. Everyone benefits from diverse and insightful points of view.

◇◇◇◇◇◇◇◇◇◇◇◇◇◇◇◇

As role models, it's important that we teach both girls and women to speak confidently and speak often.

◇◇◇◇◇◇◇◇◇◇◇◇◇◇◇◇

Mentoring, even in a professional environment, is a personal experience. The personal connections formed by mentors and sponsors lead to opportunities and promotions that are crucial for career development, and anyone can fill these roles. It's worth noting that technology provides powerful tools for connecting and expanding our networks. But access to networks doesn't replace mentoring any more than social media "likes" replace friendships.

If you're a *mentee* seeking a mentor, find men and women whose career paths align with your goals and needs. It's important that you both establish clear goals and expectations up front. For example, how will the partnership function, who will schedule the meetings, how often will you meet, and how will cancellations be handled? You will also need to establish shared expectations for communication, preparedness, feedback-sharing, and ongoing progress.

Mentor relationships are reciprocal and can be long-lasting, so make sure you make the most of your limited time together. Show your mentor you value her time by using it wisely. Avoid meeting just to catch up or asking questions you can find answers to yourself. Instead, come to her with thoughtful questions and be ready to discuss real challenges you're facing. Then, listen carefully to her recommendations and report back on your progress. She's more likely to continue to invest in you if you're acting on her input—and she sees the impact she's having on your career.

View feedback as a gift. When we get a gift, what do we say? Thank you. You have three options when you get a gift, you can accept it, reject it or re-gift it. In other words, you can use the advice, not use the advice, or pass the advice on to someone else. As a rule, be grateful and never criticize advice you get from a mentor. Women don't always get the direct input they need to be their best because coworkers may be nervous about eliciting an emotional response. In addition, women often don't give direct feedback to other women for fear of being unkind—to preserve the relationship. Make sure you don't fall into this trap with your mentor. Solicit her feedback whenever you can by asking specific questions like, "How can I improve?" and "What am I not doing that I should be?" The more you ask for and accept her feedback, the faster you'll learn—and odds are she'll respect your openness and willingness to grow.

Over time mentors can develop into sponsors who use their status and clout to create opportunities and make connections for you. Before your mentor will sponsor you, she needs to trust that you are reliable and a bet worth making. To build trust, always follow through on what you say you're going to do, and always do your very best work. When you're consistent over time, you build valuable trust with your mentor and your coworkers.

◇◇◇◇◇◇◇◇◇◇◇◇◇◇◇◇

Over time mentors can develop into sponsors who use their status and clout to create opportunities and make connections for you.

◇◇◇◇◇◇◇◇◇◇◇◇◇◇◇◇

Another approach for a mentee is to seek micro-mentoring. This is mentoring on specific competencies or skills related to one task. It involves giving and receiving feedback and may only last fifteen minutes. Think of it as a short burst of targeted advice when you need it. This may also be a good way to test the waters with a potential mentor or to help launch the more formal mentoring relationship.

If you're looking to become a *mentor*, here are some tips. First, it's never too early to be a mentor, and you don't have to be in a leadership position. Even if you're a few years into your career, you can mentor a young Millennial (or soon to be Generation Z) who just entered the workforce, or a college student who's interested in your field. You may have just experienced what she is going through and can help her take the next step.

Second, give open and honest input—even when it's hard. Look for opportunities to give your mentee specific input for improving her performance and learning new skills. Whenever possible, share your input in the moment, when it's most effective. If you hold back to protect your mentee's feelings, you're not helping her. Remember, your honest feedback will help her advance more quickly.

Third, create a sound underpinning of rich content. Expose your mentee to content on far-reaching, career-impacting topics such as executive presence, organizational culture, corporate policies, career planning, and strategic communications. When mentees are focused on these big ideas, they can comfortably lead their mentoring conversations to explore their mentor's experiences, opinions, and thought processes related to these critical issues.

Fourth, don't just mentor—sponsor! The best mentors go beyond mentorship and advocate for their mentees. Start by understanding your mentee's career goals, then think through her best path forward and how you can help. Endorse her on social media. Recommend her for a high-profile project. Introduce her to people in your network. Find ways to open doors for her and invest in her success.[8]

Finally, just as structure is essential at the start of a mentoring partnership, it's also critical at the completion of a formal mentoring relationship. Make sure you celebrate successes by sharing key lessons and celebrate what you achieved together. Explore what's next by discussing logical next steps to continue your growth. Finally, define the relationship moving forward by discussing if and how partners will stay connected, so that there's no confusion or awkwardness between them.

◇◇◇◇◇◇◇◇◇◇◇◇◇◇◇◇

Cultivating a vast and diverse network will help you build crucial relationships that provide vital support throughout your career.

◇◇◇◇◇◇◇◇◇◇◇◇◇◇◇◇

When it comes to *sponsors*, you may or may not know them. Recall that sponsors are your advocates who promote your visibility at the opportune time. Sponsor relationships usually occur organically or by informal referral. For example, let's assume that you'd like for the VP of HR to be your sponsor, but you don't know him. One solution is to reach out to him directly and set up an introductory meeting. If you're not comfortable with that, find someone who knows him and ask to be introduced or referred. Be clear on what you want from him and what you are seeking to accomplish.

Some sponsors may grow out of a mentoring relationship or you may never know who your sponsors are, but by developing your networks, you are ensuring a proliferation of potential sponsors. Cultivating a vast and diverse network both personally and through technology will help you build crucial relationships that allow you to identify appropriate and vital support throughout your career.

Studies show again and again that women want organizations with cultures that support gender diversity and inclusion, female role models, networking and mentoring opportunities, support and sponsorship from senior leaders, and work-life flexibility. It will take all of us to get to a more equal world, and we'll get there faster by helping and supporting each other.

Summary Points

- Lack of access to informal networks, such as golf, sporting events, dinner, a club, or just drinks after work, are considered structural barriers for many women.
- Selection for ingroups are largely based on bias.
- Ingroup members have higher performance ratings and report greater satisfaction with their superiors and organizations.
- Outgroup members feel left out, have more negative work attitudes, and higher levels of withdrawal behavior.
- Women cut other women to preserve the dead-even power relationship.
- Informal networks, rituals and groups are an important part of how work is structured, and women are disadvantaged if they don't participate.
- A role model is a person whose behavior, example, or success can be emulated by others, especially by younger people.
- A mentor helps you in your current position, and a sponsor helps you get your next position.

- For women, it's important to have male sponsors because men are in decision-making positions of authority, and it gives more credibility to women.
- There are many strategies for accessing informal networks, role models, mentors, and sponsors.

Reflection Questions

✓ Have you ever been excluded from a golf event? What were the reasons given? What was the outcome?

✓ Do you participate in informal networks, such as sporting events, dinners, clubs, or drinks after work? If yes, what did you do to gain access? If not, has it hindered your career in any way? What can you do to participate more?

✓ Have you ever had an experience where assumptions led to exclusion? What transpired?

✓ When have you been part of an ingroup? When have you been in the outgroup? What impact did it have on you?

✓ Have you ever had a senior female leader help your career? How about hinder your career? What did she do?

✓ Who is your role model? What is it about them that you admire?

✓ Do you have a mentor? If not, who could help you attain your goals and meet your needs?

✓ Do you mentor anyone else? What do you get out of the relationship? What has been the outcome?

✓ Does anyone sponsor or advocate on your behalf? If not, what can you do to develop these relationships?

SEVEN

Lead the Meeting, Change the Diaper

Life may not be the party we hoped for, but while we're here we might as well dance.

Jeanne C. Stein

Work-life balance is a misnomer. Every day millions of people face the difficult juggling act of managing a career and managing a life. Work alone can be all consuming, and the life part includes many facets, such as managing our family, friends, religion or spirituality, community, volunteering, hobbies, finances, and vacation and leisure—not to mention managing our own fitness, wellness, development, and future. Most people believe that it's impossible to achieve balance—rather it's about making tough choices. The better terms would be *work-life flexibility* or *work-life integration.*

As one of the most influential generations of our time, Millennials, who are in their twenties and thirties, have initiated a significant shift in today's work-life environment. These days, the big question isn't about how we obtain balance, but rather how we *integrate* our work with our life. Drawing a distinct line between our personal lives and our work lives has become something of the past, thanks to technology and our constant ability to be plugged-in. According to a recent study conducted by Ernst & Young covering 9,600 workers in eight countries, one-third of Millennials say managing their work, family, and personal responsibilities has become more difficult in the last five years. Seventy-eight percent of Millennials who work full-time are more likely to have a spouse or partner working full-time, compared to 47 percent of Boomers.[1]

◇◇◇◇◇◇◇◇◇◇◇◇◇◇◇◇

Most people believe that it's impossible to achieve balance, rather it's about making tough choices.

◇◇◇◇◇◇◇◇◇◇◇◇◇◇◇◇

As technology creeps into corporate offices everywhere, people are literally carrying their job around in their pockets. We receive emails on our cell phones, we attend meetings via Skype or webinar, we respond to client questions before bed, and we're constantly wired to our social media outlets. Combine this 24/7 work with our increased responsibilities at home, it's no wonder we desire the flexible schedule that comes with work-life integration.

Balance refers to a condition in which different elements are in equal proportions. Work-life balance revolves around mutual exclusivity between our careers and our home lives. When you leave the office at 5:00 p.m., you leave every aspect of your job at the office. You are not expected to take home work-related projects. You don't answer emails at the dinner table, you avoid your digital devices, and you respect the separation between your work and home responsibilities. Every day, you check in to the office at 8:00 a.m. and you leave at 5:00 p.m., without fail. Seems antiquated now, doesn't it?

Work-life integration, however, suggests we incorporate our work and life into one fulfilling purpose. It means having more flexibility with your schedule. If you need to take your kids to school every morning before checking in to the office—great. If you need to leave early every Wednesday to attend a class you signed up for—good for you. You can always make up the missed work hours later that night or the next day, right?

With the work-life integration philosophy, companies trust their employees to get their work done, regardless of how many hours they log in at the office or where they're getting their work done. If a company trusts their employees, and employees understand and are committed to company expectations, a flexible schedule, going back to school, or any other personal or family-related activity should never get in the way of promotion or advancement.

Seventy-four percent of Millennials say, "being able to work flexibly and still be on track for promotion" is a major concern when accepting job positions, but some companies are still resistant to a work-life integration mindset. In fact, one in six employees say they experienced negative consequences after requesting their employer permit them to have a flexible schedule. Negative consequences include losing a job, being denied a promotion or raise, being assigned to less interesting or high-profile assignments, or being publicly or privately reprimanded.[2]

◇◇◇◇◇◇◇◇◇◇◇◇◇◇◇

Younger generations are creating a shift in today's work philosophy.

◇◇◇◇◇◇◇◇◇◇◇◇◇◇◇

Why would this be? Because earlier generations continue to occupy more management positions and hold more traditional values, thus having the most influence on employee schedules and overall work environment. Baby Boomers have seldom experienced a work environment that tolerates flexible schedules and telecommuting, so they're probably less inclined to jump on board the integration train.

On the contrary, Millennials are the children of Baby Boomers—a generation consumed by their careers—and our younger generations are not eager to repeat their parent's career habits. They long for a healthier work-life relationship, one that promotes flexibility, company trust, and the ability to work from anywhere. Whether you prefer work-life balance or work-life integration, there's no denying that younger generations are creating a shift in today's work philosophy. By 2025, 75 percent of the workforce will be comprised of Millennials, so it might be wise for companies to start tailoring their rules, regulations and policies to the desires and expectations of upcoming talent.[3] In a few years, Millennials will be the ones in charge, and companies might want them on their side.

So, how does the generational shift affect women in today's work-life environment? Let's explore.

Grit and Sacrifice

Today, job and career changes are the most common sacrifices workers have made (or would be willing to make) to better manage work and personal responsibilities. More than half of full-time employees have (or would be willing to) give up an opportunity for a promotion to manage work-life. On an interesting note, given that the U.S. is the only developed country *without* paid parental leave benefits, more than one-third of Millennials would "move to another country with better parental leave benefits" versus Generation X or Boomers. They would also be more willing to move closer to family and to "take a pay cut to have flexibility".[4]

◇◇◇◇◇◇◇◇◇◇◇◇◇◇◇◇

The decisions about who works and who cares for the children are not just about sharing responsibilities.

◇◇◇◇◇◇◇◇◇◇◇◇◇◇◇◇

Lifestyle and family choices that many couples make are not negative things, but they are considered a barrier for many women because they contribute to the leadership gender gap. The decisions about who works and who cares for the children are not just about sharing responsibilities evenly, it's also about power and family dynamics, breadwinner and caregiver priorities, and lifestyle preferences and necessities—with an undertone of gender bias and role congruity perceptions.

Let's look at breadwinner and caregiver issues. Recall that 78 percent of Millennials who work full-time today are more likely to have a spouse or partner working full-time compared to earlier generations. Thus, more families have dual breadwinners, but the caregiver roles have not shifted. If a woman is the primary breadwinner in a household, she's *usually* the primary caregiver as well. Conversely, if a man is the primary breadwinner in a household, he is *rarely* the primary caregiver. Think about this. If you're trying to manage a full-time career, but also have full-time caregiver and household responsibilities, how can you possibly excel in both? The reality is that most people can't excel in both, and give everything they can just to keep it all moving.

Women are still performing most the domestic and child care responsibility in the home, even when there are two spouses working full-time. As such, if women are bearing the children—and I don't think that's changing any time soon—women will view child rearing and child care differently than men. Even if mothers are more naturally inclined toward nurturing, fathers can match that skill in other ways, such as helping with school activities, homework, grocery shopping, laundry, cooking, and cleaning. These are all mundane, but mandatory tasks. The burden should not fall on women to do everything—it's not right and it's not fair.

◇◇◇◇◇◇◇◇◇◇◇◇◇◇◇◇◇◇

Women perform most domestic and child care duties, even when there are two spouses working full-time.

◇◇◇◇◇◇◇◇◇◇◇◇◇◇◇◇◇◇

At every level, from entry to senior management, women are at least nine times more likely than men to say that they do more child care and at least four times more likely to say they do more chores. In addition, working women are 60 percent more likely than working men to have a partner who works full-time. This disparity increases at the executive level, where women are 85 percent more likely than their male counterparts to have a partner who works full-time.[5] What this means is that the vast majority of executive men have partners that stay home, yet the majority of executive women have partners that work. This makes the balancing act for women much more difficult.

This gender imbalance between work and home responsibilities also spills over to elder care. Women provide more than twice as much care not only for their own parents, but for their in-laws. This is an additional burden that needs to be shared. And, children need to see it being shared so that their generation will follow suit.

Women often respond to these work-home conflicts in a variety of ways. Some choose not to marry or have children, others choose to become "superwoman" and attempt to excel in every role, and others take leaves of absences, sick days, or choose part-time employment to juggle the conflicts. Moreover, those who take time off from their careers often re-enter at a lower level than they left, making it that much more difficult to rise in the leadership ranks.

◇◇◇◇◇◇◇◇◇◇◇◇◇◇◇

Women are more likely than men to make sacrifices in their own careers to support their partner's careers.

◇◇◇◇◇◇◇◇◇◇◇◇◇◇◇

Millennial couples split household chores more evenly than previous generations, but women under thirty still do most of the child care. Given these statistics, it's not surprising that women are more likely than men to say they make sacrifices in their own careers to support their partners' careers.

Many women I studied and interviewed shared stories about sacrifice. Some have sacrificed marriage, children, or both for their career, while others passed up promotions because of family responsibilities. Lisa, a long-time VP of sales for a pharmaceutical company, chose to forgo a husband and kids to focus on her career. She stated, "I have moved from the U.S. to Canada, to Europe, and back over the past twenty-six years. I've put in the hours and travel and I wasn't hindered by family, but I missed many milestone events in other people's lives." Lisa shared that she regretted her decisions, but felt she had no other options to advance.

One of the questions I asked my study participants was "How does being a woman impact your career aspirations, if at all?" Over 80 percent remarked that being a woman *has* impacted work-life choices they've had to make. What's interesting, is that even though Lisa sacrificed family, she felt that being a woman has not affected her career aspirations. She said, "My brain shows up at work, not my gender."

Denise worked as a senior financial advisor at Merrill Lynch for fifteen years. When she delivered her son, Matthew, she cut her hours from full-time to three days per week until Matthew was three years old. When he turned four years old, she went to four days per week, and when he reached kindergarten, she worked five days per week, but only during school hours between 8:00 a.m. and 3:00 p.m. until he completed elementary school. So, for eleven years, she worked a reduced schedule and put her career on hold.

◇◇◇◇◇◇◇◇◇◇◇◇◇◇◇◇

Even women have gender biases against other women.

◇◇◇◇◇◇◇◇◇◇◇◇◇◇◇◇

All her clients were fine with her schedule, except one female leader who felt that all advisors should work full time. Ironically, this female manager had a stay-at-home husband and a nanny. This shows that even women have gender biases against other women. What's more, is that David, a male advisor at the firm, worked the same schedule as Denise when his son was born, but received much grief about it, and after a short time, was forced to resume a full-time schedule—another example of role congruity and social expectations we have of men and women. In this case, Denise was given leeway to care for her child, but David was not allowed the same accommodations.

Women are often limited by underlying assumptions. A common example is mothers with young children. Often, women apply for leadership roles or new assignments that might require travel, but are turned down. They may have been told that there were more qualified candidates, or they were needed more in their current roles, or given some other reason as to why they didn't get the job. Her manager, and even her teammates, may assume that because of her children, she wouldn't want to travel or be committed to the job. Thus, she gets passed over because of gender stereotypes.

Even more prejudicial is the perception that women of child-bearing age are risky for hire or promotion—whether she plans on having children or not. This is what's been called the *motherhood penalty*. These underlying assumptions control the decision—the employee does not. As a result, women in general (and mothers in particular) fail to advance at rates equal to men.

◇◇◇◇◇◇◇◇◇◇◇◇◇◇

Women are not less ambitious than men. It's the cost of ambition and the struggle women face that matters most.

◇◇◇◇◇◇◇◇◇◇◇◇◇◇

The extreme demands of many 24/7 work environments today represent an impasse to many women who wish to prioritize life outside of work. As I've mentioned, women often want and value different things than men. However, women are *not* less ambitious than men. Rather, it's about the *cost* of ambition and the struggle women face in pursuing their professional goals that matters most. This is one of the major reasons why we have so few women leaders today. Women view their work more holistically—as only one piece of the pie that represents their total life experience. If they're forced to focus 24/7 on work for much of their professional lives, most women will choose not to pay that price.

Sacrifice. Struggle. Conflict. Imbalance. Bias. To overcome these obstacles, it takes one enduring characteristic—grit. I love that word. Grit is about staying focused on your goals, overcoming setbacks, working hard, strength of character, passion, perseverance, determination, fortitude, courage, tenacity, sturdiness, stamina, diligence, resilience, believing you're going to succeed, finishing what you started, and sticking with your future.

◇◇◇◇◇◇◇◇◇◇◇◇◇◇◇

Grit is a unique combination of passion and perseverance for long-term goals.

◇◇◇◇◇◇◇◇◇◇◇◇◇◇◇

The term grit has been around a long time, but it's recently been popularized by Angela Duckworth's book *Grit: The power of passion and perseverance*. Duckworth describes grit as a unique combination of passion and perseverance for long-term goals.[6] A grit mindset is about living life as a marathon, not a sprint. It's about breaking barriers at work. It's about rising to leadership. And, it's about turning the word impossible into "I'm possible."

Like emotional intelligence, doing well in school, work and life, depends much more on grit than on your ability to learn quickly or your IQ score. To integrate and manage work-life priorities, and overcome all the obstacles along the way, it takes a tremendous amount of grit—and women demonstrate it every day!

Rework Work

Work is not working for lots of workers. Recent data from the U.S. Department of Labor reports that 70 percent of women with children under eighteen years old participate in the labor market in some way, signaling a change from the days where father went off to work and mother stayed home and raised the children.[7]

Yet, more than 90 percent of women and men believe a leave of absence to handle a family matter will hurt their career.[8] This is a clear indication that employees do not feel safe nor supported when it comes to managing life outside of work. Work-life conflicts grabbed management's attention in the 1980s, largely because of the increased entry of women with dependent children into the workforce. Thus, most major organizations took actions to make their workplaces more family-friendly. But, they quickly realized that work-life conflicts were not limited to female employees with children— male workers and women without children were also facing this problem due to heavy workloads and increased travel demands. Add to this the increasing number of single-parent households, and it makes these conflicts even more arduous.

Organizations today are modifying their workplace with scheduling options and benefits to accommodate the varied needs of a diverse workforce. Here are examples of what some companies are doing to help employees reduce work-life conflicts.

- Time-based strategies—flextime, job sharing, telecommuting, and leave for new parents.
- Information-based strategies—work-life support programs, relocation assistance, elder care resources, and counseling services.
- Money-based strategies—flexible benefits, adoption assistance, domestic partner benefits, and scholarships and tuition reimbursement.
- Direct services—onsite child care, fitness center, concierge services, and free or discounted company products.
- Culture change strategies—training managers to help employees deal with work-life conflicts, training managers how to supervise employees with flexible work arrangements, and tying manager pay to employee satisfaction.

Time pressures aren't always the primary problem underlying work-life conflicts. The psychological incursion of work into the family—and vice versa—can be just as disrupting. When people are worrying about personal problems at work and thinking about work problems at home it creates conflict. This suggests organizations should spend less effort helping employees with time-management issues and more in helping them clearly segment their lives. Keeping workloads reasonable, reducing work-related travel, and offering onsite quality child care are examples of practices that can help this endeavor. Employees can also reduce interference between work and home by increasing the amount of planning they do.[9]

◇◇◇◇◇◇◇◇◇◇◇◇◇◇◇◇◇◇

Time pressures aren't always the primary problem underlying work-life conflicts.

◇◇◇◇◇◇◇◇◇◇◇◇◇◇◇◇◇◇

Work-family policies make good business sense. Would you agree with this statement? Surprisingly, this statement appears to be mostly false. At first glance, it would seem natural that these policies would increase employee engagement, productivity, and commitment. In more than half of U.S. married couples, both partners are working. Almost half of U.S. children live with a single working parent, and nearly half the workforce has elder care responsibilities. Further, employees say they want to work from home so much that 62 percent would be willing to give up social media, chocolate, vacation days, even salary increases for the benefit.[10] Now that's a sacrifice.

Yet, there seems to be a difference between policies employees say they want and those that yield positive outcomes. Research is inconsistent about the benefits of work-family policies. Some studies indicate improved employee recruitment and retention. Others have found no relationship between work-family policies and employee job satisfaction or intention to stay.

When it comes to work-family policies, human resource professionals must balance providing the benefits employees value against the organizational costs of unclear business outcomes. The good news from a business perspective is that many employees will not use many work-family benefits. Even though parents of both genders are concerned about balancing work and family, they take very little advantage of family-friendly programs, often for fear of being penalized at work. Yet, per a recent study, employees in organizations with multiple work-family policies were more likely to have positive attitudes toward their employer, whether they exercised their options or not.[11] Nonetheless, companies need to do more to foster a culture that gives employees permission to take advantage of these options.

In many cases, this requires a more holistic approach to employee programs. Take parental leave as an example. Offering it piecemeal is not enough—it needs to be available to men and women at every level. In addition, employees need to know that management supports their decisions to start families and take parental leave. One way to do this is making sure high-profile women and men take full advantage of such programs and celebrating their decisions publicly. Can you imagine the example it would set if the male president of your company took a three-month parental leave?

◇◇◇◇◇◇◇◇◇◇◇◇◇◇

At every stage, women are less eager than men to become a top executive.

◇◇◇◇◇◇◇◇◇◇◇◇◇◇

Another issue impacted by work-life concerns is the leadership pipeline. At every stage, from entry to midlevel, women are less eager than men to become a top executive, and this gap is widest among women and men in senior management. Women are more likely to cite stress or pressure of a role as a top issue, and this is not solely rooted in concern over family responsibilities. Men, too, cite balancing work and family as their main concern.[12] There are a few possible explanations: the cost and struggle of ambition matter more to women, the path to leadership is disproportionately stressful for women, and differences in the emotional intelligence competency of stress tolerance.

As women journey through their career, their path is often riddled with challenges all along the way. Add to this the additional child care and household responsibilities, and it's no wonder women don't want the added stress. Further, women value different things than men do.

One of my study participants, Diane, worked as VP of HR global learning and organizational development at a pharmaceutical company. One of the questions I her asked is, "Do you desire to be promoted to leadership or higher levels of leadership?" Her response surprised me. She had absolutely no desire to advance to the next step, Executive VP, because of the increased stress. She said it would require interfacing with the board of directors and being at their beck and call, with little to no work-life balance—and she was not willing to take that on. Yet, her male counterparts would jump at the chance.

◇◇◇◇◇◇◇◇◇◇◇◇◇◇

Women don't often desire to take on leadership roles with additional stress and pressure.

◇◇◇◇◇◇◇◇◇◇◇◇◇◇

Recall that one of the gender-specific EQ differences between men and women is stress tolerance. In general, men tend to score higher in managing and tolerating stress than women. This could be attributed to hard-wired differences or it could be due to differences in juggling multiple priorities. Whatever the reasons, women don't often desire to take on leadership roles with additional stress and pressure.

Work-life stress also takes its toll on Millennials. Why do one-third of Millennials say managing their work, family, and personal responsibilities has become more difficult in the last five years? Because many of them are moving into management at the same time they are becoming parents. Their work hours have increased over the last five years, they are twice as likely to travel overnight for business as other generations, and they are more likely to be part of a dual-career family than their Boomer counterparts. They want to work flexibly without stigmas and are willing to make tough choices and sacrifices to better manage work and home.

Given these challenges, what do employees want in today's workplace? When seeking a job, after competitive pay and benefits, being able to work flexibly, not working excessive overtime, and receiving paid parental leave were cited as important or very important across generations.

Surprisingly, nearly two-thirds of full-time employees who are parents did *not* take paid parental leave in the U.S., and over three-quarters of women indicate their spouses or partners are not eligible for paid parental leave.

Millennial parents are much more likely to take paid parental leave compared to parents of older generations when they had children. Women are more likely to take it than men, and on average, women took four and a half weeks of paid parental leave while men took just over two weeks.[13]

◇◇◇◇◇◇◇◇◇◇◇◇◇◇◇◇

Nearly two-thirds of full-time employees who are parents did not take paid parental leave in the U.S.

◇◇◇◇◇◇◇◇◇◇◇◇◇◇◇◇

What's interesting, and perhaps a sign of changing times, is that Millennials and Gen Xers are much more likely than Boomers to agree that when both parents take leave, they are more likely to equally co-parent. More women than men believe that all parents should have an equal amount of paid parental leave time, and we need both genders to take paid family leave to combat the stigma associated with leave in society.

For years working mothers have been advocating for paid family leave and flextime, with varying success, but it is only recently that more and more men have been asking for these benefits as well. As stated earlier, companies need to do more to foster a culture that gives employees permission to take advantage of these benefits without fear of penalty. The bottom line is that organizations that don't help their people achieve work-life integration will find it increasingly difficult to attract and retain the most capable and motivated employees. The message for companies: You will have a more engaged workforce and greater retention if you offer more liberal leave policies, increase the availability of flextime, and increase the number of personal days that employees can take to spend time with family.

Work-Life Strategies

Today, many companies still adhere to rigid work hours, structure, and policies. One obvious solution is to seek employers that value and promote work-life balance and offer flexible options. If no options are available at your company, request that new programs or policies be created. Companies are more responsive today to both employee and corporate pressures, and chances are others want the same things too.

It's evident that in the increasingly competitive job market, organizations need to think differently about how to attract new employees and retain existing ones. Unfortunately, many of the obvious solutions require a financial investment, such as increasing salaries, bonuses, medical benefits, or vacation days. And, if your competitive advantage in hiring simply boils down to throwing money at the problem, your hires are quite possibly going to jump ship when a higher offer or benefits package is put in front of them.

So, how can an organization increase its benefits without increasing its budget? Many startups and technology companies look to add fun into the mix—billiard tables, foosball tables, nerf guns, happy hours, and pizza Fridays are some examples. But, these won't necessarily appeal to all types of employees, and it may not be a sustainable option.

The Executive Education program at MIT Sloan School of Management took a different approach by introducing flex-time.[14] Working directly with their human resources department, they launched a remote work pilot for their team of thirty-five employees. The program has several key principles:

- Everyone is encouraged to work remotely at least two to three days per week.
- Wednesdays are the "work in the office if you physically can" days.
- You don't need to work a strict nine-to-five schedule, but be mindful of regular business hours and don't expect others to match your unique working hours.
- Don't feel that you need to be connected 24/7.

This foundation proved instrumental in having the team understand the opportunities and responsibilities in having a flex-time schedule. After the six-month trial period, they surveyed the team to determine if this arrangement was a viable and successful long-term benefit. The survey found that 100 percent of the team said they would recommend working remotely to other departments.

The financial cost was negligible as they simply added a benefit that did not increase their personnel budget. They found both tangible and intangible bottom-line benefits to their flex-time program. For example, their employees report feeling less stressed simply because, for some, they reduced or eliminated a grueling commute. Thus, they saw less absenteeism. This is consistent with a 2014 survey on workplace flexibility by the Society for Human Resource Management, which found that one-third of companies saw a decrease in absenteeism after they implemented flex-time policies.[15]

MIT's flex-time program also delivered financial gain in the form of increased productivity, regardless of the weather. Boston is well-known for its harsh winters. However, their team members could put in full, productive days from their homes, without the stress of driving in the snow or having to take delayed mass transit options.

◇◇◇◇◇◇◇◇◇◇◇◇◇◇◇

Traditional work practices, like required office hours, can come off as a lack of trust for employees' ability to get the job done.

◇◇◇◇◇◇◇◇◇◇◇◇◇◇◇

Most surprising is how the program has impacted employee trust. Peter Hirst, director of the program states, "When we were first launching the program, we didn't realize how the program communicates the trust we have for our staff. We trust our people to be professionals and understand what needs to be done, regardless of where they work." It's easy to forget how traditional work practices—like required office hours—can often come off as a lack of trust for employees' ability to get the job done. When they surveyed their staff, 62 percent recorded an improved feeling of trust and respect.[16] Based on this statistic alone, it's clear that people who feel trusted will get their work done efficiently while improving overall morale and company culture. Even though their journey into flex-time is relatively new, they expect that offering flex-time will have a meaningful financial impact on their ability to retain and recruit high-quality employees.

Regarding women and their disproportionate share of domestic and child care duties, here are some strategies to consider. Research shows that when men do their share of chores, their partners are happier and less depressed, conflicts are fewer, and divorce rates are lower.[17] They live longer too. Studies demonstrate that there's a longevity boost for men and women who provide care and emotional support to their partners later in life.[18] But, the greatest positive impact may be on the next generation. Research in numerous countries reveals that children of involved fathers are healthier, happier, and less likely to have behavioral problems. They are also more likely to succeed in school and, later, in their careers.

When children see their mothers pursuing careers and their fathers doing housework, they're more likely to carry gender equality forward to the next generation. And when we make headway toward gender equality, entire societies prosper.

◇◇◇◇◇◇◇◇◇◇◇◇◇◇◇◇

When fathers equally share housework, their daughters were less likely to choose stereotypically female occupations.

◇◇◇◇◇◇◇◇◇◇◇◇◇◇◇◇

A powerful study led by the University of British Columbia psychologist Alyssa Croft showed that when fathers shouldered an equal share of housework, their daughters were less likely to limit their aspirations to stereotypically female occupations.[19] What mattered most was what fathers did, not what they said. For a girl to believe she has the same opportunities as boys, it makes a big difference to see Dad doing the dishes.

Research over the last forty years has consistently found that in comparison to children with less-involved fathers, children with involved fathers have higher levels of psychological well-being, better cognitive abilities, higher levels of educational and economic achievement, and lower delinquency rates.[20]

From an emotional intelligence perspective, some EQ competencies improve as well. These children tend to be more empathetic and socially competent. But, these EQ benefits aren't limited to just the children. Parents benefit too. For men, participating in child rearing fosters the development of patience, empathy, and adaptability. For women, earning money increases their decision-making ability, their bargaining power, protects them in case of divorce, and provides important financial security in later years, as women often outlive their husbands.[21] Not to mention that their confidence gets a boost, as well as their independence.

It's a fact that sometimes women prefer to stay home full-time with the children and willingly forfeit their careers. Sometimes it's a necessity that women stay home, such as the need to breast-feed. Sometimes women are forced to stay home due to pressures from their partners or families. And, sometimes it's adherence to gender stereotypes based on the couple's own biases. Regardless of the reasons, women who choose a professional path should have the same opportunities as men and be supported in their efforts.

There is no doubt that when men and women are in roles that are incongruent to stereotypic expectations, that they face intense social pressures from family, friends, and coworkers. For men, it can be especially difficult to buck these stereotypes. Nonetheless, if we desire more equality, we need to be comfortable in our skin, be true to our values, and be confident in our decisions and actions. Society needs to embrace and support men who share responsibilities, and men need to let go of their ego when it comes to child care and household chores, and see that sharing responsibilities as an equal partner will reap tremendous rewards in their relationship.

In chapter five, we discussed unconscious bias, and how these hidden, reflexive preferences shape our world views and affect how welcoming and open a workplace is to different people and ideas. One solution is to make sure you proactively and consistently communicate your desires to advance, travel, or take a new assignment—especially if you have children. This type of communication will eliminate ambiguity and help put to rest any biases or assumptions made about you.

◇◇◇◇◇◇◇◇◇◇◇◇◇◇

We must make a conscious effort to break gender patterns and assumptions if we are to ever reach equality.

◇◇◇◇◇◇◇◇◇◇◇◇◇◇

It's promising that the household division of labor is split more evenly with Millennials, but remember that they grew up watching their parents who probably adhered to more traditional roles of caregiving. Therefore, their attitudes are based on their childhoods of watching their mothers care for the children while their fathers earned the wages. To counter this, we must make a conscious effort to break these patterns and assumptions if we are to ever reach equality.

The good news is that Millennial men appear more eager to be real partners than men in previous generations. One study in over 1,000 adults asked participants to rate the importance of various job characteristics. Among Millennials, 82 percent said "having a work schedule that allows me to spend time with my family" was very important.[22] I am very encouraged by this data, and believe that we are moving in the right direction.

In a 2015 *New York Times* article by Sheryl Sandberg and Adam Grant, they suggest that to make gender parity a reality, we need to change the way we advocate for it.[23] I completely agree. The usual focus is on fairness—to achieve justice, we need to give women equal opportunities. They state that we need to go further and articulate why equality is not just the right thing to do for women, but the desirable thing for us all.

The women's suffrage movement in the late nineteenth century provides a good case study. States did not grant voting rights when women campaigned for justice; suffrage laws got passed only when women described how having the right to vote would enable them to improve society. Similarly, during the civil rights movement, Martin Luther King, Jr. was careful to emphasize that racial equality would be good for everyone. Many men who support equality hold back because they worry it's not their battle to fight. It's time for men and women alike to join forces in championing gender parity. It's for these reasons that we must empower more women at work, and empower more men at home.

◇◇◇◇◇◇◇◇◇◇◇◇◇◇◇◇◇◇

The more parity there is at home, the more parity there will be at work.

◇◇◇◇◇◇◇◇◇◇◇◇◇◇◇◇◇◇

Perfect fifty-fifty equality between partners is hard to define and sustain at any given moment, but the pendulum should swing back and forth regularly. The more balance there is at home, the more balance there will be at work. Another way of putting it—the more parity there is at home, the more parity there will be at work. It's important to note that work-life balance or work-life integration is not just a women's issue, it's a people issue, and it benefits everyone—men, women, and organizations.

For women, it's a daily struggle to try and do it all—and many women try. Women want to be helpful, women want to be supportive, and women want to give their whole selves—and there's certainly nothing wrong with that. In the words of Brené Brown, we must remind ourselves that as women "We are enough." It's okay to be vulnerable because being vulnerable is not weakness, it's the measure of courage.[24]

When Nora Ephron presented the 1996 Wellesley commencement speech addressing the issue of women having both a career and family, she said, "It will be a little messy, but embrace the mess. It will be complicated, but rejoice in the complications. It will not be anything like what you think it will be like, but surprises are good for you. And don't be frightened; you can always change your mind."[25] Indeed, for many women, life may not be the party we hoped for, but while we're here we might as well dance.

Summary Points
- Millennials want a healthier work-life relationship, one that promotes flexibility, company trust, and the ability to work from anywhere.
- Lifestyle and family choices contribute to the leadership gender gap.

- Women perform most domestic and child care duties, even when there are two spouses working full-time.
- Most executive men have partners who stay home, yet the majority of executive women have partners who work.
- Millennial couples split household chores more evenly than previous generations, but women under thirty still do most of the child care.
- Women are not less ambitious than men. It's the cost of ambition and the struggle women face that matters most.
- Grit is a unique combination of passion and perseverance for long-term goals. It takes grit to integrate and manage work-life priorities and overcome obstacles.
- Organizations should spend less effort helping employees with time-management issues and more in helping them clearly segment their lives.
- Nearly two-thirds of full-time employees who are parents did not take paid parental leave in the U.S.
- There are many strategies to help reduce work-life conflicts for both men and women.

Reflection Questions

- ✓ How do you manage work-life priorities? What's working and not working?
- ✓ Does your spouse or partner work full-time? How have you divided the household and child care duties, if applicable? Is it an even split, or do you do more or less?
- ✓ In your company, have you seen a shift in attitudes about work-life balance or work-life integration? Has your company changed any policies or added new programs?
- ✓ When you leave the office, does your work stop or does it continue into the evening? What can you do reduce competing work-life priorities?

✓ Have you ever requested a flexible schedule or telecommuting option from your employer? If so, what was the response? If not, what do you think the response would be?

✓ Have you ever made a job or career change to better manage work and personal responsibilities? If not, would you? What are the costs and benefits to you?

✓ Have you made sacrifices to manage your life and career? Have you made sacrifices for your spouse or partner's career? What was the outcome?

✓ Have you ever been denied a promotion or assignment because of assumptions or biases? What transpired? What did you do?

✓ Have you ever taken a leave of absence from your company, such as parental, personal, or medical leave? What was the outcome? If not, would you be willing to take a leave if necessary?

✓ Does your company offer work-life programs and benefits? Have you taken advantage of them? Why or why not?

EIGHT

Are We Limiting Ourselves?

*What lies behind us and what lies ahead of us are tiny matters
compared to what lies within us.*
Ralph Waldo Emerson

We are not born holding ourselves back. Just as many young girls as boys aspire to be astronauts, doctors, inventors, artists, pilots, professors, firefighters, attorneys, marine biologists, professional athletes, or even President of the United States. When we were children, our aspirations were limitless and anything seemed possible. When you were young, what did you dream of being when you grew up? Is it what you ended up doing?

Childhood aspirations are shaped by the people, standards and social expectations that surround us. When we're small, most of us have a limited idea of what's out there, so our dreams are shaped by what we're exposed

137

to. Our families greatly influence our outlook on life. If we look up to one family member in particular, we tend to be drawn to their career as we want to be like them. And, it's not just our relatives' roles at work that can influence children's aspirations. The gender roles that our parents take on at home can also dramatically impact our childhood career dreams.

In the last chapter, we discussed how a father's behavior around the house seems to be a predictor of his daughter's career aspirations beyond what he might be publicly endorsing or saying about gender roles. If fathers talk about supporting gender equality but don't take on equal roles in domestic tasks, then this sends conflicting signals to their daughters—which lead daughters to place more weight on their fathers' actions rather than their words.

◇◇◇◇◇◇◇◇◇◇◇◇◇◇◇◇

We are not born holding ourselves back.

◇◇◇◇◇◇◇◇◇◇◇◇◇◇◇◇

By contrast, as fathers demonstrated their beliefs in gender equality by taking on an equal distribution of domestic tasks, their daughters would select roles that are more gender neutral or even male-stereotypic, such as a scientist or athlete. Their decisions; however, are important as it could have a major impact on their paychecks down the line. Girls who aspired to traditionally female-dominated occupations were far more likely to earn lower wages in their first jobs, since stereotypically female jobs tend to pay less.[1] And, these stereotypically male or female preferences that children exhibit during childhood continue into (and have a profound effect on) our adult lives.

So, what happened to those childhood dreams? Over time, through the socialization process, girls are both positively and negatively reinforced to be compliant, cooperative, supportive, unassertive, risk averse, avoid conflict, and fit in. Women learn that confidence and leadership ambition are inversely linked to their overall likeability and acceptance. We are consistently taught to aim lower than men, and as a result, we do.

Hanging Up Our Heels

In study after study, starting in junior high school, if you ask boys and girls, "Do you want to lead—lead your junior high class, lead your high school class, lead your club in college, lead a team or company you join as an adult?", more males than females respond yes, and it's one of the reasons we have a world where so few of the top corporate jobs are held by women.

The dramatic shift in mindset from *anything is possible* to *limited possibilities* speak to the power of socialization and the very real pressures imposed on women throughout their lives. The barriers to leadership that we've discussed so far—role congruity and gender bias, structural obstacles, and work-life issues—accumulate and can interfere with a woman's ability to see herself and be seen by others as a leader. It's no surprise then that because of the mixed social and cultural messages, expectations, and reinforcement, that women often hold themselves back.

A 2012 report by McKinsey showed a startling statistic.[2] They interviewed two hundred female executives across various industries in positions of directors, vice presidents, and senior vice presidents. These women were successful and adapted to the male environments in which they operated and overcame extraordinary challenges through stamina and sheer grit. When they were asked, "Do you desire to be part of the C-suite?" 59 percent of the women did *not* aspire to C-level leadership, such as Chief Executive Officer, Chief Financial Officer, or Chief Operating Officer.

The reasons they gave were, "When you see it up close, it's not clean at the top. Motives are not always enterprise-related, and it's more about personal agendas." Also, "My ego aspires to make it happen, but my authentic self is not sure if it's worth it. It would require me to do more and more politics, and I don't want to. I don't enjoy that."[3] These attitudes are common among women and contribute to the leadership gap.

Even among the most successful women who were interviewed, more than half felt they held themselves back from accelerated growth. Most said they should have cultivated sponsors earlier because a sponsor would have pushed them to take more risks. Too often, these women said, they did not raise their hands or even consider stretch roles. Another interesting finding is that more women than men reported they would likely move into (or be willing to) take support positions—thus perpetuating the leadership imbalance.

◇◇◇◇◇◇◇◇◇◇◇◇◇◇◇

Women need to shift their thinking from "I'm not ready" to "I want to learn and grow from this opportunity".

◇◇◇◇◇◇◇◇◇◇◇◇◇◇◇

A recent article in the *Orange County Business Journal* brings this to life.[4] Tanya Domier nearly turned down a job leading one of Orange County's largest private companies. She was president of Advantage Solutions' marketing division when the founder of the company suggested the promotion. She said, "I have no interest in being CEO—I have three little boys and a husband, and there's an appreciable difference between being the number three person in the company, which I am today, and the number one person," said Domier.

A few years later, the company went on the sales block. The founder's prodding escalated and a few board members said to her, "Tanya, you're crazy. This is a once-in-a-lifetime opportunity…you're going to stay for the next deal anyways, why wouldn't you want to be the CEO?" She went home, talked to her family, and decided to throw her hat in the ring. She said, "It was the best decision I have ever made."

Tanya attributes her reluctance to a phenomenon that's been widely discussed. Rarely has there been a man who had been offered a promotion that said, "I'm not ready." Unfortunately, it's a rather common trait of women who are offered the next spot to say, "Oh, I don't think so," "I'm not quite ready," "I still have a lot to learn," or "I have other priorities." An internal report at Hewlett-Packard revealed that women only apply for open jobs if they think they meet 100 percent of the criteria listed. Men apply if they think they meet 60 percent of the requirements.[5] Women need to shift their thinking from "I'm not ready" to "I want to learn and grow from this opportunity." No one goes into a job totally prepared for it. As Wayne Gretzky said, you miss 100 percent of the shots you don't take.

Tanya shares that "I had no aspirations to be CEO—none. I didn't ever question my strengths; it was very important to me to have a successful family. And I felt like I was in such a great position of juggling being a mom and a wife and the president of marketing that I felt like I was going to have to make tradeoffs in my family life to be able to get the top job, and it wasn't worth it to me. What I didn't realize is there were no tradeoffs, because I already worked a ton. Being number one wasn't any harder than number three. It was just different. And in some ways, it's easier because you do have a little bit more control over your schedule. So, it is interesting. I call myself an accidental CEO."[6] Tanya was just named the *Journal*'s Business Person of the Year in the services category.

◇◇◇◇◇◇◇◇◇◇◇◇◇◇◇◇

The top three occupations for women are administrative assistant, teacher, and nurse—all are staff roles.

◇◇◇◇◇◇◇◇◇◇◇◇◇◇◇◇

Women enter the workforce at equal or greater numbers than men. Starting at the middle-manager level and moving all the way to the C-suite, women start to fall off precipitously by either shifting from line roles to staff roles, self-selecting out of the workforce, or simply stop trying and just settle in. What this means is that most women never reach the vice president, president, or C-level positions, and the exodus of highly educated women is a talent drain on companies hoping to compete.

At the director level, women either stay there, or begin to shift toward staff roles. Back in chapter one, we discussed that the top three occupations for women are administrative assistant, teacher, and nurse—all are staff roles. A staff role provides support for an organization, such as legal, human resources, and customer service, whereas a line role has profit and loss responsibility and is focused on core operations. Line jobs are less flexible than staff jobs, so as women form families, staff jobs look more appealing, and women know that line jobs carry more pressure. The downside of this strategy is that C-suite executives and other senior leaders are promoted more often from line roles than from staff roles.

Another way women potentially limit themselves is by doing *office housework*. What might this mean? It's getting the coffee, taking the notes, picking up the donuts, helping new hires, cleaning out the refrigerator, planning the holiday party, and all the other behind-the-scenes work that helps a company run smoothly. The issue here is these are time consuming activities that women volunteer for, often don't get recognized, and cause women to miss opportunities. The person taking copious notes in the meeting almost never makes the stand-out point. On the other hand, men tend to volunteer for activities that are more public and visible that do get recognized, such as serving on cross-functional teams or showing up at optional meetings.

Someone must carry out these administrative tasks—and just as happens with housework at home, that someone is usually a woman. Unfortunately, these communal contributions often get overlooked, taken for granted, or simply disappear. So, why do women volunteer for these activities? Because women want to be helpful and supportive—and that's a wonderful trait.

◇◇◇◇◇◇◇◇◇◇◇◇◇◇◇◇

The bottom line is that having people help both behind the scenes and in public is essential for any business.

◇◇◇◇◇◇◇◇◇◇◇◇◇◇◇◇

In keeping with deeply held gender stereotypes, we expect men to be ambitious and results-oriented, and women to be nurturing and communal. When a man offers to help, we shower him with praise and rewards. But, when a woman helps, we feel less indebted. She's communal, right? She wants to be a team player. The reverse is also true. When a woman declines to help a colleague, people like her less and her career suffers. But, when a man says no, he faces no backlash. A man who doesn't help is "busy;" a woman is "selfish." Because of this double standard, women pay a professional penalty for their presumed desire to be helpful.

The bottom line is that having people help both behind the scenes and in public is essential for any business. Research shows that teams with greater helping behavior attain greater profits, sales, quality, effectiveness, revenue, and customer satisfaction. In their quest to care for others, women often sacrifice themselves. For every one thousand people at work, eighty more women than men burn out in large part because they fail to secure their own oxygen masks before assisting others.[7]

Talking to Ourselves

In the next chapter, we will explore gender differences in many aspects of both life and work. When it comes to communication, there are numerous ways that we are different. Let's look at how we talk about and describe our successes and failures.

Henry and Brenda have worked tirelessly on a large-scale project for the past six months, and have just completed it. At a recent meeting, they were invited to roll out their new project to the sales team. After their presentation, they received much praise on the new initiative. Henry responds with, "Thanks, I worked really hard on this and it was tough going," then provides details about his efforts the past several months. Brenda responds to the praise by saying, "We got really lucky, and the team that worked with us on this project was just fantastic!" Can you see the difference in their responses?

When it comes to *success,* men tend to point inward (taking the credit themselves) attributing it to their innate skills and talent. Women point outward (giving others credit) attributing it to external factors, such as, "I had a great team," "It was good timing," or "I got lucky." Now, let's look at the other end of the spectrum. When it comes to *failure*, men point outward (blaming others or external factors), saying things such as, "I didn't try that hard," or "I wasn't that interested." As you may have guessed, women behave exactly the opposite. Women point inward (blaming themselves), attributing failure to an inherent lack of ability or lack of effort.[8]

◇◇◇◇◇◇◇◇◇◇◇◇◇◇◇

Giving others credit and acknowledging the team is a good thing, but it can't come at the expense of your own self-respect and self-regard.

◇◇◇◇◇◇◇◇◇◇◇◇◇◇◇

The way we internalize and communicate success and failure is a real issue. For women, it creates self-doubt, insecurity, and affects our self-esteem—not to mention confidence in our abilities to take on future projects or challenges. If we are always giving credit for our successes to others, then we never get the chance to truly own our accomplishments based on our own knowledge, skills, and qualities. Neither approach is perfect. Men need to be more thoughtful about acknowledging the team and others, and women need to take ownership and accountability for their own achievements.

Another concern pertains to perception. What messages are we sending our leadership teams and colleagues if our successes are always due to other people or other factors? What does it say about your efforts and ability to accomplish tasks? What does it say about your leadership skills? For men, what messages are they sending? At best, it conveys that they are confident, independent, and can get the job done. At worst, it conveys that they are selfish. It's important to note that giving others credit and acknowledging the team is a good thing, but it can't come at the expense of your own self-respect and self-regard.

When it comes to negative self-talk, it's no surprise that women are much harder on themselves than men. When a man and woman each receive negative feedback, the woman's self-confidence and self-esteem drop to a much greater degree.[9] Even when a compliment is given, women tend to deflect praise or minimize their accomplishments. In addition, consistently attributing failure to ourselves, even when it's not our fault, wreaks havoc on our confidence. Even before we try, we often tell ourselves, "I can't do that," "I wouldn't be good at that," "I'm not ready for that," or "I'm not experienced enough for that." These self-imposed limits lead us to inaction, which preserves our inexperience, which reinforces our self-doubt. We must break this vicious circle by letting go of negative self-talk.

For many women, self-doubt is a form of self-defense. To protect ourselves from being disliked for being too successful, we question our abilities and downplay our achievements, especially in the presence of others. We put ourselves down before others can. We are our worst critic, and we need to be kinder and gentler with ourselves.

◇◇◇◇◇◇◇◇◇◇◇◇◇◇◇◇◇◇

For women, focusing on confidence and assertiveness are arguably the most important to advance your career.

◇◇◇◇◇◇◇◇◇◇◇◇◇◇◇◇◇◇

From an emotional intelligence perspective, recall that overall, men score higher than women in confidence and assertiveness. However, this doesn't mean that all women lack confidence and assertiveness, and it doesn't mean that you can't improve in these areas. In chapter three, I provided numerous EQ strategies to help bolster these qualities. Of all the EQ competences, for women, focusing on confidence and assertiveness are arguably the *most important* to help you advance your career.

Here's the critical concept—confidence and assertiveness are *skills*—not elusive genes you're either born with or without. While qualities such as confidence, leadership, vulnerability to stress, empathy, and others, are partly influenced by genetics, these are fluid and flexible life skills that can be developed with awareness, focus, and practice.

Men score higher in confidence and assertiveness because they are socialized to be confident and assertive. These are qualities we expect in men—to be confident, assertive, driven, decisive, results-oriented, competitive, and even aggressive. We expect women to be unassertive, supportive, caring, kind, sensitive, people-oriented, and nurturing. These social expectations are nothing but gender stereotypes—there are many women who are decisive and competitive, and many men who are supportive and sensitive. Yet, these stereotypes are at the core of why women are held back, and why women hold themselves back.

Regarding leadership, we explored agentic leader qualities in chapter five. These are male-related qualities that both men and women associate with being a leader. These opposing social expectations strongly communicate that women are ill-suited for leadership roles and sets women up for inherent conflicts as they advance. For example, it's difficult for a female leader—or any leader for that matter—to be both confident *and* unassertive, aggressive *and* sensitive, or results-driven *and* nurturing. As noted earlier, research shows that when it comes to leadership skills, although men are more confident, women are more competent.

◇◇◇◇◇◇◇◇◇◇◇◇◇◇◇

Confidence trumps competence.

◇◇◇◇◇◇◇◇◇◇◇◇◇◇◇

Here's the rub. It's been shown by researchers at the University of California, Berkeley, that team members who speak up and appear more confident, are perceived by others as competent to lead, even if they lack competence in the subject matter.[10] Even though they lacked skills, the most dominant personalities were rated the highest for such qualities as general intelligence, conscientiousness, dependability, and self-discipline. At the same time, subjects perceived less outspoken team members as having less desirable traits, giving them high scores for being conventional and uncreative. These findings suggest that dominant individuals can ascend group hierarchies and attain influence simply by appearing confident and speaking up. For women, these are important findings because—while this may be troublesome—confidence trumps competence. So, to appear more confident and improve your own reputation, simply speak up.

We hold ourselves back by lacking confidence, not raising our hands, and not speaking our minds. I witness this every week in class. In the MBA courses I teach, the young women don't speak up and don't raise their hands as often as the young men. Given that my doctoral research focused on women and leadership, I am sensitive to gender dynamics in the classroom. Just this week, Anna, one of my students, wanted to talk outside of class. She shared with me that she's been struggling the past few weeks. This came as a big surprise. Of the six women in the class, she comes across as one of the most self-assured and outspoken. However, she said she suffers from social anxiety and a lot of self-doubt. After talking for a few minutes, I realized it was a confidence issue. She does not see herself as others see her. Because of her self-doubt, she holds back and doesn't share her opinions. I reassured her that her contributions are valuable, that she's on equal footing with her classmates (they are not superior to her), and that she truly belongs—her eyes filled with tears. Sometimes we just need a little encouragement.

◇◇◇◇◇◇◇◇◇◇◇◇◇◇◇◇

Women tend to judge their performance as worse than it is; men judge their performance as better.

◇◇◇◇◇◇◇◇◇◇◇◇◇◇◇◇

We internalize the negative messages we get throughout our lives—the messages that say it's wrong to be outspoken, aggressive, more powerful than men—and we consistently underestimate ourselves. Multiple studies show that women tend to judge their own performance as worse than it is, while men judge their performance as better than it is. For example, assessments of medical students in a surgery rotation found that when asked to evaluate themselves, the females gave themselves lower scores than the males, despite faculty evaluations that showed the women outperformed the men.[11]

Unrelenting negative messages make us fearful—and fear is at the root of so many of the barriers that women face. Fear of not being liked. Fear of being excluded. Fear of making the wrong choice. Fear of not being a team player. Fear of drawing negative attention. Fear of overreaching. Fear of being judged. Fear of failure. Fear of being a bad mother, wife, or daughter. Without fear, women can pursue professional success and personal fulfillment—and freely choose one, or the other, or both. I believe that it's nearly impossible not to internalize these messages, at least to some extent, but the good news is we have control to change the way we think about these internal obstacles.

Career Limiting Moves

Much has been written about women's personal branding and image. This includes how you look, how you sound, what you say, and how you act. Inappropriate behavior in any of these areas can lead to career limiting moves, or CLMs, as I like to call them. Often, these are unconscious mistakes that women make at work, and most of the time we're oblivious to the perception we're giving to others.

Let's start with executive presence. Men naturally have what we define as executive presence—height, deep voice, non-emotional, matter-of-fact style of speech, and space-occupying. If a six-foot tall man stands next to a five-foot-three woman at the front of the room, we naturally look to the male as the leader (because of gender and height biases). Women can't do anything about their height, the pitch of their voices, or that they're smaller in stature than most men. So, how do women get around this problem and convey executive presence?

When speaking in public, women must take command of a room, especially if the audience is male-dominated or there are mostly male speakers. Women simply don't command the kind of attention that men do, so we must take control. Too often, I see women speak too softly, fidget, cross their feet, touch their arms, play with their hair, avoid eye contact with the audience, and use fillers, tags, or disclaimers in their speech. These behaviors not only detract from executive presence—an audience could tune out your message altogether or perceive you as unprofessional and not credible.

Women need to use language that gives power, not drains power. This includes what we do with our voices, our speech patterns, and our speaking habits. Many of these habits start in childhood and carry over into adulthood. One of the most common behaviors that takes away our power is phrasing statements as questions by using inflection of our voice—and women do this significantly more than men. For women, it's a safe way of making a statement or expressing an idea without being perceived as too direct or pushy.

For instance, "When I finish this task, the project will be complete?" This is clearly a statement, but by phasing it as a question, it opens the possibility for others to comment, add additional information, or express their concerns about the project—it also sounds like you are unsure of yourself. If you're truly interested in other's opinions, a better approach would be to make your statement, "When I finish this task, the project will be complete." Then, add a tagline after your statement, such as, "I'm interested in your thoughts." Here's another example, "I think that's great?" To the listener, it's unclear whether you think it's great or not, and it doesn't express much conviction. If each of these questions were phrased as statements, it would sound more powerful.

◇◇◇◇◇◇◇◇◇◇◇◇◇◇

Women need to use language that gives power, not drains power.

◇◇◇◇◇◇◇◇◇◇◇◇◇◇

Another language subtlety that drains power are the words we use. Women use qualifiers or hedges—a linguistic tool to soften the tone of our content and hedge a statement. Women do this to avoid coming across as too aggressive and to convey humility and politeness. Examples of hedges are, "I *just* want to check in," "I *just* want to follow-up," "If it's not *too* much trouble," "I'll *try* my best," "I *hope* for the best," and other hedge words including "might," "maybe," "sort of," "kind of," "could be," and "perhaps." For instance, "When she *kind of* talks like this, she *perhaps* doesn't sound like she knows what she's talking about, *maybe*." These language nuances are even found in the pledges of our largest youth organizations—Boys and Girls Scouts of America.[12]

The Boy Scout pledge: "On my honor I *will* do my best to do my duty to God and my country and to obey the Scout Law; to help other people at all times; to keep myself physically strong, mentally awake, and morally straight." Here's the Girl Scout pledge: "On my honor, I will *try* to serve God and my country, to help people at all times, and to live by the Girl Scout Law." The Boy Scout pledge sounds like it has more conviction—they *will* carry out their pledge. On the other hand, the Girl Scouts will *try* to carry out their pledge. There has been much debate within these organizations about their pledges. The Girls Scouts thought by using *try*, instead of *will*, they were being more honest and holding the girls to a more realistic standard.[13] Whichever your preference, which one sounds more confident?

Disclaimers are another example of linguistic tools that women use to weaken their statements and sound less authoritarian. Disclaimers are phrases that precede a statement, but discount its content or importance. The word *but* often bridges the disclaimer and the statement. For example, "I'm not the expert here, *but*…," "I could be wrong, *but*…," "This might not make a lot of sense, *but*…," "You've probably already thought of this, *but*…," or "I'm not sure if this is right, *however*…" To men, these words often convey that women are ignorant or uninformed.

In addition, women use tags at the end of their statements to turn them into questions, such as, "Don't you?", "Correct?", "Right?", "Okay?", "You know?", and "Don't you think?" To men, these words convey, "I need your help." or "I need your assurance."[14] Each of these verbal techniques serves the purpose of involving others in the decision-making process, and appearing humble and polite—yet, they undermine a woman's message and hinder her ability to share her ideas clearly and confidently.

◇◇◇◇◇◇◇◇◇◇◇◇

As with gender stereotypes and leadership, how we talk poses a double bind for women.

◇◇◇◇◇◇◇◇◇◇◇◇

Because men got to the business workplace before women, it is natural that the "first language" of business is the masculine way of speaking. The masculine language is full of declarative statements, such as "I will," "I know," and "I am." The language is objective, to the point, and focuses on facts more than feelings. His direct, more forceful kind of speech sounds confident, competent, and authoritative—important aspects of the male culture where status and power are highly valued. In the female culture, maintaining relationships matters more than status. Power is shared more horizontally than vertically. Thus, the feminine style of language has speech structures that maintain flatness, so women use more questions than declarative statements, and use hedges, disclaimers, and tags more than men.

What's interesting is that a woman who uses this type of language may be very confident, but she's using these speech patterns to level the power in the relationship (especially with other women) and avoid being perceived as superior. This is the same process that we discussed in chapter six, called the power dead-even rule.[15] This rule also partly explains why women credit others for their own successes. Women tend to be more comfortable being part of a group when accepting credit for accomplishments, ideas, and opinions.

As with gender stereotypes and leadership, *how we talk* poses a double bind for women. If a woman speaks according to feminine culture, she may be viewed as lacking confidence, being unassertive, and not being leader-like. Or, she may not be heard at all as in the case of unintentional invisible bias. But, if a woman speaks according to masculine culture, she may be seen as too aggressive and, once again, not being leader-like.

Both men and women can and do speak both languages. Being aware of these differences enables us consciously to use whichever is more effective in each circumstance. Taking someone literally, rather than translating what may be appropriate in their gender culture, can lead to judgment, misunderstanding and frustration. It is true that more words soften a message, but fewer words make it more memorable. If your message is important, try to say it in as few words as possible. In my years of pharmaceutical sales, we were taught to be as direct and concise as possible to convey our messages clearly to customers. One motto I used personally is, "Brevity is beautiful." It's a fact that short sounds more confident than wordy.

◇◇◇◇◇◇◇◇◇◇◇◇◇◇◇◇

More words soften a message, but fewer words make it more memorable.

◇◇◇◇◇◇◇◇◇◇◇◇◇◇◇◇

Avoiding office politics is another potential career limiting move—and I'm guilty of this myself. First, politics in an organization consists of activities that are not required as part of an individual's formal role, but that influence, or attempt to influence, the distribution of advantages and disadvantages within the organization.[16] Second, most people have never been trained on how to use political behavior effectively. The business of politics is the business of relationships and understanding the quid pro quo (something in exchange for something else) inherent in every relationship.[17] It's impossible to completely avoid office politics because it's how work gets done.

There are two main problems with politics at work. First, organizations are made up of individuals with different values, goals, and interests. This sets up the potential for conflict over the allocation of limited resources—such as departmental budgets, office space, project responsibilities, and salary adjustments. Second, and perhaps the most important, is the realization that most of the "facts" used to allocate the limited resources are open to interpretation. Since decisions relating to people are rarely cut and dry, other factors come into play, such as attitude, potential, likeability, loyalty, familiarity, ability to perform under pressure, and so on. It's in this large and ambiguous middle-ground where politics flourish—and people will use whatever influence they can to taint the facts to support their goals and interests.

For women, this is a complete turn-off. This kind of brokering of deals makes women uncomfortable and they find it a little smarmy. Men, on the other hand, are more comfortable with the concept of "You scratch my back, and I'll scratch yours." This may sound familiar to you, as it was discussed in chapter two. It's transactional leadership that focuses on the exchanges that occur between leaders and their followers—and is more commonly associated with men. Politics is one of the facets of the corporate world I dislike the most. The backstabbing, the finger pointing, the jockeying for position, the kissing up, the playing favorites, the inequities, and the self-promoting.

In addition, political behavior moderates the effects of ethical leadership. Men are more responsive to ethical leadership and showed the most citizenship behavior when levels of both politics and ethical leadership where high.

Women are just the opposite and appear most likely to engage in citizenship behavior when the environment is consistently ethical and apolitical.[18] Unfortunately, politics are part of organizational life and deciding not to play is deciding not to be effective. So, my message to women is that you must engage, at least to some extent.

◇◇◇◇◇◇◇◇◇◇◇◇◇◇◇◇

Politics are part of organizational life and deciding not to play is deciding not to be effective.

◇◇◇◇◇◇◇◇◇◇◇◇◇◇◇◇

Professional business attire is an area that has long been problematic for women at work. On one hand, women have many more fashion choices than do men. On the other hand, more choices lead to more areas of gray. We've evolved from the days of buttoned up, formal attire we saw in the 1980s, but the workplace casual trend has made it more difficult. For a man, it's simple—dress shirt, slacks, jacket, and optional tie. For women, determining whether to wear pants or dress, jacket or sleeveless, heels or flats, how high the skirt should go, and how low the blouse should go—are not always easy decisions. Thus, some women have made the mistake of blending business attire with cocktail attire. A study on executive presence by the Center for Talent Innovation showed that senior executives listed twice as many appearance blunders committed by women than men.[19] Notable appearance blunders for women included unkempt attire—83 percent said it detracts from executive presence, and too-tight or provocative clothing—73 percent said it detracts from executive presence.

It's a fact that women are judged more harshly on their appearance than men. It's also a fact that inappropriate attire diminishes your professional power, and has ruined many a career. Executive presence depends on getting three things right: appearance (how you look), communication (how you speak), and gravitas (how you act). These elements interact to generate that aura of authority that sets leaders apart, and are critical to your success at every step in your career journey. Leadership roles are given to those who look and act the part. Top jobs often elude women because they lack executive presence or underestimate its importance. Presence alone won't get you promoted—but its absence will impede your progress, especially if you're female or a person of color. Another interesting finding showed that demonstrating emotional intelligence contributed 61 percent to a woman's executive presence, and 58 percent to a man's executive presence.[20]

As mentioned throughout this book, women have certain advantages when it comes to gender-specific emotional intelligence competencies, as do men. Women score higher than men in empathy, interpersonal relationships, and social responsibility. There is also small, but statistically significant differences that give women an advantage in emotional self-awareness and emotional expression. Historically, these skills have not been valued in the workplace as much as male EQ skills. However, times are changing. As I mentioned earlier, women's gifts are particularly suited to the demands of today's workplace. These skills include building and managing relationships, having a preference for direct communication, leading from the center rather than the top, comfort with diversity, and the ability to integrate multiple concepts and draw information broadly.

◇◇◇◇◇◇◇◇◇◇◇◇◇◇◇◇

Women's gifts are particularly suited to the demands of today's workplace.

◇◇◇◇◇◇◇◇◇◇◇◇◇◇◇◇

In addition, women are more likely to possess leadership characteristics that are predominately effective in contemporary organizations—such as transformational leadership—as compared with their male counterparts. This type of leadership emphasizes intrinsic motivation and follower development, engenders trust and loyalty, improves engagement and productivity, leads to higher retention rates, and ultimately maximizes shareholder value.

Despite these facts, many women minimize or downplay these skills rather than taking advantage of them. Use your empathy to connect with your colleagues and customers, leverage your interpersonal relationships to enhance team building and collaboration, put words to the emotions that you observe in others to show that you can read the room, identify and express your own emotions, and act on your desire to be a good corporate and social citizen. These traits would benefit any organization—and will boost your executive presence as a bonus.

Unlimited Strategies

In this chapter, we've discussed various ways that women hold themselves back for a myriad of reasons—including mixed social and cultural messages, opposing gender expectations, positive and negative reinforcement, and gender culture influences. Let's look at some strategies to help overcome these self-imposed limits.

We began with a discussion about our childhood ambitions. You may dismiss those childhood aspirations as unrealistic now that you're an adult with responsibilities and bills to pay, but that role reflected what you enjoyed doing and who you were at that time. Those childhood dream jobs are a window into our passions and talents. Identifying and understanding those passions are key to improving our performance and enjoyment of the jobs we currently do, even if they aren't specific to the careers we dreamed of as kids. Looking back might help you identify aspects of your job that you love, or it might put you on a completely new path.

I cited the fact that women begin to shift from line roles to staff roles as they advance. Even though line jobs can be less flexible and carry more pressure, if you aspire to be in a leadership position, it's important that you pursue a line role because leaders are promoted more often from these roles. Also, take note of the experiences of executive women who said they've held themselves back by not cultivating sponsors soon enough, not raising their hands, and not considering stretch roles. Don't be afraid to ask for the help you need, for what you want, and to take on new challenges and responsibilities— these activities often lead to positive outcomes.

◇◇◇◇◇◇◇◇◇◇◇◇◇◇◇◇

Don't be afraid to ask for the help you need, for what you want, and to take on new challenges and responsibilities.

◇◇◇◇◇◇◇◇◇◇◇◇◇◇◇◇

We discussed the concept of office housework, and the fact that women volunteer for behind-the-scenes activities that don't get recognized far greater than men do. One suggestion is to not always volunteer. While these activities are supportive and helpful, let other women and men contribute. If you oversee selecting people for these duties, assign tasks rather than asking for volunteers. This will ensure an even gender distribution, ensure that the support work is noticed and valued, and ensure that no one person will be overburdened.

Here's an example of what one female manager did. She worked in a consulting firm and was passed over for a promotion because her helping and support activities, which took up her time, were not recognized by the firm. So, she found more efficient ways to help. Instead of meeting one-on-one with dozens of junior colleagues, she began inviting mentees for group lunches. This saved her time and created a support network for them to help one another. Rather than handling questions reactively in time-consuming phone calls, she wrote an FAQ manual and shared it with colleagues. When clients made unreasonable requests, instead of saying she was too busy, she explained that it would stretch her team past the breaking point. By explaining that she was protecting others, she could say no, but still seem giving and caring. After making these changes, she was promoted to partner.[21] Most organizations regularly assess individual accomplishments. Why not track acts of helping as well? As stated earlier, having people help both behind the scenes and in public is essential for any business, and the research shows that teams with greater helping behavior reap many positive organizational benefits.

Every now and then everyone has some self-doubt. Those are the moments when we need someone, like trusted colleagues, sponsors, mentors, family, and friends, to just push us in the pool knowing we will swim. Self-doubt and negative self-talk can be debilitating to a woman's career and progress in life. If you are early in your career, you've already demonstrated that you are competent in certain areas, and just like emotional intelligence, as you age, those competencies will improve and grow. No one has all the answers at work. Know that your contributions are valuable, that you have opportunities and options available to you, and that you belong.

◇◇◇◇◇◇◇◇◇◇◇◇◇◇◇◇◇◇

Give yourself permission to fail, because it's the only way you'll succeed.

◇◇◇◇◇◇◇◇◇◇◇◇◇◇◇◇◇◇

Whatever you choose to tackle in work and life will stem from your confidence. Simply put, confidence is crucial to anyone's ability to lead and succeed. For women, it's helpful to focus less on people pleasing and perfectionism and more on action, risk-taking, and accepting failure. Here's an acronym that may help. FAIL = *First Attempt In Learning.* If we could view failure in this way, as simply a recurring learning opportunity, it won't seem so scary. Give yourself permission to fail, because it's the only way you'll succeed.

Because men and women view success and failure differently, look for opportunities to celebrate women's accomplishments, and point out when women are being blamed unfairly for mistakes. Although women are often penalized for promoting themselves, you can lift other women, and they can do the same for you. For example, when you introduce female coworkers, highlight their credentials and accomplishments. You might say, "Julie was in charge of our most recent product launch, and it generated more sales than any other initiative this year." That's going to get someone's attention, and right off the bat, will positively change the perception of your colleague.

Assertiveness has been a recurring topic in many chapters of this book. From women not speaking up in meetings, to not raising our hands, to EQ gender differences. Per *Merriam-Webster*, assertiveness is defined as:

disposed to or characterized by bold or confident statements and behavior. *Wikipedia* defines it as: the quality of being self-assured and confident without being aggressive.

It's helpful to imagine a Venn diagram with two overlapping circles. One circle is aggressive and the other circle is passive. In the middle where the two overlap, you'll find assertiveness. If you push what *you* want it's considered aggressive. If you give in to what *others* want, it's considered passive. The key is finding balance between the two. For women, being too aggressive is generally not the issue, but being too passive is. It's critical that you be your own marketer, and request (or even fight for) the things you really care about—whether it's more work-life balance, a promotion, a salary bump, more travel and responsibility, or just to have more input on your team.

◇◇◇◇◇◇◇◇◇◇◇◇◇◇

Given the exchange relationship of politics, think about what you want from the other person.

◇◇◇◇◇◇◇◇◇◇◇◇◇◇

To boost your executive presence, you must act and sound in a way that gives you power. I've taught presentation skills for many years; here are some suggestions. Speak louder and project your voice (the audience should not be straining to hear you). In general, both men and women speak too softly when they present. Slow your rate of speech and allow the audience to follow what you are saying (paced speech is perceived as confidence). Think of CEOs and presidents, their speeches are never rushed, and they take their time with each sentence. Pause and breathe between phrases, this will help you eliminate fillers (um, uh, like, you know, etc.). For example, instead of inserting open spaces with fillers, simply use silence. It's much more powerful.

Eliminate hedges, disclaimers, tags, and use downward intonation (voice must go down at the end of sentences). Again, think of CEOs and presidents, when presenting they make lots of statements and rarely ask questions (or phrase their statements as questions). Remember to vary the pitch of your voice and use it to emphasize key points—it's also more engaging to hear a varied speech rather than a monotone one. Project confident body and facial language by standing evenly on both feet, relaxing your hands by your sides (and using for gestures), and making eye contact with the audience. If you can implement even a few of these techniques, it will go a long way in enhancing your presence and projecting confidence.

To help with office politics, approach situations as you would any negotiation. Take the time to find out what the other person needs, what you have to offer, and how you can facilitate a win-win situation. Remember that women negotiate cooperatively, and men negotiate competitively. If it's important to you, don't be afraid to assert yourself—if you don't ask, you don't get. Also, given the exchange relationship of politics, think about what *you* want from the other person. The other party will not only expect this from you, they will appreciate the fact that you've thought it through, and will make the discussion much easier.

Finally, a quote by Marianne Williamson—often attributed to Nelson Mandela—illustrates the meaning of courage.[22]

"Our deepest fear is not that we are inadequate.
Our deepest fear is that we are powerful beyond measure.
It is our light, not our darkness that most frightens us.
We ask ourselves, who am I to be brilliant, gorgeous, talented, fabulous?
Actually, who are you *not* to be?
You are a child of God.
Your playing small does not serve the world.
There is nothing enlightened about shrinking so that other people won't feel insecure around you.
We are all meant to shine, as children do.
We were born to make manifest the glory of God that is within us.
It's not just in some of us; it's in *everyone*.
And as we let our own light shine, we unconsciously give other people permission to do the same.
As we are liberated from our own fear, our presence automatically liberates others."

For women, playing small does not serve the world, and shrinking so others won't feel insecure only perpetuates the lack of power. If more women took ownership and pride in their achievements, it would empower and liberate so many others. We are not born holding ourselves back. It's true then that what lies behind us and what lies ahead of us are tiny matters compared to what lies within us.

Summary Points

- More men than women want to lead, and it's one of the reasons that so few of the top corporate jobs are held by women.
- Starting at the middle-manager level and moving all the way to the C-suite, women start to fall off precipitously.
- The top three occupations for women are administrative assistant, teacher, and nurse—all are staff roles.
- Women limit themselves by doing office housework—behind-the-scenes, time-consuming activities that often don't get recognized.
- Men and women talk about and describe their successes and failures very differently.
- Focusing on confidence and assertiveness are arguably the most important to help you advance in your career.
- Gender stereotypes are at the core of why women are held back, and why women hold themselves back.
- Women use language and linguistic techniques to avoid being perceived as too direct or pushy, and to level the power in relationships.
- Many women minimize or downplay their emotional intelligence skills rather than taking advantage of them.
- There are many strategies to help women overcome self-imposed limitations.

Reflection Questions

- ✓ When you were young, what did you dream of being when you grew up? Is it what you ended up doing? Why or why not?

✓ Have you ever limited yourself in your career (intentionally or unintentionally)? If so, how and why?

✓ Do you want to lead? At what position or level? If given the opportunity, how high would you go? If you don't want to lead, why not?

✓ Have you ever taken a stretch role? If not, do you want to take on a stretch role with more responsibility? Why or why not?

✓ Are you currently in a line or staff role? Which do you prefer? Where do you want to be?

✓ Do you do any office housework? What types of activities? How often? Have these activities helped or hindered your career progression? What could you do differently?

✓ How do you communicate your success and failure? How has this been received by others? What messages have you been sending?

✓ Do you engage in negative self-talk or self-doubt? If so, how often and why? What do you say and think of yourself? What can you do to let go of these negative thoughts and behaviors?

✓ Do you consider yourself confident? Assertive? If not, what keeps you from using these skills? How have these impacted your career? Your life? What are you willing to do to increase your confidence and assert yourself more?

✓ Do you display executive presence? If not, why not? What can you do to sound more confident and clear?

✓ What words and speech patterns do you most use to communicate? Do you phrase your statements as questions? Use hedges, disclaimers, or tags? Does your language give power or drain power?

✓ Do you engage in or avoid office politics? Why or why not? Has it helped or hindered your career? What are you willing to do to increase your effectiveness?

NINE

Why Does S/he Do That?

People take different roads seeking fulfillment and success. Just because
they're not on your road doesn't mean they've gotten lost.
Dalai Lama

S teve is always on the move. It seems he spends more time walking the
office floor than in his office doing work. Two or three times every
week, Steve pops into his boss's office, as well as other leaders in
the department, asks what they're working on, casually mentions what he's
working on, and gets caught up on the latest company and industry news. This
all seems so simple and innocent—and it is.

Now, let's compare this to Cathy's behavior. Cathy is a colleague of
Steve's in the same department and they share the same manager, Dale. Cathy
stays in her office all day, working away on her projects, and hopes that Dale

and the other department leaders will notice how committed, diligent and consistent she is in her work output.

Three months down the line, Dale has a senior-level position that has opened on his team. Steve and Cathy have similar backgrounds and tenure, so they both apply for the job. However, Dale already has a candidate in mind, and after only one round of interviews, he gives the job to Steve. Dale is confident in Steve's ability to perform the new role because he's familiar with Steve's past projects and accomplishments. He feels that he has a good relationship with Steve and can trust him because he has a better sense of who Steve is compared to Cathy.

Sound familiar? This type of scenario plays out every single day, in every single industry across the globe. In this scenario, both Steve and Cathy are doing what is perfectly acceptable and natural in their respective gender *cultures*. In an office environment, men tend to walk the floor and consistently message what they're doing to the leadership teams. This is normal and even expected in the male culture. In sharp contrast, women tend to stay in their offices, working away on their own, hoping their good work will speak for itself. This is normal in the female culture. But, look at the outcome. When a promotion became available on Dale's team, he felt much more comfortable with Steve because Steve had been in his office nine times in the past three months and Cathy had not. Neither Steve nor Cathy were aware of the other's gendered behavior. They were doing exactly what they've been taught to do their entire lives—and what they're most comfortable with.

Gender Culture

You may scratch your head and ask, "Why does s/he do that?" Why does the opposite gender act in a way that makes no sense or seems absurd to you? It's because people do things that make sense to *them*. Both men and women are trying to do the right thing, but by two different sets of rules that define what right is. It is not about rights or wrongs, it's simply about *difference*.[1] By having an awareness and appreciation of these differences, and understanding the intent of the other gender, it can have a significant impact on your individual success, as well as your organization's ability to manage employee talent. In fact, unique talents and skills of both genders provide a natural complement that can improve the productivity, innovation, and economic growth of your organization.

Gender identity is an important part of the unchanging core of our personalities, and it is firmly established for both sexes by the age of three.[2] Children learn how boys and girls "should" act from the way their parents, caregivers, and teachers treat them; by observation of adult behavior; through peer pressure; and through nursery rhymes, cartoons, television, video games, magazines, books, and movies. Although we live in the same society, males and females are raised in unique and distinct cultures. This culture starts at birth and carries into adulthood.

For nearly all of us, it started with pink or blue blankets. As infants, we are spoken to, coddled and treated differently. From the moment we come into this world, adults project their own beliefs, assumptions, expectations, and prejudices onto the child's behavior—such as the belief that boys are tough, independent and aggressive, and girls are fragile, dependent, and nurturing.[3] This kind of disparate treatment throughout childhood teaches boys and girls to behave in gender-conforming ways. Thus, the seeds for divergence in sex roles are planted very early.

◇◇◇◇◇◇◇◇◇◇◇◇◇◇

Although we live in the same society, males and females are raised in unique and distinct cultures.

◇◇◇◇◇◇◇◇◇◇◇◇◇◇

Let's look at how children play. Boys play games centered on conflict and competition (think GI Joe, cops and robbers, war games, or any sports). In these games, boys learn how to win and lose, get to a goal, take risks, not to show emotions, and play with people they do not like. Boys are also taught that when the game is over, you are friends again. How many times have you seen boys verbally or physically attack each other during a game, then happily go for pizza and soda afterward? Let's look at men at work. How many times have you seen men viciously and verbally attack each other in a meeting, then say, "Want to grab a drink?"[4]

In contrast, girls play games centered on relationships, getting along, and avoiding conflict (think dolls, tea parties, dress up, or playing house). In these games, girls learn how to build relationships, work cooperatively, take turns, communicate, and do what is fair for all with an even distribution of power. They also learn that the process is more important than winning or getting to a goal.[5] Think back to a time when you were playing dolls with a girlfriend. You most likely placed the dolls in a variety of creative scenarios, with lots of planning and scheming that lasted for hours. Now, think about how it ended. Have you ever lost at a game of Barbies? You *can't* lose—it's not possible because it's about the process.

On both the playground and in the classroom, there is a subtle reinforcement of "appropriate" behavior for boys and girls. These different standards enhance a boy's skill in dealing with competition and power, but diminish these traits in girls. For example, boys are encouraged (and allowed) to freely speak out in the classroom, teaching boys to compete by getting their ideas heard first. Girls are often scolded when they speak out and are told to raise their hands instead, teaching them to be compliant and less powerful. By doing this, teachers unknowingly promote our culture's typical female values of girls following rules, waiting their turn, and being polite, and promote typical male values of verbal competitiveness, aggressiveness, and even impoliteness.

To compound the issue that boys and girls receive vastly different messages, they also play separately. Gender segregation occurs because boys and girls have radically different play styles, perhaps stemming from biological differences as well as disparate socialization during infancy and toddlerhood. These same-sex playgroups from the ages of six to ten create powerful socializing environments in which boys and girls become differently acculturated. As a result, boys and girls essentially grow up in different worlds.[6] It's during this period that male and female sex roles become solidified into the distinctive patterns that we see today.

As adults, we carry these early lessons into the workplace. In fact, men and women approach virtually *every aspect* of business differently. We have differences in the way we work within a structure, network, conduct meetings, work in teams, communicate, negotiate, take risks, address conflict, respond to stress, make decisions, problem solve, prioritize, process and interpret information, and finally, how we lead. The example of Steve and Cathy showed differences in how we network in the office.

◇◇◇◇◇◇◇◇◇◇◇◇◇◇◇◇◇◇

It's no coincidence that the lessons we're taught as kids translates into key EQ skills as adults.

◇◇◇◇◇◇◇◇◇◇◇◇◇◇◇◇

Now, armed with the knowledge of the lessons we learn as children, let's take another look at the gender-specific EQ competencies that we see globally. Recall that, overall, men score higher than women in areas of self-confidence, assertiveness, and stress tolerance. Women outperform men in areas of empathy, social responsibility, and interpersonal relationships. There were also small differences that gave men an advantage in independence and problem solving, and women an advantage in emotional self-awareness and emotional expression. It's no coincidence that the lessons we're taught as kids translates into these key EQ skills as adults. You might be asking yourself, "Are these gender differences due to nature or nurture?" The answer is yes. Let's explore further.

Gender and the Brain

I don't think it comes as a surprise to anyone that men and women are wired differently. These variations shape how men and women gather and process information, which in turn influences what we notice, what we value, and our behavior. It's important to note that the biological differences discussed here refer to general gendered tendencies. Meaning that not all men are one way and all women are another. In fact, research suggests that about 20 percent—one in five—is hardwired more like the opposite gender.[7]

Gender differences are first informed by nature (science), then by nurture (socialization)—influenced by family, friends, education, culture, media, and the environment.

The right side of our brain is responsible for artistic development, creativity, intuitive thought, and visual and spatial relations. It deals with the emotional and abstract and helps us see shapes and patterns holistically. The left side is responsible for logic, reasoning, and analytical skills. The two hemispheres are connected by the *corpus callosum* that allow one side to communicate with the other.[8] However, there are some stark differences in our neurobiology.

For women, the centers that control language and emotional responses are on *both* sides of the brain. Women have more specialized communication cells, and a thicker corpus callosum allowing more communication and cooperation between the hemispheres—which leads to better verbal articulation (we're adept at using words to calm as well as attack). Because of the intricate wiring, emotions are better integrated with our verbal abilities, making us more fluent at expressing our feelings to others. Emotions are also linked with our memories, so women are adept at remembering details of events. Put another way, women's brains come with lots of RAM. Men's brains are more compartmentalized like little boxes that don't overlap. This is how a man can focus on something for hours (like watching TV, playing video games, or fishing).

◇◇◇◇◇◇◇◇◇◇◇◇◇◇

Gender differences are first informed by nature, then by nurture.

◇◇◇◇◇◇◇◇◇◇◇◇◇◇

Women typically have a larger *anterior cortex* than do men, which scientists attribute women's superior ability to integrate and arrange memories and emotions into mixed patterns of thought. In her book, *The First Sex*, anthropologist Helen Fisher explored differences between the sexes in how they think. She says that "Women tend to think contextually and holistically.

They tend to think in webs of factors, not straight lines."[9] When women think, they collect more information from their environment, like a radar picking up signals across a wide spectrum, and arrange their thoughts into more complex patterns. They see more relationships between different elements and weigh more variations before they make their decisions.

On the other hand, men tend to focus on a specific issue, omit extraneous data, and move in a more step-like fashion toward the goal (using the left side of their brain) like a laser focusing on a single point in depth. This is advantageous when solving a problem expeditiously, but men may not see alternative viewpoints which would require a literal shift to a creative mindset (the right side of their brain). Both are perfectly good ways of thinking. The important point is that men and women were built to put their heads together to solve problems and innovate—which benefits organizations at all levels, especially in leadership.

In *The Female Vision*, Helgesen and Johnson refer to this as well. They say that women see broad-spectrum—for example, by picking up nonverbal communications or integrating their work and lives. Men are singularly focused on achievement and their career.[10] Women typically value meaningful relationships and meaningful work first, then value position and salary second—and assess it by drawing from their own core values. In our society, the male way of thinking is unjustifiably more valued, but forward-thinking companies like Google and other technology companies are starting to see and value the female way of thinking more.

In *A Whole New Mind*, Daniel Pink outlines how society has moved from the Information Age to the Conceptual Age over the last century.[11] The abundance of information, global outsourcing, and technological automation has caused a shift in the nature of work that has put a premium on relationships—and on the female way of thinking. The industrial and information ages valued analytical skills and the ability to follow predefined rules and procedural manuals. These skills are essential, but no longer sufficient. The ability to create and empathize, recognize patterns, and make meaning, will determine who flourishes and who flounders. Different aptitudes, such as "high concept" and "high touch" are now valued. High concept is the ability to direct patterns and opportunities, create a satisfying narrative, create artistic and emotional beauty, and combine seemingly unrelated ideas into a novel invention. High touch is the ability to empathize with others, understand the subtleties of human interaction, find joy in oneself and elicit it in others, and the pursuit of purpose and meaning.

◇◇◇◇◇◇◇◇◇◇◇◇◇◇◇◇

Women's brains come with lots of RAM.

◇◇◇◇◇◇◇◇◇◇◇◇◇◇◇◇

The emphasis on these strengths in the new age bode well for women and align with their hard-wired abilities. Today, businesses are seeking more broad-based ways of thinking and seeing to compete. Deans of universities are emphasizing the value of liberal arts education to think horizontally and connect the dots to be innovative. In Thomas Friedman's book, *The World Is Flat*, he outlines how the global competitive playing field is being leveled.[12] Around the year 2000, there was a massive investment in technology, an explosion in software like email and search engines, and computers became cheaper, allowing intellectual work and capital to be delivered from anywhere in the world—and by anyone. By connecting all knowledge centers on the planet together on a single global network—individuals can now collaborate and compete in real-time on all different kinds of work.

So, how does this global shift affect businesses and individuals? The skills you currently possess, for the most part, can be outsourced to someone in another country who can perform those skills faster, better or cheaper than you. In fact, anything that can be digitized can be outsourced. For you and your company to remain competitive in this global environment, it is essential that you can see broadly, think broadly, and develop deep relationships with others. Friedman says, "Those who create value through leadership, relationships, and creativity will transform the industry. Companies that don't have the leadership, flexibility and imagination to adapt and keep up with speed of change, will fail like the dot.com bust of the 1990s."[13] Your emotional intelligence skills are key to building quality relationships, and it's what will set you apart.

There are other areas of the brain that are distinct between men and women. The *hippocampus* serves as the center for memory and emotion and is larger and more active in women. This explains why women are usually better at expressing emotions as well as recalling intricate details from the past. Thus, women tend to have richer, more intense memories of emotional events than do men and can recall and link to past events more readily.[14] The *prefrontal cortex*, as discussed in earlier chapters, is not only larger in women, but also develops earlier in girls than in boys. It's the part of our brain that controls judgement, decision making, and consequential thinking. The *amygdala*, located in the limbic system, is best known for regulating our fight or flight response to fear, danger, or stress. There's a high degree of hormonal activity—and it's known as the emotional center of our brains. The amygdala is larger and more active in men's brains than in women's and affects how we deal with stress, risk, conflict, and decisions.

◇◇◇◇◇◇◇◇◇◇◇◇◇◇◇◇

Your EQ skills are key to building quality relationships, and it's what will set you apart.

◇◇◇◇◇◇◇◇◇◇◇◇◇◇◇◇

These biological differences can be seen in imaging methods that measure cerebral blood flow. These include functional MRI, as well as PET and SPECT scans that require radioactive isotopes to work. These show gender differences in what we notice, what we value, and how we connect the dots or tell a story. Daniel Amen and his team showed that overall, women's brains are much more active than men's. However, men's brains showed greater activity in targeted regions associated with visual perception, form recognition, and tracking objects through space (such as a football thrown down the field). A potential downside of the high activity in women's brains is that it leads to more rumination which can create self-doubt and second-guessing. It can lead to being self-critical and can even create perfectionism due to overthinking—so this needs to be kept in check.

On average, men have more *gray matter* in their brains and women have more *white matter*. Gray matter provides the neural energy required to perform functions that take place in a single area of the brain; white matter distributes and integrates the information in different parts of the brain which enables mental activities to take place in the left and right hemispheres at the same time.[15] Let's take driving as an example. If you look at an image of a man's brain while he's driving, it will be pinging away or lighting up in one area of his brain. If you look at an image of a woman's brain performing the same activity, her brain is lighting up all over the place like a pinball machine. This is the primary physiological reason that women are more likely to bring right-brain resources, such as intuitive knowing, to left-brain situations simultaneously.

Finally, a discussion about neurobiology and gender would be remiss without a discussion about hormones. Hormones are chemical messengers that produce specific behavior, but the relationship is reciprocal—hormones influence how we act, and our actions influence hormone release.

Women's ovaries produce two main hormones—*estrogen* and *progesterone*. Although these are not produced in the brain, they can affect behavior. During the first half of the menstrual cycle there is an increase in estrogen, which is associated with a state of well-being characterized by optimal energy level, elevated mood and enthusiasm, outward and social, creativity, clarity of thinking, sharp memory, and the ability to concentrate.[16] This is the best time to initiate new projects and collaborate with others. At mid-cycle (ovulation) women are most receptive to others and new ideas, and there's a rise in left hemisphere activity—particularly verbal fluency. This is a good time to pitch new ideas, communicate and give feedback to others.

During the second half of the menstrual cycle there is an increase in progesterone causing women to be evaluative, intuitive and reflective, and there's an increase in right hemisphere activity. This is a good time to reflect on projects and assess what needs to be changed or adjusted. At the end of the cycle, a falling progesterone level causes a disruption in the fuel supply of glucose to the brain—the brain is the most fuel-demanding organ in the body. This decrease in "brain fuel" contributes to the most common psychological and emotional symptoms of PMS (irritability, rage, depression, tension, anxiety, confusion, fatigue, memory lapses, inability to concentrate, and decreased stress tolerance).[17] During the first day or two of menstruation, many women feel an urge to organize their work spaces and tie up loose ends. This is a good time to get things in order, be patient with yourself and others, and rest, if needed. Although an employer is not going to know the time of a woman's menstruation, it's important for women to be aware of their cycle, so they can uniquely contribute at each phase.

◇◇◇◇◇◇◇◇◇◇◇◇◇◇◇◇

When stressed, men tend to withdraw and women prefer to talk it through.

◇◇◇◇◇◇◇◇◇◇◇◇◇◇◇◇

Oxytocin, a hormone released from the pituitary gland, plays an important role in how women respond to stress. When confronted with danger, the amygdala triggers a fight or flight response for both men and women, but women are more prone than men to ask for help. When faced with stressful situations, women tend to seek the company and support of other women, or become protective and caring toward their children. The male hormones *testosterone* and *vasopressin* help reduce stress in men, but this also inhibits oxytocin release in stressful situations. In addition, too much oxytocin in men can reduce testosterone levels, thereby increasing their stress. Thus, men tend to withdraw or shut down when stressed, whereas women prefer to talk it through or "tend and befriend" as it's been called.[18]

Both men and women produce testosterone, but men typically produce twenty to thirty times more than women do. As you know, testosterone is known to fuel aggressive behavior, but it also drives men's competitiveness, creativity, intellect, feelings of success, and their ability to develop and execute ideas. And, it's the right level of testosterone that's essential for men to cope appropriately with stress. Though women produce it, the hormone does not have the same stress-reducing properties as in men, and this is when oxytocin comes to the rescue.

◇◇◇◇◇◇◇◇◇◇◇◇◇◇

*Men and women live in different worlds
biologically, culturally, and socially.*

◇◇◇◇◇◇◇◇◇◇◇◇◇◇

In my volunteer work, I speak to colleges and high schools to educate students on a wide range of topics related to diversity. Chad, one of the speakers, is a female-to-male transgendered individual. He shares a story about hormones that I find fascinating. Prior to his transition, he recalls the chatter in his head and the fact that his brain never seemed to stop processing. When he received his very first shot of testosterone in the doctor's office years ago, he felt an overwhelming sense of calm and immediately felt more confident and happy—like an anti-depressant, even though he wasn't taking anything else at the time. He also noticed that the chatter in his head went away completely. I asked him if he saw any differences in how he communicated or changes in his ability to focus. He said he feels like he talks less now (and in a lower tone), and that he has trouble multitasking like he used to be able to do, and gets stressed if he has more than one task at a time. As time passed, he noticed other differences from the testosterone. In addition to the physical changes, he realized that he seldom cries anymore. Instead of crying, he finds himself getting angry, and shares an anecdote about developing a case of road rage.

This is a powerful story about the impact that hormones have on our ability to gather and process information, focus, communicate, cope with stress, deal with conflict, and even affect our confidence level. Due to differences in brain anatomy, hormones, and how we're raised, it's clear to see that men and women live in two different worlds both biologically and culturally, and our differences are due to both nature (science) and nurture (socialization).

Organization Structure

As we learned from the games children play, boys are taught lessons about how to live in a *hierarchy* or vertical structure, and girls are taught how to live in a *flat* or horizontal structure. As adults, these practices carry into the workplace. In *Hardball for Women*, Pat Heim outlines these key differences. Men prefer to work in a hierarchical structure—having a clear leader at the top, with many layers in between, and a clear pecking order and line to advancement. Roles are clearly defined with status and power emphasized. This structure is both goal-focused and linear-focused, with a directive communication style, meaning that men are more comfortable giving the answer instead of group discussion or dialogue.[19] This explains why many men are comfortable working within a military structure.

The hierarchical military model was built by men for men going all the way back to the Industrial Age. It's a competitive, machine-like environment based on order, efficiency, speed of decision making, individual performance, and the pursuit of measurable goals. Because this structure aligns well with the way men naturally think and act, it makes it difficult for them to consider their workplace and their performance in it from any other perspective.

Male-led companies don't question the type of structure because they simply don't recognize it. Same goes with society. This hierarchy has been supported, practiced, and refined for over two hundred years, and in the eyes of many, this male-designed model is still the most effective and efficient way of conducting business and leading and managing people.[20] While this may have been proven true in the past, we now exist in a rapidly changing global business environment where we can't afford to leave the talents of half the workforce unrealized.

◇◇◇◇◇◇◇◇◇◇◇◇◇◇◇◇

Men prefer hierarchical structure that is goal and linear focused.

◇◇◇◇◇◇◇◇◇◇◇◇◇◇◇◇

In comparison, women prefer to work in a flat structure that is process-focused and multi-faceted. This structure encourages collaboration, teamwork, and communication cross-functionally. It also implies equality among everyone, and the notion that "We're all in this together." Talking it over through discussion and involvement is the preferred communication style in a flat structure—just as girls perfected in their games of house, dolls, and dress-up.[21] This process-focused, team-oriented approach also serves as the foundation of the transformational leadership style discussed in chapter two.

Because equality is emphasized, power would be evenly distributed in a horizontal structure. Recall the discussion about the power dead-even rule. Since women have been taught that relationships are the most important, women learn to keep the power even to preserve the relationship. If a woman rises in power, other women may act to undermine her to bring her back down to even. We also saw how women soften their language with other women (and men) to build rapport and not be perceived as superior to others.

There are other key distinctions between the male goal-focused structure and the female process-focused structure. Since men are generally more comfortable giving the answer, they cut straight to the bottom line first. They will only backfill and give other options if needed. In contrast, women tend to give options by talking it over first, and then present the bottom line. As you can imagine, this can frustrate the other gender. If a male is only looking for an answer to a problem, he doesn't want to hear about other options or alternatives. To him, this is unnecessary information that distracts from the overall goal which is to solve the problem. However, a female prefers to dialogue and fully explore the issue. To achieve this, she both sees and gives alternatives to solve the problem through discussion.[22] This is a big part of the reason why women's ideas are often ignored by men—because men see it as explaining too much, or not being focused, or not getting to the point—so they tune women out. On the flip side, women may get frustrated because men refuse to listen to other approaches, or can't focus on more than one issue at time, or can't multitask as she would.

◇◇◇◇◇◇◇◇◇◇◇◇◇◇

Women prefer flat structure that is process and multi focused.

◇◇◇◇◇◇◇◇◇◇◇◇◇◇

Since most companies still have hierarchies, women need to be mindful not to jump the chain of command, and to communicate directly if you have an employee who jumps the chain. If an individual complains or seeks guidance from their boss's superior, they may be doing so to challenge authority. Men who are uncomfortable with having a female boss, might also attempt this maneuver. This is one of the most valuable lessons I learned years ago from one of my bosses. He told me point-blank to "never break the chain of command". At first, I wasn't sure what he meant by this, then realized that he considered hierarchy and pecking order to be the most important in the way he led his team. I quickly learned to run everything by him first, and to never go above him as it could damage our relationship, and make him perceive me as disloyal.

However, I've been on the other end of this as well. I've had male direct reports who did go above me. My boss at the time, Dave, was warm and welcoming to everyone. Ed would approach Dave, and Dave was more than happy to listen and offer advice. However, this made it difficult for me to manage Ed because he felt comfortable going to Dave whenever an issue arose. The critical factor here was Dave's response to Ed. At the first meeting, Dave should have asked Ed, "Have you spoken to Shawn about this?", and sent him back down the chain of command. Dave continued to meet with Ed on a periodic basis, which undermined my authority. I eventually asked Dave to tell Ed to come to me first, so I can have the first shot at addressing the problem. Once I communicated this, our relationship improved and the chain of command was again intact.

Teams and Meetings

A team meeting has been scheduled for tomorrow at 2:00 p.m. To prepare himself for the meeting, Bob stops by the offices of Joe, Bill, and Todd, who will also be at the meeting, to discuss meeting topics, get alignment and agreement, and address anticipated concerns. Megan has also been invited to this meeting. Megan prepares herself for the meeting by researching some facts and figures, printing copies of key documents, and jotting down notes. When the meeting begins, Megan quickly realizes from the discussion that prior decisions have already been made and she feels a bit lost and unprepared.

What might be going on here? Its gender culture once again. Meetings are one of the most visible areas where we see gender differences play out. Because men live in a hierarchy, and position in the hierarchy is important, men tend to get their ducks in a row and build alignment *before* the meeting to avoid being influenced in public situations (and to save face).[23]

◇◇◇◇◇◇◇◇◇◇◇◇◇◇

Men build alignment before meetings to avoid being influenced in public.

◇◇◇◇◇◇◇◇◇◇◇◇◇◇

Women, in sharp contrast, bring their ideas and discussion points to the meeting expecting to dialog with everyone involved, but unbeknownst to her, the substantial part of the meeting has already occurred. Again, both are doing what is perfectly acceptable in their respective gender cultures, and completely unaware of the other's actions. What's the result? The obvious result is women are often left out of the loop on key decision-making and rapport-building opportunities. Another consequence is if the essential parts of meetings consistently occur before all team members have a chance to weigh in, then decisions are being made based on suboptimal and incomplete information—without the contribution of multiple perspectives.

It's important for women to be aware of this behavior to avoid resistance in meetings, and increase the chances that her ideas will be supported. To do this, women need to invest some time before the meeting to explain her ideas and the personal advantage to each team member in supporting her. Women are often surprised that they must go through this process of extra effort because it doesn't exist in the flat female culture. They ask, "What's the point of having a meeting if you don't do business there?" or "Why not just have everything out in the open?" It may feel slimy and political to some women, but in the male culture, it serves a strong purpose.

How we conduct ourselves *during* the meeting is also very different. Just as in the classroom where boys are encouraged to speak out and girls are told to raise their hands, we see these same behaviors as adults. Men speak at length in a declamatory voice, tend to interrupt and dominate the conversation, and resist being influenced in public. Women generally speak briefly, phrase their points or statements as questions, wait their turn, and smile more.[24] Take notice next time you are in a meeting. If you think about the different cultures, it makes perfect sense. Men are jockeying for position, and women are trying to preserve and respect relationships. What's the result? Men verbalize and share their ideas more often than women in meetings, and appear as confident and decisive leaders. I use the word "appear" deliberately, because it's about *perception*. Women may also be confident and decisive leaders, but they don't always come across that way based on these subtle gender behaviors.

◇◇◇◇◇◇◇◇◇◇◇◇◇◇◇◇◇

Women speak briefly, wait their turn, and smile more than men in meetings.

◇◇◇◇◇◇◇◇◇◇◇◇◇◇◇◇◇

We also have different definitions of what it means to be a good *team player*. Men grow up learning to sacrifice themselves for the good of the team and carrying out the agenda of those above them.[25] This definition focuses on doing what is necessary even if you disagree with the boss and the decision he or she makes. Women grow up attempting to find a win-win situation to meets everyone's needs. For them, doing good work as an individual means being a good team player. This definition focuses on supporting others, sharing information, and being willing to listen to ideas that may be different than yours. For example, in the spirit of open dialogue, a woman may question her boss's idea so she can offer additional ideas that could help the team. A male boss may perceive this as insubordination because she questioned him and didn't do what he told her to do. This is an all-too-common trap for women. To maintain a smooth relationship with your boss, the best solution would be to adopt the male approach and do what the coach asks, but then hold true to the female view and offer your own insights and perspective. You could say, "I've done what you've told me, and I've written up a couple of strategies that I think could even broaden your approach."[26] By doing this, you don't have to give up your bright ideas. You may have to adhere to your boss's wishes first before you try to add your own. Your boss will likely appreciate this approach as well.

Recall the discussion about office housework from chapter eight. These are the behind-the-scenes activities that women volunteer for which help a company run smoothly, but often don't get recognized. This is an example of women doing good work as an individual and trying to be a good team player. In these types of activities, women serve as the team glue—connecting people to avoid reinventing the wheel, helping individuals communicate with each other, or getting new hires up-to-speed. However, it's human nature not to notice when things go well, and we take it for granted. Unfortunately, relational work is not seen as strategic or important in many organizations. Technical skills are more valued, so "women's work"—the fostering of social connections and communication—often disappears. But, what is a leader? Is it not someone who can move a team forward? By smoothing operations, connecting people, and offering win-win solutions, that's *exactly* the role that women are taking when they provide this type of support. It's important that women get credit for this valuable work and talk about it to their bosses so they too can recognize its importance.

Communication

Now, let's look at how we communicate. Men tend to (excuse the bluntness here) make things up, and women tend to provide too many details. What this means is that if a man does not know the answer to something, he either says that he knows the answer or he makes up an answer—which is consistent with men's risk-taking behavior. In contrast, women fully disclose all their positive and negative ideas and are honest about what they *don't* know.

For example, a man may look at a job description, see one or two items that applies to him, and tell the hiring manager that he is qualified and can do the job. A woman, on the other hand, may look at a job description, see all but one item that applies to her, and tell the hiring manager that she does not have experience in that one area. Of course, this is a simplified example, but it is effective in illustrating general differences. What's the result? Statistics show again and again, that men are offered jobs and promotions more often than women because men *ask* for jobs and promotions more often than women.

◇◇◇◇◇◇◇◇◇◇◇◇◇◇◇◇

Women disclose their ideas and are honest about what they don't know.

◇◇◇◇◇◇◇◇◇◇◇◇◇◇◇◇

Men cover their underlying fears with a tough exterior even though they have the same worries that women do. They do not admit what they don't know. Saying that they know the answer when they don't, works more often than not because if they don't know how to do something, they go find out. This tactic instills confidence in a man's ability. When we act as if we're in charge, that's often exactly what happens.

Nicki, one of my MBA students, has worked as an administrative assistant in the Los Angeles Unified School District for eight years. She shared a story with me about a younger male colleague who was recently appointed to a director-level position. He had worked there for less than a year, and prior to his promotion, she had little interaction with him. When his promotion was announced, he came to Nicki for help on how to approach an issue that was to be part of his new role (and that he told his new boss he knew how to solve). The options seemed so clear to her, but he couldn't see it. Over the years, she's encountered this type of interaction many times. It frustrates her to see others continually get promoted, yet they come to her for solutions to their problems. It was this incident that prompted Nicki to further her education and pursue her MBA.

A woman's agenda is more personal, so she has no qualms about expressing her shortcomings. After all, she is being open, honest, and transparent—all valued qualities in the relationship-based female culture. If her boss asks her to perform a new job that she doesn't know how to do, she may say, "I don't have any experience with that. We could ask another department to help, but that may not resolve it. We could call in a consultant. But to be perfectly honest, I'm just not sure." Does this sound like the voice of a competent and knowledgeable employee?

The critical factor here is that men don't know any more than women—they just act as if they do. This approach makes men appear as confident and capable employees and opens the door to many more opportunities. If women could learn to speak with assurance, and send the message, "Don't worry, it's under control," or "No problem, I've got this," their bosses would be more likely to turn to them for bigger responsibilities. Try this: When asked a question about how you'd accomplish a goal, just give it your best shot. Say what makes sense to you and leave it at that. If you don't know, make it up and act as if you know—you can figure it out later.[27]

◇◇◇◇◇◇◇◇◇◇◇◇◇◇◇

Men don't know any more than women— they just act as if they do.

◇◇◇◇◇◇◇◇◇◇◇◇◇◇◇

Men and women use different verbal language. As mentioned earlier, men have a command and control style of leadership, which is directive focused—giving commands and telling others who, what, when, where, and how to accomplish a task. Instead of directing others, women's leadership style and language focuses on involvement, using phrases such as "We can…", "Let's do…", or "As a team…" This is language that gets others to do what they want and need without being confrontational, and thus reducing the risk of conflict.

Recall from the last chapter the way women talk—using language and softeners that equalize relationships, but often drains power—this contrasts with men who use language that conveys power and status in the hierarchy. Also, recall our discussion about how men and women talk about and describe successes and failures. These language differences result in very different perceptions by others, and very different outcomes.

Not surprisingly, we also differ in our nonverbal communication. In general, women communicate nonverbally much more than men do, and pick up on nonverbal cues more often than men. These gestures include nods, smiles, head tilts, body posture, and facial expressions. For example, let's look at how we listen to each other. Picture a man and a woman in conversation. Women lean forward, smile, tilt their head, and often nod during the conversation to tell the speaker "I hear you," "Keep going," or "I'm with you". However, this does not necessarily mean she agrees with what is being said, but is simply encouraging the speaker to continue. In contrast, men generally sit back in their chair, maintain stoic looks on their faces, hold their heads upright, and nod *only* when they agree with what is being said.[28] Watch this the next time you see a conversation between genders.

What's the possible perception of these different approaches? First, it can confuse cross-gender communication. If a woman nods in a conversation with her boss, then later differs with him, he may see her as switching positions or wishy-washy. If a man sits there with little facial and body expression, he may be perceived as not paying attention, not caring, or in disagreement. Second, if a woman is nodding and smiling consistently, she may appear agreeable to everything, as a pushover, or not very decisive. If a man sits there listening, then nods once or twice in agreement, he will likely appear more decisive and confident. Now, does this mean that a woman is indecisive because she continually nods during a conversation? Of course not. But, it's a common perception. I can relate to this because I am a nodder and head tilter. I always have been, and I wonder how many times I've come across as too agreeable or indecisive because of my behavior in conversations. Again, these gender differences are not about rights and wrongs—these are just variant styles of communication based on gender-specific culture, but they can and do elicit different impressions.

Risk-Taking, Conflict and Negotiation

Most people have observed (or experienced themselves) differences in how men and women approach risk-taking, and the amount of risk they are willing to endure. John Bates with Executive Speaking Success, is a TED speaker and coach. He's trained hundreds of speakers for TED, TEDx and corporate events. In searching for TEDx speakers, he found that when TEDx asked ten men in U.S. and Europe to speak, nine of them said yes. They also asked ten women in U.S. and Europe to speak, and nine of them said no. When asked why they responded no, the women cited not being "expert" enough, they had too much going on, and feeling too "braggy". These responses are typical and reflect many factors.

Women tend to be much more calculated in their risk-taking and decision making than men. As we learned from differences in brain anatomy, women problem-solve using divergent thinking, or viewing things in a larger context. Women consider other people, their family, their health, finances, safety, quality of life, and future commitments. Women also ask more questions, seek alternative solutions, and worry more about details. The downside of divergence is that it takes more time and can make women more hesitant in their decision-making process. Men tend to just "jump in" and see what happens, processing information quickly, asking fewer questions, and worrying less about details than moving forward. Therefore, men problem-solve using convergent thinking, or zeroing in on a specific issue for resolution. This can translate into taking greater risk, but the downside of rapid convergence is missing opportunities, such as better and more creative solutions.

◇◇◇◇◇◇◇◇◇◇◇◇◇◇◇◇

Women problem-solve using divergent thinking; men problem-solve using convergent thinking.

◇◇◇◇◇◇◇◇◇◇◇◇◇◇◇◇

You may recall the study published in the *British Medical Journal* in December 2014, that made quite a splash in the media. The researchers behind the study, from Newcastle University, note that sex differences are well documented when it comes to risk-seeking behavior and emergency hospital admissions. Men are much more likely than women to be admitted to an emergency department after accidental injuries, as well as being more prone to sporting injuries and fatal traffic collisions. Some of these differences may be attributable to cultural and socioeconomic factors, such as males may be more likely to engage in contact and high risk sports, and males may be more likely to be employed in higher risk occupations. However, sex differences in risk-seeking behavior have been reported from an early age, raising questions about the extent to which these behaviors can be attributed purely to social and cultural differences.

The study evaluated the number of Darwin Awards given to men and women over a twenty-year period (1995-2014). The Darwin Awards is an annual hall of fame commemorating those considered to have died in exceptionally stupid ways. The class of risk—the "idiotic" risk—is qualitatively different from those associated with, say, contact sports or adventure pursuits, such as parachuting. Idiotic risks are defined as senseless risks, where the apparent payoff is negligible or non-existent, and the outcome is often extremely negative and final. Wendy Northcutt, of the Darwin Awards, describes the awards' rationale: "In the spirit of Charles Darwin, the Darwin Awards commemorate individuals who protect our gene pool by making the ultimate sacrifice of their own lives." The analysis shows that, of 318 cases, 282 of the awards were given to men, with just thirty-six awarded to women. Therefore, the study reports a statistically significant finding of men making up 89 percent of Darwin Award winners.[29] The researchers consider this finding to support the hypothesis that men are more likely than women to engage in foolish behavior and seem to make little or no real assessment of the risk. They just do it anyway—often at risk to their own health or finances. The researchers conclude it is puzzling that males are willing to take such unnecessary risks—perhaps simply as a rite of passage, in pursuit of male social esteem, or solely in exchange for bragging rights.

Of course, not all risk-taking decisions end negatively, and there are countless examples in our history of great accomplishments because of risk. For some women, saying no to risks could point to a lack of confidence, but that's not the case for all. Women are less willing to fail than men, and are generally put off by self-promotion, which explains the "braggy" comments in the TEDx example. What's the result of this risk-taking difference? Saying no means *no opportunity*. Therefore, the women who probably would have been fantastic TEDx speakers, did not get the chance to share their knowledge and expertise to make a positive impact on others. Although it's great to avoid a Darwin Award, the world *needs* more women to say yes.

Conflict is a central concept in both gender cultures—the male culture is centered on direct competition and conflict; the female culture is centered on relationships and avoiding conflict. Conflict, an inherent element of competition, means we disagree about something. Friendship, on the other hand, means we're in harmony. Even when girls play spontaneous competitive games like hopscotch or jump rope, they do not compete directly with one another. These are turn-taking games in which there's no expressed goal and no strategy for winning. If one girl gets tired or stops playing, it doesn't come at the expense of another girl's failure, as it would in direct competition where there is always a winner and a loser.

◇◇◇◇◇◇◇◇◇◇◇◇◇◇

Conflict is a central concept in both gender cultures.

◇◇◇◇◇◇◇◇◇◇◇◇◇◇

Girls are taught not to fight, but we haven't learned what to do with our stifled angry feelings if we feel slighted. In fact, we take it personally and rarely forget a slight because relationships are just too important for us. We've learned not to compete, not to speak up, not to draw attention to ourselves, and most definitely not to act more powerful than others. Boys have learned different lessons. They have become accustomed to experiencing conflict, have much practice settling disputes, and can distance themselves personally when attacked.[30] As mentioned earlier, their hardwiring also lends itself to less emotional attachments. Because of these early lessons, as well as a larger prefrontal cortex and less testosterone, women gravitate toward win-win situations so they can keep relationships intact. The practice in turn-taking and indirect competition can be an advantage in the modern workplace where bolstering relationships, such as leading a diverse team or getting more customers, are placed at a premium.

To deal with conflict that's appropriate for each culture, men and women use different negotiation styles. There are two general approaches to negotiation—*distributive bargaining* and *integrative bargaining*—which differ in their goal and motivation, focus, interests, information sharing, and duration of relationship.[31] Distributive bargaining seeks to divide up a fixed amount of resources and operates under zero-sum conditions, that is, any gain I make is at your expense, and vice-versa. In other words, it's a win-lose situation. This type of bargaining is common when there's a fixed pie. For example, high sales performers get a larger piece of the bonus pie, which means that lower sales performers receive less of a bonus payout.

Integrative bargaining seeks one or more settlements that can create a win-win solution, allowing both parties to leave the table feeling they have achieved a victory—whereas distributive bargaining leaves one party a loser. As discussed in chapter five, in negotiations women tend to value relationship outcomes more than men, and men value economic outcomes more than women. Because of this, men negotiate competitively, and women negotiate cooperatively. Not surprisingly, men utilize distributive bargaining more often than women, and women use integrative bargaining more often than men.

◇◇◇◇◇◇◇◇◇◇◇◇◇◇◇◇◇

Men utilize distributive bargaining; women utilize integrative bargaining.

◇◇◇◇◇◇◇◇◇◇◇◇◇◇◇◇◇

In terms of organizational behavior, integrative bargaining is preferable to distributive bargaining because it preserves and builds long-term relationships. For this to succeed, both parties need to be open with information and candid about concerns, sensitive to the other's needs and trust, and maintain flexibility. Because these conditions seldom exist in organizations, negotiations often take a win-at-any-cost dynamic.

Women's own attitudes and behaviors can hurt them in negotiations. Managerial women demonstrate less confidence than men in anticipation of negotiating and are less satisfied with their performance afterward, even when their outcomes are similar to men. Women are also less likely than men to see an ambiguous situation as an opportunity for negotiation—unduly penalizing themselves by not engaging in negotiations that would be in their best interests. Some evidence suggests that women are less aggressive in negotiations because they are worried about backlash from others. What's interesting though, is that women are more likely to engage in assertive negotiation when they are bargaining on behalf of someone else than when they are bargaining on their own behalf.[32] In the female culture, these behaviors make sense. Demonstrating less confidence in anticipation of negotiation, and being less likely to see negotiation as an opportunity, are due to the desire to avoid conflict. Worrying about backlash from others, and negotiating more aggressively for others rather than ourselves, are to preserve our all-important relationships.

Gender Culture Strategies

Like everyone else, I've known that men and women were wired differently which cause us to act in distinct ways. But for many years, other than physical appearance, reproductive capability, and a few behavior variations, I thought that we were more alike than unalike. But, the more research I've done over the years, the more I've come to realize that men and women have biologically, culturally and socially distinct approaches to nearly everything in work and life. It's amazing that we find commonality at all.

We have discussed that both men and women are trying to do the right thing, but by two different sets of rules about what they believe right is. There are significant differences in the way we conduct ourselves in the workplace, and our gendered behavior impacts other's perception of us—which impacts promotion and advancement for women.

Women are not as content in today's workplace as men are. From the boardroom to the conference room, women feel valued differently than men. They feel dismissed for their ideas and excluded from events and opportunities for advancement. They often state they must work harder than men do just to prove themselves half as good, and often feel doubted for their competence and commitment. I heard these many times from my research participants. In fact, the number-one complaint women have in the workplace is not feeling *valued* or *appreciated,* because men often misread women's intentions, misinterpret their actions, and fail to recognize their strengths. The same goes for women; they often misread men's intentions and behaviors because they don't understand what compels men to think and act as they do.

On the other hand, men are generally comfortable in today's corporate culture. They assume and expect that women want to engage in work as they do—whether in prioritizing issues, solving problems, participating on teams, making decisions, or leading others. His main blind spot is not being aware of how his behavior in this male-designed environment affects women. Her main blind spot is assuming that men's behaviors are intentional.[33] Our challenge at work isn't in our ability to do our jobs; it's in our inability to authentically engage with the other gender.

◇◇◇◇◇◇◇◇◇◇◇◇◇◇

Our gendered behavior impacts other's perceptions of us.

◇◇◇◇◇◇◇◇◇◇◇◇◇◇

Now that you have this awareness, what can you do? First, reassess what the opposite gender is really trying to communicate and simply hear the message differently. In short, reinterpret the intent behind the actions.[34] This will require that we observe and listen more closely, and not rely on our initial assumptions or stereotypes. For instance, let's go back to the meeting example with Bob and Megan. Bob met with other men prior to the meeting to align and avoid surprises. Megan realized at the meeting that she was left out of key decisions that were made. Armed with the knowledge of gender culture, she could have met with Bob first to brief him on what she planned on discussing at the meeting and get his input. She could say to Bob beforehand, "I want to prevent you from being blindsided. Here's what I plan on covering at the meeting. What are your thoughts?" This would have gone a long way in helping him feel at ease in his culture, she would have been part of the decision-making process, and it would have helped ensure acceptance of her ideas. Note—if you have a male boss, it's extremely important that you go through this same exercise and obtain his buy in and commitment before a meeting—you won't have a prayer if you try to do it during the meeting.[35]

A second strategy is to modify your behavior to be in sync with the other person. In other words, be empathetic and put yourself in their shoes. Do what works in the other person's gender culture. Since women grew up in a process-oriented culture, as opposed to the goal-oriented male culture, they prefer to explore issues and options through dialogue.[36] If you're a male working with females on a project, it's imperative to flex your style and not rush the process or push them to "cut to the chase". They are getting to the same bottom line as you, they just have a different means of getting there. Flexing would allow women to fully contribute, express their ideas and feel listened to, help you to see alternatives you may have missed, and would likely lead to a better solution. If you're a female working with males on a project, it would be helpful if you modify your style and get to the bottom line quickly—and only provide additional information if asked for it. This may seem incomplete to you, but it's rarely necessary to share all the knowledge you have on a topic. This would keep him engaged, lessen the chance of him tuning out, and help you to be viewed as more self-assured and credible in his eyes.[37]

Third, talk about your gender differences and what is happening. Discuss ways that you can best work together that is congruent with your respective gender norms. Unless everyone in business around the world reads this book, other gender books, or attends a gender training, it's unlikely that your colleagues will have knowledge of these gender dynamics. By sharing what you've learned here, even in small part, you can begin a dialogue. Using gender-savvy language—terms like hierarchy and flat culture, goal- and process-orientation, and talking it over versus getting to the bottom line— takes what was invisible or unconscious and turns it into an entity that can be actively managed.[38] It's okay to say to your male boss, "I don't need you to solve this problem. I just want to process through my options with you."

If you're a male boss, you can say, "What do you think you ought to do about that?", or "Do you think that's the best solution?", or "Do you see any alternatives?"[39] This will go a long way to help her process the problem, and help you see that she's perfectly capable of solving her own problems.

◇◇◇◇◇◇◇◇◇◇◇◇◇◇◇◇◇◇

By sharing what you've learned here, even in small part, you can begin a dialogue.

◇◇◇◇◇◇◇◇◇◇◇◇◇◇◇◇◇◇

Recall the discussion about meetings and how we differ in our behavior. Men dominate most conversations and share their ideas more often than women. If you get interrupted, you could say, "I'd like to finish my thought before we move on." If you want to contribute, but are having trouble getting a word in edgewise, just jump in. You don't always need to raise your hand or wait to be called on by the meeting leader. If you don't jump in occasionally, the team will never get a chance to hear your brilliant ideas, and meetings are often the best time to showcase your knowledge, confidence and leadership.

Finally, when it comes to negotiation, gender stereotypes are accurate for some women, but not all. The simple fact is that women can't expect something they don't ask for. So, if economic outcomes are valued, it's necessary to behave more aggressively. If social outcomes are valued, it's necessary to behave cooperatively. Men and women need to know that it's acceptable for each to show a full range of negotiating behaviors. Thus, a female negotiator who behaves competitively and a male negotiator who behaves cooperatively need to know that they are not violating gender culture expectations.

Recall that women use more integrative bargaining which seeks one or more settlements that can create a win-win solution. To achieve a win-win outcome, it helps to put more issues on the table. The more negotiable issues introduced, the more opportunity for trade-offs. In addition, focusing on the underlying interests of both sides rather than on specific issues, helps you focus on what the other side really wants and why. When both parties are focused on learning and understanding, it yields higher joint outcomes than those in which parties are more interested in their individual bottom-line outcomes.

Negotiating a win-win does not mean compromise, as compromise reduces the pressure to bargain integratively. After all, if your opponent caves in easily, no one needs to be creative to reach a settlement. People then settle for less than they could have obtained if they had been forced to consider the other party's interests, trade-off issues, and be creative. A classic example is two sisters arguing over who gets an orange. Unknown to them, one sister wants the orange to drink the juice, whereas the other wants the orange peel to bake a cake. If one sister gives up the orange, they won't be forced to explain their reasons for wanting it. They could each have the orange because they want different parts.

◇◇◇◇◇◇◇◇◇◇◇◇◇◇

Our differences are a source of strength, not weakness.

◇◇◇◇◇◇◇◇◇◇◇◇◇◇

Recognize that a sameness mindset about the genders in organizational culture and leadership maintains the status quo and limits diversity. It causes us to talk past each other and misread each other's intentions. It also leads us to make uneducated assumptions that may be completely off the mark about the meaning and motivations behind the behavior of others. The only way to overcome this mindset is through education and awareness that each gender is unique, and recognizing and valuing our differences. Our differences are a source of strength, not weakness—and we need to start viewing them as such.

A greater understanding can only lead to a greater appreciation for each other and the realization that our differences can be very complementary. I hope that we learn not to expect each other to think and behave the same, to understand other's behaviors and motivations, to appreciate our differences, and to find greater success and satisfaction at work and in our personal lives. This knowledge can help you predict and maximize potential, not just in your interpersonal interactions, but at the team and organizational levels as well.

As the quote at the beginning of this chapter reads, "People take different roads seeking fulfillment and success. Just because they're not on your road doesn't mean they've gotten lost." The next time you wonder to yourself, "Why does s/he do that?", remember that men and women do things that make sense to them, and are likely behaving in a way that is acceptable and natural in their respective gender culture. Be mindful that subtle gender differences can lead to different perceptions across many aspects of business. Let's work together in gender partnership to appreciate and value our collective differences.

Summary Points

- Boys play games centered on competition and conflict; girls play games centered on relationships and avoiding conflict.
- Boys learn to live in a hierarchy with the most powerful person at the top; girls learn to live in a flat culture with an even distribution of power.
- The lessons we're taught as kids translates into key EQ skills as adults.
- Due to differences in brain anatomy, hormones, and how we're raised, men and women live in two different worlds both biologically and culturally, and our differences are due to both nature and nurture.
- Men are goal-focused with a command and control leadership style; women are process-focused and lead by involvement.
- Men and women conduct themselves differently before, during, and after meetings.
- Men tend to make things up; women tend to provide too many details.
- Men problem-solve using convergent thinking; women problem-solve using divergent thinking.
- Men utilize distributive bargaining; women utilize integrative bargaining.
- There are many strategies to help both men and women navigate and overcome gender culture differences.

Reflection Questions

✓ What games did you play as a child? What did you like about these games? What games did you not like playing? What lessons did you learn from the games you played?

✓ What emotional intelligence skills do you think you're highest in? Are these skills consistent with the games you played growing up, or the lessons you learned as an adult?

✓ How do you react when you're stressed? Do you shut down, go off by yourself, talk to others, or some other method? Does this strategy help manage your stress? If not, what can you do to better manage it?

✓ Do you prefer to work in a vertical or horizontal organization structure? What do you like about this structure?

✓ When you communicate your ideas to others, do you tend to present options and alternatives first, or do you present the bottom line first? How is this communication style received by others?

✓ How do you conduct yourself in meetings? Do you share your ideas? Do you raise your hand? Do you get interrupted? How have these behaviors helped or hindered you?

✓ When you are listening, what nonverbal behavior do you exhibit? Do you nod or tilt your head, smile, or use facial expressions? How are these behaviors received by others?

✓ Do you consider yourself a risk-taker? When presented with opportunities, do you say yes or no more often? What is keeping you from taking more risks in your work and in your life?

✓ How do you address conflict? Do you tackle it head on? Do you avoid it? Do you try to collaborate or compromise? Has this conflict style worked for you?

✓ What is your attitude toward negotiation? Do you hate it? Do you enjoy it? Do you see it as an opportunity? Do you generally negotiate toward a win-lose or win-win outcome? Do you consider yourself a good negotiator? If not, what can you do to improve it?

PART III
Next Steps

TEN

Diversify or Die

Never act until you have clearly answered the question:
"What happens if I do nothing?"
Robert Brault

Whether global organizations have asked themselves the above quote or not, it's clear that many have not acted when it comes to diversity, and organizations across all sectors have yet to jump on the bandwagon. However, in recent years, some forward-thinking companies have invested significant efforts and resources toward improving diversity and inclusion (also known as D&I). And, this trend is on the rise.

First, let's define D&I. Diversity is the collective mixture of differences that includes individual and organizational characteristics such as values, beliefs, experiences, backgrounds, and behaviors. Inclusion is the achievement of a work environment, in which all individuals are treated fairly and respectfully, have equal access to opportunities and resources, and can contribute fully to the organization's success.

The fact is, as a global society, we are becoming more diverse every day. We see it in our workplaces, in our churches, in our communities, and in our schools. For the first time in the U.S., the 2014 Census Bureau showed that racial and ethnic minorities now surpass non-Hispanic whites as the largest group of American children under five years old—which means that Caucasian kindergarteners are now in the minority for the third straight year. This marked a milestone in a trend toward a more diverse U.S. that's projected to continue. Births outnumbered deaths for all ethnic and racial groups last year except for non-Hispanic whites, and in the decade through 2022, Hispanics will make up about 80 percent of growth in the workforce.[1] It's too early to tell how these shifts will play into the nation's economic and social future, but if demographics are destiny, the U.S. is fated to change.

Because of our expanded demographics, society is becoming increasingly intolerant of a lack of diversity in their companies. There is also more corporate pressure on companies than ever before to examine their business practices and take action. As mentioned in the introduction, in March 2015, eBay agreed to nominate one additional woman to its board of directors in response to mounting public pressure for diversity, and in 2013, Twitter appointed its first female board member after it became a target of intense criticism for its all-male board.

◇◇◇◇◇◇◇◇◇◇◇◇◇◇◇◇

Society is becoming increasingly intolerant of a lack of diversity in their companies.

◇◇◇◇◇◇◇◇◇◇◇◇◇◇◇◇

Both developed and developing countries are undergoing an unprecedented demographic transition, one that calls into question traditional assumptions about the characteristics of the working-age population. At the beginning of the twentieth century, the world had 1.7 billion people. Due largely to advances in science, public health, sanitation, and education in both developed and developing countries, that number surged to six billion by the century's end. That number reached seven billion by 2011, and the United Nations estimates the population will reach nearly eleven billion by the year 2050.[2]

Life expectancy has increased in all countries; thus, we are living longer and working longer. The U.S. age distribution has been the classic population "pyramid," in which each younger generation outnumbered the next older generation. In a revolutionary change, the U.S. population pyramid is turning into a population "pillar," with roughly equal-sized generations at all ages.[3] Meanwhile, the contrast between birth rates in developed countries and developing countries is stark. Birth rates have declined in countries like the U.S. and Europe, and are surging in Africa and Asia. For example, the older population in Europe is expected to be more than twice the size of the younger population by the mid-twenty-first century. The high birth rates in developing countries means an increase in migration across borders to find employment. This means that the global workforce will need to employ a higher proportion of older people, thus increasing age diversity. It also means employing more women in countries where it has traditionally been low, and tapping the work skills of a wide range of diverse employees.

Diversity and Discrimination

Diversity in the workplace is a growing concern in many countries, and this concern extends beyond the ramifications of international population trends. Simply put, shifts in the nature and location of economic activity are combining with social and demographic trends to increase the role of nontraditional workers, particularly women, in the paid workforce. At the same time, international support for human rights is blurring traditional patterns of workplace discrimination based on religion, social class, caste, disability, sexual orientation, race and ethnicity, age, and gender.

In 1948, the United Nations created the Universal Declaration of Human Rights. The declaration consists of a preamble and thirty articles, setting forth the human rights and fundamental freedoms without any form of discrimination to which all men and women, everywhere in the world, are entitled.[4] The declaration assures every person, as a member of the human society, specific economic, social, and cultural rights. These rights are characterized as indispensable for human dignity, and the declaration indicates that they are to be realized "through national effort and international cooperation."

The rights most relevant to employment include the right to Social Security, the right to work, the right to equal pay for equal work, the right to rest and leisure (I interpret this as work-life integration), and the right to a standard of living adequate for health and well-being. Although the articles were designed to fit together harmoniously, there is potential tension between the articles that assure freedom of cultural and religious expression and those that assure equality in the workplace. For example, defined gender roles for women and men at home, can also spill over to behaviors at work. Saudi Arabia's constitution includes no statement of equality related to gender, race or ethnicity; it declares, "The state protects human rights in accordance with the Islamic Shari'ah," When these gender expectations create limitations on behaviors between men and women, they challenge the principles of equality and fairness in the workplace.

Another example is the ban on wearing religious attire and religious symbols at work. Some countries ban Muslim women from wearing hijabs or burkas to work. Opponents of such laws criticize them as limiting freedom *of* religion and religious expression. Proponents claim that they promote a secular society and assure freedom *from* religion in schools and in the workplace and therefore guaranty equality in the public arena. This is the same principle that applies to the separation of church and state.

The right to equal pay for equal work (also called equal remuneration) legislation that requires employers to pay women equally for their work as they do men, is by far the most common form of antidiscrimination legislation throughout the world. Taking equal remuneration into account, in addition to anti-sexual harassment and equal rights legislation, more than three-quarters of countries offer some form of protection based on gender.

◇◇◇◇◇◇◇◇◇◇◇◇◇◇◇

Increasing numbers of women in the workplace may be the most important component of diversity in most of the world.

◇◇◇◇◇◇◇◇◇◇◇◇◇◇◇

Despite the prevalence of laws based on gender, it wasn't until 2009 that President Barack Obama signed the first major legislation—the Lilly Ledbetter Fair Pay Act—closing a loophole in the U.S. legislation related to equal pay for equal work, making it easier to sue for wage discrimination. Lilly Ledbetter worked for nineteen years at a Goodyear plant in Alabama and sued after she found she was paid less than her male counterparts. The battle reached the Supreme Court, which ruled against her in a five-to-four decision. The high court's decision was based on the principle that a person must file a discrimination claim within 180 days of a company's initial decision to pay a worker less than another worker doing the same job. Since Ledbetter realized the discrepancy after nineteen years of working there, she could not have possibly sued within this timeframe. Under the new bill, every new discriminatory paycheck would extend the statute of limitations. President Obama said that the bill "is by no means a women's issue, it is a family issue."[5] It's important to note that in most cases of gender discrimination women constitute the group that needs protection., but the laws in most countries can be applied to men as well because they prohibit discrimination regardless of gender.

Increasing numbers of women in the workplace may be the *most important* component of diversity at the national level in most of the world, not only because of their strengthened presence, but also because their changing roles have simultaneous effect at home and work. Changes in the age composition of the working-age population may also change women's share of the labor force. For instance, the share of women in the labor force may increase even more in countries where populations are growing older, as women tend to live longer than men. In these cases, many women need to support themselves in the absence of a husband, and others seek paid activity outside a home that no longer contains children. In either circumstance, where women's educational attainment equals or exceeds men's, employers in most countries can expect challenges to practices that favor men at all levels of the workforce, including supervisory or executive positions.[6] Women have been increasingly active economically in most regions. Thus, women's activity rates are increasingly similar around the world, except in Middle Eastern and North African countries where society invests less in girls' education and constrains women's roles outside the home.

Women's increased participation in the labor force is the product of several social and economic changes, but one of the biggest reasons is that in most countries outside Africa, large numbers of women have achieved control over their fertility, thus expanding their opportunities for education and employment. As a result, both advocates and policy makers are addressing employment-related barriers, such as negative attitudes toward employed women, unfavorable policies regarding family and child care, part-time employment, maternity benefits, and maternal and paternal leave.

◇◇◇◇◇◇◇◇◇◇◇◇◇◇◇◇◇

Women's paid employment increases investment in children—and thus in the future labor force.

◇◇◇◇◇◇◇◇◇◇◇◇◇◇◇◇◇

In fact, global economic development policy now makes fostering women's employment opportunities a priority in developing countries. World Bank economists have concluded that countries that limit women's employment lose as much as a percentage point of potential annual growth through inefficient allocation of productive resources.[7] In addition to the economic benefits of turning dependents into producers, researchers have shown that women's paid employment increases investment in children—and thus in the future labor force. Women who have other choices for their lives also tend to limit their childbearing, bringing fertility rates down so that the future labor force is of a size that the national economy can more readily absorb.

Most democratic and nondemocratic countries today ban job discrimination that is related to gender, race and ethnicity, and some go further and forbid discrimination based on other characteristics like age, social class, physical and mental disability, sexual orientation, HIV status, and pregnancy. Although the declaration has been ratified or accepted by 167 countries, quite a few states either did not sign it or do not enforce it in their laws. Many countries have inadequate legislation; others have appropriate legislation but limited enforcement. Often the obstacles for implementation are traditions and long-existing cultural practices that are discriminatory. An example of this would be the different types of biases mentioned in chapter five, including role congruity expectations, agentic leader beliefs, and gender stereotypes. These deep-seated attitudes toward men and women at work and as leaders, are very real today. The bottom line is that employees who are treated unfairly are less productive, less satisfied, and less loyal to their organizations, which results in reduced organizational income.

Given these facts, why does discrimination still exist in our global organizations? Because the behavior is embedded in deeply engrained prejudicial perceptions that color our evaluation of other people's skills, abilities, and talents. In other words, if one is prejudiced, say against older people, he or she will make a series of inaccurate and often prejudicial assumptions (they are slow, old-fashioned, lack technical skills, etc.). Operating from a mindset that affects perception of reality, an employer is not likely to objectively determine the prospective employee's real qualifications—for example, a woman's ability to manage an engineering team—and is less likely to hire her for a management job. Decisions that are propelled by prejudices tend also to perpetuate them: The employer may never realize the potential economic loss for his or her business by not hiring that women (such as her unique talents, her vision, her teamwork, or her ability to understand female customers).

Numbers Don't Lie

Diversity doesn't mean employing people who have different upbringing, education, preferences in clothes and food, or hair color. That just illustrates individual, benign differences which make all people unique. True diversity at work means employing people based on group memberships that are visibly different from whatever is considered "mainstream" in society. This group affiliation can have practical or even detrimental consequences in people's lives, such as limited job opportunities, promotion prospects, and unfair treatment in the workplace. In other words, it is about being susceptible to employment consequences as a result of one's association within or outside certain social groups.[8] For example, growing up in rural China would create barriers to employment, whereas growing up in urban China would give a job seeker a significant advantage in the job market; being a man in Japan would be associated with more and better job opportunities than being a woman; and belonging to the lower castes in India would be a disadvantage in the workplace compared with belonging to the upper castes.

There is now overwhelming evidence of a strong business case for diversity and inclusion. Diversity has emerged as a business-critical factor in the ability to innovate, attract clients, and retain and cultivate the best talent amidst a changing population and often unpredictable business conditions. Employers could lose their competitive advantage if they do not utilize the wide range of skills and talents offered by women, racial and ethnic minority groups, older adults, people with disabilities, and other minorities.

◇◇◇◇◇◇◇◇◇◇◇◇◇◇

There's a strong correlation between corporate financial performance and gender diversity.

◇◇◇◇◇◇◇◇◇◇◇◇◇◇

An often-cited study by Catalyst found that *Fortune* 500 companies with the highest representation of women board directors attained significantly higher financial performance, on average, than those with the lowest representation of women board directors—in particular, those with three or more women board members had stronger than average performance. Companies with the highest percentage of women board directors achieved 53 percent higher return on equity, 42 percent higher return on sales, and

66 percent higher return on invested capital.[9] They also found that the link between women board directors and corporate performance held across industries—including consumer staples, healthcare, industrials, information technology, and materials. A separate study examined fifteen years of data on the management teams of S&P 1500 firms, and found that more women in top management improved the performance of firms that were heavily focused on innovation—these firms produced $44 million more in revenue with females in the C-Suite.[10] These studies demonstrate a strong correlation between corporate financial performance and gender diversity. It's worth pointing out that the relation between the percent of women on boards and financial performance has been extensively researched, and there are some studies that refute these claims.

Another study showed that better problem solving, decision making, and increased creativity are positively associated with diversity. Researchers measured twenty-eight teams on a wide variety of diversity characteristics (gender, age, race) at a company in Germany, and found that the more diverse teams performed better on highly complex tasks (such as technology and engineering) than homogeneous teams. This result was related to the wider range of thinking processes and increased creativity from the diverse teams.[11]

When it comes to innovation, diversity wins again. Using employee data from Denmark, researchers found robust evidence that diversity in workforces' cultural backgrounds, education, and demographic characteristics is an important source of firm innovation among white-collar occupations. More ethnically diverse workforces correlated with firms' greater likelihood of applying for patents, having a higher number of overall patent applications, and a wider range of patenting technological fields.[12] The reason for this is that people from different backgrounds see problems and solutions from different perspectives, and that richness of ideas leads to stronger outcomes, making diversity a proven ingredient of creativity and innovation.

Customer satisfaction is also strengthened by diversity. The employee demographics of most companies today still do not reflect the diversity in our communities. JC Penney chose to hire a wide range of diverse employees to better serve their communities. In an analysis of more than 700 JC Penney stores, researchers found that store employees matching or mirroring the race and ethnic makeup of their communities positively affected customer satisfaction, productivity and ultimately earnings—attributing more than $69 million dollars in revenue to this "racioethnic representativeness."[13] In addition, other studies have shown an increase in employee satisfaction, higher morale, increased competitive advantage, and enhanced corporate image—all as a result of having a more diverse and inclusive workforce.

◇◇◇◇◇◇◇◇◇◇◇◇◇◇◇◇

If innovation is the Holy Grail, then diversity should be a company's unrelenting quest.

◇◇◇◇◇◇◇◇◇◇◇◇◇◇◇◇

The Center for Talent Innovation researched global corporations and found that those with diverse leaders yielded additional benefits to individuals. Employees reported that they were 60 percent more likely to see their ideas developed, 75 percent more likely to see their innovation implemented, 70 percent more likely to have captured a new market in the past year, and 87 percent more likely to feel welcome and included in their teams.[14]

However, they found that when leadership lacks innate or acquired diversity, or fails to foster a speak-up culture, fewer ideas with market potential make it to market. Ideas from women, people of color, LGBT (Lesbian, Gay, Bisexual, Transgender) and Millennials were less likely to win the endorsement they need to go forward because 56 percent of leaders don't value ideas they don't personally see a need for—a veritable chokehold when an organization's leaders are predominantly Caucasian, male, heterosexual, and come from similar educational and socioeconomic backgrounds. In short, the data strongly suggest that homogeneity stifles innovation—and 78 percent of their survey sample work for such a company. They concluded that innovative capacity resides in an inherently diverse workforce where leaders prize difference, value every voice, and manage rather than suppress disruption. If innovation is the Holy Grail, then diversity should be a company's unrelenting quest.

The Corporate Executive Board studied global corporations and found that diverse and inclusive workforces demonstrate more discretionary effort, greater retention, greater team commitment, and more collaboration among teams. George Chavel, CEO of Sodexo, one of the companies they studied, said that, "It is diversity and inclusion that is differentiating us as an organization and establishing our competitive advantage in the marketplace."[15] Nick Colucci, CEO of Publicis, told the Healthcare Businesswomen's Association that, "We have done an engagement survey inside my organization every year for the past five years. Teams that are diverse, usually led by women, have the highest engagement scores and coincidentally, have the best performance financially too. It's an absolute truism in our organization that diverse teams lead to a more engaged work population and better performance."[16]

LGBT employees are disproportionately impacted when organizations lack D&I. In the U.S., you can still be fired for being gay or transgender in more than half of the states. As of 2017, thirty states have yet to adopt legislation expressly prohibiting firing or refusing to hire an individual based on their sexual orientation or gender identity. Nearly two-thirds of LGBT Americans report having experienced discrimination in their personal lives, and of those, 47 percent report experiencing discrimination in the workplace.[17] Thus, fear of negative repercussions keep more than half of LGBT workers in the closet. They fear that coming out and being their authentic selves might limit advancement opportunities, they have more distrust of their organizations, and feel more isolated. Even worse, such workers are less productive, and talented employees are leaving workplaces where they don't feel welcome.

◇◇◇◇◇◇◇◇◇◇◇◇◇◇◇◇◇◇

In the U.S., you can still be fired for being gay or transgender in more than half of the states.

◇◇◇◇◇◇◇◇◇◇◇◇◇◇◇◇◇◇

There are tangible benefits for organizations that enact LGBT policies in the workplace. Employers will get the most out of their employees when they feel included and are "out" to their coworkers and supervisors. Being able to acknowledge one's sexual orientation is beneficial in the following ways: 70 percent of "out" employees deem themselves very loyal to their employers, 64 percent are more satisfied with their job and rate of promotion, 30 percent are more productive, and "out" employees exhibit better mental and physical health compared to closeted employees.[18]

The Human Rights Campaign's Corporate Equality Index is the national benchmarking tool on corporate policies and practices pertinent to LGBT employees. In 2002, only thirteen out of 319 corporations surveyed (less than one in twenty) earned perfect ratings of LGBT inclusion. By 2017, 517 out of 887 major businesses (more than one in two)—spanning nearly every industry and geography—earned a top score of 100 percent and the distinction of "Best Places to Work for LGBT Equality".[19] Further, every single company on *Fortune* magazine's list of the "100 Best Companies to Work For" includes sexual orientation in their nondiscrimination policy, and more than half of these companies include gender identity in their nondiscrimination policy. As more and more businesses are realizing, nondiscrimination policies, benefits and other practices that include LGBT workers are essential as they compete for talent and customers.

So, based on all this data, strong evidence shows that diverse workforces perform better than majority-male white workforces. Such astounding numbers can partly be attributed to the fact that, in general, diversity drives innovation. This may be because having a well-managed, diverse team brings together varied perspectives that lead to more dynamic analysis and problem solving. Specifically, having a gender-balanced team fosters an environment that nourishes innovation and collaboration more than a one-gender team.

When most people think about diversity at work, they generally think about race and ethnicity. Even if a company is diverse in race, age, sexual orientation, and disability, they may *not* be gender diverse—it could still be predominantly male. To fully leverage D&I and all the benefits discussed here, it's important to ensure that your diversity initiatives include gender.

Diversity Explorers

There are a growing number of companies across a variety of industries that have invested considerable resources to be more diverse and inclusive. Some experts have even asked if this is going to be the year of diversity in business—and all indicators seem to say yes. This topic has been raised in the public eye and is now front and center in most human resources and talent management initiatives. And, research proves that companies with great diversity outperform their peers by a significant margin. If you aren't taking this topic seriously, you should be.

The technology industry has a problem with gender and race diversity—and they know it. Technology has been under intense media scrutiny and public pressure from civil rights and labor activists since 2013. The table below shows you why.

COMPANY	EMPLOYEES	% MALE EMPLOYEES
Amazon	132,600	61%
Microsoft	114,000	73%
Intel	106,700	75%
Apple	98,000	68%
Google	57,100	69%
Qualcomm	27,000	80%
Facebook	14,495	68%
LinkedIn	9,900	58%
GoDaddy	5,000	76%
Twitter	3,860	66%

Data from company websites 2016

Most of the world's biggest technology companies—ten are shown here—are made up primarily of Caucasian and Asian men. The average for these companies is 70 percent men and 88 percent Caucasian and Asian. The percentage of other types of race or ethnicity makeup approximately 10 percent or less across the board. Some of these companies, admittedly, had not looked closely at their diversity until they were forced to a few years ago—and they were shocked at what they found. Now, many are taking significant strides to be more diverse and inclusive as they recognize the validity and benefits they could gain if they employ a wider range of workers.

The U.S. Equal Employment Opportunity Commission requires all companies with one hundred or more employees to file an EEO-1 report—a compliance survey mandated by federal statute and regulations. The survey requires company employment data to be categorized by race/ethnicity, gender and job category. The agencies also use the EEO-1 report data to support civil rights enforcement and to analyze employment patterns, such as the representation of women and minorities within companies, industries or regions. Some companies post their EEO-1 reports and openly share their diversity data on their websites; other companies have yet to be transparent.

◇◇◇◇◇◇◇◇◇◇◇◇◇◇◇

Most of the world's biggest technology companies
are made up primarily of Caucasian and Asian men.

◇◇◇◇◇◇◇◇◇◇◇◇◇◇◇

Although Google is not the largest tech company, it has shown significant influence in the industry by the very fact that after tech was called upon to release demographic data, Google was the first to respond with numbers in May 2014. Sixteen others soon followed. Google has also made a significant financial investment toward D&I. So far, they've invested $265 million supporting local programs by external partners, and focusing on diversifying their own workforce. You may have heard about or seen the unconscious bias training and research they freely shared on their Work platform. Over 65 percent of Googlers have participated in these workshops, and all new

Googlers and managers are trained in it.[20] Research shows that simply raising awareness about unconscious bias can lead to more conscious decision making.

Amazon has several affinity groups which provide critical inputs and insights about where the company should focus its diversity efforts. The Amazon Women in Engineering affinity group hosts the annual AmazeCon conference, Amazon's internal conference on gender diversity. Amazon also supports STEM (science, technology, engineering, math) education through a variety of programs to encourage girls to seek careers in the sciences. In addition, they created Amazon Circles in coordination with the launch of *LeanIn.org* in 2013. They built on the idea of peer mentoring groups by adding a senior advisor so that participants can benefit from both perspectives.[21]

Microsoft has several initiatives in place to try and recruit top diverse talent. Their executive recruiting team has a strategic and proactive focus on prospecting diverse talent; they recognize and encourage technical women by sponsoring awards and scholarships; they support computer science education and opportunities for women and minority students by partnering with traditionally female, black, and Hispanic universities; and they encourage girls and diverse students to study computing through their DigiGirlz program and their high school minority student day and summer internship program.[22]

Intel has gone a step further. Danielle Brown, Chief Diversity Officer, said, "Intel is committed to setting the industry standard for a diverse and inclusive workplace culture."[23] They seem to be putting their money where their mouth is too. In January 2015, they set an ambitious goal to be the first high tech company to reach full representation of women and underrepresented minorities in their U.S. workforce by 2020—and they committed $300 million to support this goal. They're also tracking hiring, retention, and pay parity. They plan to address all pay gaps in accordance with their usual practice, with the aim of reaching 100 percent pay parity.

◇◇◇◇◇◇◇◇◇◇◇◇◇◇◇◇

*Intel is committed to setting the tech industry standard
for a diverse and inclusive workplace culture.*

◇◇◇◇◇◇◇◇◇◇◇◇◇◇◇◇

Of course, technology companies aren't the only ones focusing on diversity. Companies such as SAP, L'Oréal, Aetna, Sodexo, BAE systems, Pfizer, Deloitte, and Wells Fargo have been at it for quite a while. However, despite the efforts, most global organizations remain ineffective at building a diverse and inclusive workforce, and their employees concur. In a global labor market survey of over nine thousand employees, most did not agree that diversity is well represented in their organization, nor did they agree that divergent perspectives are valued.[24] It's difficult to change corporate culture, especially in large companies. Everyone knows that being more diverse and inclusive is the right thing to do, yet getting people to think differently, and actively driving them toward making change is difficult in any organization—especially ones with thousands of people. Let's explore some strategies that may help.

Diversity Strategies

Not so long ago, merely mentioning that companies should take diversity and inclusion into account when hiring would raise eyebrows. But that started to change when the Hudson Institute's landmark Workforce 2000 study forecasted that the American workforce would become much more diverse in the new millennium—and companies that couldn't adapt would risk losing their competitive edge. The report was right on the money, and that trend is only continuing as women and people of color constitute 70 percent of new entrants to the workforce.

Many organizations have responded by creating a new executive position—Chief Diversity Officer (CDO)—with the sole responsibility of promoting workforce diversity. Just a decade ago, this position was almost unheard of, but today, approximately one in five *Fortune* 1000 companies have diversity leaders. These CDOs are implementing comprehensive programs to help their company boost diverse recruitment, help those employees advance, implement diversity training, and even forge relationships with diverse vendors. These efforts help build morale, reduce employee turnover, and build stronger relationships with customers in diverse communities—ultimately boosting a company's success.

Over the last ten years, CDOs have made great strides in reshaping the corporate landscape. Because women have often come up against barriers themselves, it's no surprise that some of them have become the country's most influential diversity leaders. And, they're making progress from every conceivable angle—some are CDOs in *Fortune* 500 companies, some have launched their own training and consultancy firms, and still others are working within the nonprofit sector.

These types of diversity efforts are what's known as *diversity management*, which refers to the voluntary organizational actions that are designed to create greater inclusion of employees from various backgrounds into the formal and informal organizational structures through deliberate policies and programs. Effective diversity management means dealing with the collective mixture of all workers, not just the recent additions to the workforce or to the majority population. For example, consider a jar of red jelly beans and assume you will add some green and purple jelly beans. Many would believe the green and purple represent diversity, but diversity is the resultant mixture of the jelly beans. When faced with a collection of diverse jelly beans, most managers do not address diversity; instead, they address how to handle the last jelly beans added to the mixture.[25] In other words, the true meaning of diversity suggests that if you are concerned about racism, you include all races; if you are concerned about gender, you include all genders; or if you're concerned about age, you include all age groups. The mixture should be all inclusive.

◇◇◇◇◇◇◇◇◇◇◇◇◇◇◇◇◇

Chief Diversity Officers have made great strides in reshaping corporate culture over the last ten years.

◇◇◇◇◇◇◇◇◇◇◇◇◇◇◇◇◇

Because diversity management can create competitive advantages in areas such as recruitment, retention, marketing, problem solving, and innovation, it is not limited to the HR function—it is a systematic organization-wide effort based on the premise that for organizations to survive and thrive, there is an inherent value in diversity. Diversity efforts can be viewed on a continuum: Equal employment opportunity legislation means it is against the law to discriminate, affirmative action programs mean that companies need to take positive steps to ensure equal opportunities, and diversity management is proactive and aimed at promoting a diverse and heterogeneous workforce.

One important pitfall for organizations to avoid is the ASA (attraction-selection-attrition) cycle. Conventional HR practices tend to produce and perpetuate homogeneity in the workforce because of this cycle. Typically, individuals are *attracted* to organizations that appear to have members with similar values to their own. In turn, organizations *select* new members who are like their existing members because their hiring continues to make everyone feel comfortable. Recruiting practices then emphasize hiring people from sources that have historically been reliable and selecting candidates whose characteristics are similar to those employees that have been successful in the past. Thus, employees who do not fit in well with the dominant organizational culture eventually leave or are fired, creating a selective *attrition* process that supports and maintains a workforce that is homogenous.[26]

Recall the discussion in chapter five about hiring based on organizational fit. The ASA cycle is the reason why many organizations look for fit in their hiring, and the reason fit is perpetuated. Fit causes us to be biased in favor of the dominant types of workers in an organization (such as Caucasian and Asian men in technology), and biased against anyone who doesn't fit the mold (such as African American or Latina women applying for positions in tech). In the long run, this trend is unhealthy for organizations in that it limits their talent pool, their long-term growth, and their ability to adapt to environmental changes and tap into new markets. We should not be hiring based on fit, and we need to remove this characteristic from our recruiting criteria.

It's important to remember that diversity representation in the workforce is only the initial step toward workplace inclusion. Inclusion reflects the extent to which employees perceive that they are part of the communication systems, informal networks, and decision-making processes. Therefore, increasing diversity representation and achieving inclusion is a two-stage process with each stage affecting the other in a circular way. The first stage is *reactive*: Organizations are recruiting and employing a more diverse workforce. The second stage is *proactive*: Organizations are investing efforts in active diversity management with the aim of enhancing inclusion and fostering organization effectiveness.

◇◇◇◇◇◇◇◇◇◇◇◇◇◇◇◇

We should not be hiring based on fit, and we need to remove this characteristic from our recruiting criteria.

◇◇◇◇◇◇◇◇◇◇◇◇◇◇◇◇

Questions an organization could ask at the first stage are, "Are we able to attract diverse talent?" and "To what extent do we reflect our client base?" Questions at the second stage could include, "To what extent do our policies and practices attract and retain well-qualified and diverse individuals?", "Is our organizational culture inclusive and culturally competent?" and "To what extent are employees from different identity groups participating in formal and informal networks and actively involved in the decision-making process?" For organizations to become truly inclusive, it is not enough that they have policies and guidelines in place; there needs to be a deep conviction in the importance of inclusion. This level of commitment to diversity and inclusion can only come from the very top of the organization.

For most organizations, they should look at developing at least a five-year strategic D&I plan. Michàlle Mor Barak, professor at University of Southern California and diversity researcher, has outlined an inclusive workplace model with four distinct levels.[27] An inclusive workplace is an organization that is not only accepting and utilizing the diversity of its own workforce (level I), but is also active in the community (level II); participates in state and federal programs to include population groups such as immigrants, women, and the working poor (level III); and collaborates across cultural and national boundaries with a focus on global mutual interests (level IV). Diversity strategies at level I and II are most common, followed by level III and IV with expanding circles of inclusion.

Here are some inclusive workplace strategies at level I that companies can apply to their own workforces:

- *Leadership involvement*—Create a top-level focus and strategy at the CEO, COO, CHRO, and CDO level. Assign a top executive the responsibility for leading and sponsoring the diversity program, and create a diversity council or committee of employees from various departments and levels within the organization.
- *Policies and procedures*—Create a diversity mission statement, anti-discrimination policies, corporate values, and behavioral standards that reflect D&I.
- *Education and training*—Offer unconscious bias or sensitivity training workshops to increase diversity awareness and skill building, and to help employees understand the need for, and meaning of, valuing diversity.
- *Performance and accountability*—Establish diversity goals, quotas and metrics. Develop action plans to meet the goals of specific business units and the organization and hold managers accountable to these goals by linking diversity performance to compensation. Ensure supplier diversity.
- *Work-life balance*—Offer flexible work arrangements such as telecommuting, job sharing, working at home, and part-time work assignments to accommodate diverse needs and lifestyles of employees.
- *Career development and planning*—Establish career development and planning initiatives for women and underrepresented groups to ensure fair promotion opportunities for high-potential employees and to increase diversity representation in managerial level jobs.

- *Employee networks*—Create affinity or employee resource groups (ERGs), as well as mentoring programs, to empower employees of diverse backgrounds.
- *Communication*—Provide transparent diversity-related communications internally and externally, and utilize company-wide diversity engagement surveys.

In recent decades, the public expectations for corporate "good citizenship" behaviors have not only increased, but have changed. The more the public hears of corporate greed and corruption, the less patience it has for corporate indifference and unethical behavior. This sentiment was heightened because of the global economic crisis of 2008 and generated a very cynical public view of corporate greed and its consequences for both people and the environment—as illustrated in the 2015 movie *The Big Short*. Thus, there is a strong expectation today among the public (and employees within companies) for corporate policies that recognize the importance of the local community and the larger society.

Hence, the idea of corporate social responsibility (CSR) has grown in popularity and is one of the criteria used to assess the *Fortune* 500 annual list of "World's Most Admired Companies." The idea of CSR expands a company's responsibilities beyond its traditional economic shareholders to that of multiple stakeholders, including the community. Employees and consumers today are more socially aware and savvy about their power to influence corporate citizenship behavior than generations past.

Here are some inclusive workplace strategies at level II to help organizations improve CSR and connect with their communities:

- *Community support*—Make charitable contributions, support diverse professional associations, support educational or cultural institutions, provide health services for women and children, or participation of company leaders on boards of minority organizations.

- *Students and youth*—Provide corporate internships for students, mentoring programs for youth, tutor children in local schools, or sponsorship of school programs.
- *Career development*—Provide job skills training to women and underrepresented minorities, or conduct diversity career fairs for the community.
- *Communication*—Provide transparent communication about specific CSR activities on company website, annual report, and shareholder and financial meetings to report dedication and commitment to CSR goals.

The combination of business globalization, worker migration, and workforce diversity creates a challenge for companies engaged in international business. Many companies, such as IBM, GM, BP, Nestle, and Novartis operate in more than fifty countries. Of the one thousand largest industrial companies in the U.S., seven hundred expect their growth abroad to exceed their domestic growth in the next five years.[28] The inclusive workplace sees value in collaborating across national borders and identifying global mutual interests. For example, the exclusionary organization will send local employees on international assignments to strictly enforce a company's values and norms overseas, whereas the inclusive workplace will hire local managers and give autonomy to its international branches.

◇◇◇◇◇◇◇◇◇◇◇◇◇◇◇

Since there are many types of diverse groups in the workplace, the easiest place to start with is gender.

◇◇◇◇◇◇◇◇◇◇◇◇◇◇◇

As shown here, the trend toward globalization and diversity is increasing, and the goal to promote more inclusive environments will continue to be an enduring principle. But, how it is executed may look very different over time. Even diversity as we consider it now is becoming more diverse. One of the D&I trends that's becoming increasingly important is intersectionality, or recognizing that people are multifaceted. This may shift how ERGs are organized and defined. Consider, for example, a gay female veteran. Which ERG would she choose? Women's, veterans, or LGBT? Per a recent piece in the *Washington Post*, "Why Intersectionality Can't Wait," overlapping identities can create "profound invisibility" and need to be acknowledged to promote full inclusion and equity.[29]

Since there are many different types of diverse groups in the workplace, the easiest place to start with is gender. Gender encompasses most other types—such as a young female Millennial, an African-American veteran, or a transgender female with a disability. As stated earlier, increasing the numbers of women in the workplace may be the *most important* component of diversity at the national level in most of the world.

D&I change must come from the top, and it must be believed in the middle. Change also must be incentivized, meaning that people should see and believe that diversity drives the bottom line from their own experience. There's no question that diversity takes work—it requires awareness, it requires understanding, it requires empathy, it requires behavior change, it takes listening, and it takes time. But, if you put in the hard work, you'll have much more robust outcomes for both yourself and your organization—the result being a more equal workplace and better performing company. The payoff is well worth the effort.

If organizations choose to do nothing in response to the global population shifts, and don't adapt to meet the changing needs of a wide range of diverse employees, they risk losing their competitive edge, or worse, becoming obsolete. Although employees no longer stay at one company for life, the decisions that are made about who is hired, developed, and promoted endure for years. As such, a forward-thinking mindset is a mandate for business executives today. As we'll explore in the next chapter, the Millennial generation are seeking companies who are truly diverse and inclusive, or at least moving in that direction.

Summary Points

- Diversity is the collective mixture of differences that includes individual and organizational characteristics such as values, beliefs, experiences, backgrounds, and behaviors.
- Inclusion is the achievement of a work environment, in which all individuals are treated fairly and respectfully, have equal access to opportunities and resources, and can contribute fully to the organization's success.
- Both developed and developing countries are undergoing an unprecedented demographic transition.
- Life expectancy has increased in all countries; therefore, the global workforce will need to employ a higher proportion of older people.
- The right to equal pay for equal work was by far the most common form of antidiscrimination legislation throughout the world.
- Discrimination still exists in global organizations because the behavior is embedded in deeply engrained prejudicial perceptions.
- There is now overwhelming evidence of a strong business case for diversity and inclusion.
- Most of the world's biggest technology companies are made up primarily of Caucasian and Asian men.
- Diversity management is the voluntary organizational actions that are designed to create greater inclusion of employees from various backgrounds into the formal and informal organizational structures through deliberate policies and programs.
- There are several inclusive workplace strategies to help both individuals and organizations maximize human potential.

Reflection Questions

- ✓ What demographic groups do you consider yourself a member of? For example, gender, age/generation, race/ethnicity, sexual orientation/ gender identity, veteran, disability?

✓ What is the demographic makeup of your organization overall? What is the demographic makeup of your company's management and leadership teams?

✓ Have you ever experienced or observed workplace discrimination? What occurred? What was the outcome? How did it affect you?

✓ Do you experience any gender expectations at home or work that challenge the principles of equality and fairness in the workplace? How have you worked through it?

✓ Have you worked with diverse individuals or teams? Was your experience positive, negative or neutral? What were the outcomes?

✓ Are you a member of any affinity groups or ERGs at work? Have these groups been helpful to you as an individual, or in your career? If yes, how so?

✓ Does your company hire based on fit? If so, what has been the outcome?

✓ Does your company exhibit corporate social responsibility (CSR) by creating or supporting programs for the community? If so, how have they focused on the local community or society? Have you ever participated in these programs?

✓ Does your company have any diversity and/or inclusion strategies in place (e.g., diversity metrics, policies, benefits, or training)? If so, what is your impression of them? Have you participated in any programs? Have they been effective?

ELEVEN

Could Millennials Save the Day?

If you want something you've never had, you must be willing to do something you've never done.
Thomas Jefferson

I magine a diverse workgroup of a dozen people who have been assigned a project in an accounting firm. They've met for the first time as a team, and are discussing communication preferences for follow-up. Herbert, a seventy-one-year-old accountant, asks the team to provide him a hard copy of each of their respective plans, and wants to schedule more face-to-face meetings. Virginia, a fifty-nine-year-old controller wants to schedule calls with each team member to discuss their plans in-depth. Brad, a forty-two-year-old auditor requests that the team emails their plans so he can review them. And, Katy, a twenty-six-year-old analyst wants the team to text her their thoughts about next steps.

This is an oversimplified, but great way to show some of the drastic distinctions between each generation. In this case, Herbert, part of the Veteran generation, prefers written communication. Virginia, part of the Baby Boomer generation, prefers telephone communication. Brad, part of Generation X, prefers email. And, Katy, part of the Millennial generation, prefers texting.

Today, there are four generations working side-by-side in the workplace. As discussed in the last chapter, people all over the world are living and working longer. The World Health Organization shows that men and women who are healthy at age sixty will on average be physically capable of working until they are in their mid-seventies.[1] In the U.S., those aged sixty-five and older are working more than at any time since the turn of the century, and today's older workers are spending more time on the job than did their peers in previous years. As of May 2016, this represented 19 percent of Americans (nearly nine million people) who reported being employed full- or part-time—continuing a steady increase that dates to the year 2000.[2] Given the rise in workers ages, by the year 2020, there will be five generations working side-by-side. And, data shows that half of all working adults between ages fifty and sixty-four say they will delay retirement, and another 16 percent report they never expect to stop working.[3]

◇◇◇◇◇◇◇◇◇◇◇◇◇◇◇

By the year 2020, there will be five generations working side-by-side.

◇◇◇◇◇◇◇◇◇◇◇◇◇◇◇

Each generational cohort has unique descriptors and drivers that influence their behavior and attitude, which help explain why its members act the way they do. Note that there is no consensus as to the precise start and end dates for each generation (especially the newest ones), therefore I've used the most commonly published dates for each group. The *Veterans* (also known as Traditionalists) were born before 1945, the *Baby Boomers* were born between 1946 and 1964, *Generation X* were born between 1965 and 1980, and *Millennials* (also known as Generation Y) were born between 1981 and

2000.[4] The youngest generation who have not yet entered the workforce, are *Generation Z*, born after the year 2000.

The Veterans comprise senior Americans who were born prior to World War II. The number of total U.S. births for this generation is 47 million.[5] They came of age during the Great Depression and the war—experiences that had a lasting impact on their development and worldviews. They are generally seen as civic minded due to their military service and upbringing during conservative times. This generation grew up with rotary phones, and since technology was in its infancy, they prefer face-to-face and written communication. What's important about technology, is as it came into existence, it helped define how each generation would come to communicate and collaborate—thus establishing their relative technological comfort zone.

The Baby Boomers grew up in a time of much prosperity after WWII, and represent a staggering 76 million people.[6] Baby Boomers were raised in overcrowded public schools in the late 1950s and 1960s, and television provided them graphic depictions of every event ranging from Cambodian death camps to the lunar landing. They were rebellious and questioned all that had mattered to previous generations as they entered college and young adulthood. The formative events for Baby Boomers included the Vietnam War, the Cold War, Watergate, the Cuban missile crisis, and the JFK assassination.[7] They were also influenced by the Civil Rights Movement, the Women's Movement, and grew up in a time of free love and personal freedom.

◇◇◇◇◇◇◇◇◇◇◇◇◇◇◇

A hallmark of Gen X is the flood of women who entered the workforce during the 1980s.

◇◇◇◇◇◇◇◇◇◇◇◇◇◇◇

Although it doesn't get much attention, Generation X were raised in technology—from televisions, video games, microwave ovens, and VCRs, to the very first cell phones in 1973 and personal computers in 1975. Gen X, raised in the 1970s and 1980s represents 55 million U.S. births.[8] They saw the national debt soar, a struggling economy, and their families experience record-breaking divorce rates. They also experienced the AIDS epidemic and the Challenger space shuttle disaster. Because so many American systems crumbled in their youth, they dislike taking orders and are comfortable challenging authority.[9] A notable hallmark of Gen X is the flood of women who entered the workforce during the 1980s.

Millennials or Gen Y are not simply an extension of Gen X. Raised in the 1990s and 2000s, their parents are largely the Boomers and they are 66 million strong.[10] They currently range from seventeen to thirty-six years of age, with half of the generation early in their professional lives. They witnessed further advances in technology with the advent of the internet in 1990, camera phones, text and instant messaging, and a wide-range of social media. Formative events include globalization, the September 11th terrorist attacks, non-traditional families, and increased diversity. They also experienced an increased focus on the child, and schoolyard violence and bullying. Per the U.S. Census Bureau population estimates released in April 2016, Millennials have *now surpassed* Baby Boomers as the nation's largest living generation as young immigrants expand its ranks. They number 75.4 million, surpassing the 74.9 million Baby Boomers—whose generation are older and their numbers shrinking as the number of deaths among them exceeds the number of older immigrants arriving in the country.[11]

Finally, Gen Z were born in 2001 and continue today, making this cohort sixteen years of age and younger. We're over half-way into this newest generation, and have yet to see the exact size and unique characteristics that will define its personality—although its estimated to be a sizable 69 million people (before immigration) which could eclipse the Millennials as an economic force.[12] There's no doubt that a significant aspect of this generation is the widespread usage of the internet from a young age, and a more positive view of globalization and diversity than previous generations. Members of Gen Z are typically thought of as being comfortable with technology, and interacting on social media websites for a significant portion of their socializing.

Gen Why

Why is there so much hype about Gen Y? This generation has garnered much attention in the past decade, partly because they are the biggest generation since the Baby Boomers, and partly because they have unique work preferences, attitudes, and practices. Since most people start work between the ages of eighteen and twenty-three, Millennials entered the workforce starting in 2000. Those in the first half of this generation experienced the 2008 Great Recession first hand. They graduated college and were eager to enter the workforce, but faced a declining job market, stiff competition, and sky-high student loan debt. Thus, many Millennials were unemployed, forced to take entry-level jobs outside of their desired field, and moved back home. Trends we had not seen in previous generations.

Looking at workers between mid-twenties and early-thirties (the age bracket most impacted by the recession), the unemployment rate is consistently above the national overall level of joblessness since the recovery. Even more concerning is the fact that this gap is now wider than it was in 2009, suggesting the current recovery has not spread to younger workers as previous recoveries did. Census data show that only about 63 percent of Millennials were working in 2012, compared with 70 percent of the similar age bracket in 1990.[13]

◇◇◇◇◇◇◇◇◇◇◇◇◇◇◇◇◇

Millennials are straying from historic patterns and spending less on big-ticket items.

◇◇◇◇◇◇◇◇◇◇◇◇◇◇◇◇◇

It's likely that many Millennials will be unable to make up this lost ground because early adulthood is when productivity is greatest and pay raises more significant. A depressed starting salary means a worker will likely earn much less for the rest of his or her career. Because of massive student loan debt, limited employment opportunities, and stagnant wages, Millennials are straying from historic patterns—spending less on big-ticket items such as suburban homes and new cars—changes that have a negative impact since these items power the U.S. economy.

Younger Millennials, those who began their job hunts as the economy was recovering, are moving out. Census data show that the share of eighteen to twenty-four-year-olds living with their parents dropped in 2014 for the second consecutive year. But by comparison, the share of twenty-five to thirty-four-year-olds living at home rose. The fact that Millennials are staying home longer, and appear to have lost interest in purchasing cars and homes is the byproduct of the recession, which has left more than a temporary scar. It seems to have fueled a permanent generational shift in their spending habits and tastes.

Given that the theme of this book is *perception,* it's fitting that Millennials—more than any other generation—have been the subject of both positive and negative perceptions (or misperceptions). Can you think of some common characteristics of Millennials? What is your personal view of this group? Let's examine both admirable and less flattering characteristics.

POSTIVE PERCEPTIONS	NEGATIVE PERCEPTIONS
High self-esteem (trophy kids)	Entitled (trophy kids)
Confident	Lazy
Technology savvy/Social media driven	Self-centered
Socially responsible	Narcissistic
Not motivated by money	Money-driven
Multitaskers	Multitaskers
At ease with diversity at work and home	High maintenance
Intolerant of organizational lack of diversity	Easily bored/Short attention span
Ambitious	Lacks ambition
Challenge status quo	Question/Challenge authority
High expectations for themselves and others	No respect for chain of command

Hard-working	Lax work ethic
Entrepreneurial	Lax attire
Frequent & proactive communication style	Direct communication style (no filter)
Value real-time candid feedback	Can't take negative feedback
Value recognition	Wants constant recognition/Personal attention
Open and eager to learn new things	Expects immediate response
Seek meaning in their work	Frustrated with others' lack of tech skills
Value work-life integration & flexibility	Impatient
Value collaboration and teamwork	Wants to advance without putting in the work
Prefer flat structure (not hierarchy)	Pampered/Spoiled
Creative and innovative	Whiny
Resourceful	Needy
Persistence/Determination	Lack interpersonal skills
Global perspective	Lack loyalty/Job hoppers

As you can see, there are as many positive as negative characteristics that describe this sizable group. Some perceptions are in direct opposition to one another—such as not motivated by money *and* money-driven, ambitious *and* lack of ambition, and hard-working *and* lax work ethic. Multitasking is considered both a positive skill (ability to address many things at one time) and negative skill (giving only partial attention to many things at one time), so it is in both columns.

Whether they're labeled as whiny, lazy and spoiled, or creative, resourceful and hard-working, much has been said about Millennials. There is some truth to both sides of this coin. For example, the increased focus on the child by their Baby Boomer parents caused many Millennials to have high self-esteem and confidence, but also a sense of entitlement and lax work ethic. After all, these are the kids that were given a trophy for just showing up and "participating." It's important to note here that whatever the outcomes may be from the extra attention, it was not caused by the Millennials, but rather their doting and devoted parents that helped create such an environment.

◇◇◇◇◇◇◇◇◇◇◇◇◇◇◇◇

There are as many positive as negative characteristics that describe Millennials.

◇◇◇◇◇◇◇◇◇◇◇◇◇◇◇◇

As a professor, I have been pleasantly surprised. The majority of my MBA students are in this generation. I expected them to be self-centered, lack interpersonal skills, and not be willing to put in the work needed on their reading and assignments. By contrast, they are willing to work hard, are hungry to learn, and they care about each other. They devote extra time to help each other with classes, they attend each other's social events, and are very collaborative. Perceptions that I've found to be true is their resourcefulness and need for feedback. During class discussions on any given topic, they instantly pull-up additional information on their devices, which helps enhance discussion. In addition, they value relevant and timely feedback about what and how they're doing—I see this as a positive trait as it shows that they are open and willing to try new things to improve.

One exercise that we do early in the semester assesses their job satisfaction motivators. Because no job is perfect, we often must make trade-offs—one job may pay well, but provide limited opportunities for advancement; another may offer work we enjoy, but have poor benefits. Out of twenty-one job factors, I ask them to rank-order their top five attributes. In over one hundred students, the top five factors that contribute to their job satisfaction are:

1. Compensation and pay
2. Meaningfulness of their work
3. Career development and advancement opportunities

4. Flexibility to balance life and work issues
5. Independence and autonomy

This shows that Millennials are generally driven by intrinsic motivators—factors such as achievement, responsibility, recognition, work itself, advancement, and growth. Except for compensation which is an extrinsic motivator, all the other key job attributes center on factors that are intrinsically rewarding, and are consistent with many of the positive perceptions of this group.

At a recent conference, I met Kathy, CEO of an upstart software company based in San Francisco. Her twelve employees are all Millennials. She shared with me that after a week of travel, she returned to the office one Friday afternoon to find the entire staff gone. After a few text messages, she learned that they collectively decided to leave work early to donate blood. Of course, she couldn't be upset at this behavior. It simply highlighted the importance of social responsibility in their lives and their need to give back. Not surprisingly, many Millennials seek companies that demonstrate corporate social responsibility as well, as discussed in chapter ten.

◇◇◇◇◇◇◇◇◇◇◇◇◇◇◇◇◇◇

Millennials tend to donate, volunteer, campaign, and be more actively engaged than other generations.

◇◇◇◇◇◇◇◇◇◇◇◇◇◇◇◇◇◇

This holistic and philanthropic view of the world can be seen in the popularity of crowdfunding websites that have sprung up in the past few years, such as Kickstarter, GoFundMe, and Indiegogo. Crowdfunding is the practice of funding a project or venture by raising monetary contributions from many people—primarily through the Internet. These projects are driven by individuals and cover a wide range of interests, such as artistic and creative projects, medical expenses, travel, or community-oriented social entrepreneurship projects. It's a form of crowdsourcing and alternative finance for many, and in 2015, it was estimated that over $34 billion was raised this way worldwide.[14] Compared to other generations, Millennials tend to donate, volunteer, campaign, and be more actively engaged with social, environmental, or political affairs more often.

Because of the premium they place on flexibility and autonomy, we're seeing shifts not only in current roles, but in the willingness to take on future roles as well. For example, some law firms are struggling to understand these new values. The traditional lawyer path is long and arduous—finish law school, pass the Bar exam, work excessive weekday hours, work weekend hours, and log years in the firm trying to make partner. Millennial men just out of law school see this and realize they don't want the rigorous lifestyle—and are not willing to follow the same path. Senior partners can't understand why these young men are unwilling to embrace the traditional route. Older men need to see that the status quo will not work for their younger counterparts, and if they desire to build their firms for the future, they must try to accommodate Millennial preferences.

As mentioned in chapter seven, Millennials have initiated a significant shift in today's work-life environment. For them, the question isn't about obtaining balance anymore, but about integrating their work with their life. Millennial couples split household chores more evenly than previous generations, even though women under thirty still do most of the child care. And, Millennial men appear more eager to be real partners than men in previous generations. In fact, three-quarters of Millennials are more likely to say they'd be a stay-at-home parent if it made financial sense for their family, more than Gen X and Boomers.

◇◇◇◇◇◇◇◇◇◇◇◇◇

Forty-four percent of Millennials would like to leave their current employers in the next two years.

◇◇◇◇◇◇◇◇◇◇◇◇◇

Due to their financial struggles during the recession, almost across the board, Millennials are more likely than other generations to say the economy has impacted their decisions regarding the timing of having children. Almost a third of Millennials cited a lack of confidence in the general economy, and they cited the following more than other generations regarding the timing of having children: personal debt, student loan debt, difficulties in finding work after college, and living with their parents after college.

In Deloitte's 2016 Millennial study, they collected the views of nearly 7,700 Millennials working full-time representing twenty-nine countries around the globe.[15] They identified a key area that is consistent with one of the perceptions—that Millennials lack loyalty and are job hoppers. Forty-four percent of Millennials (that's twenty-three million people) say if given the choice, they would like to leave their current employers in the next two years, and two-thirds (that's thirty-five million people) expect to leave by 2020. A perceived lack of leadership skill development and feelings of being overlooked are compounded by larger issues around work-life balance, the desire for flexibility, and a conflict of values. For employers, this exodus of talent will be a major issue moving forward.

When it comes to values, Millennials and businesses are aligned for the most part, but have mismatched purposes. Millennials want businesses to focus more on people (employees, customers, and society), products, and purpose—and less on profits. They recognize that businesses need to have financial success to survive, but believe these other factors are key to long-term success. Nearly two-thirds of Millennials think that businesses should put employees first by focusing on satisfaction, fair treatment, well-being, development, growth, and ironically—loyalty. More than half believe that companies should have a solid foundation of trust, integrity, honesty, and ethics, and that customer loyalty and satisfaction should be a priority. High-quality products, innovation, attention to the environment, and corporate social responsibility also rank high.

◇◇◇◇◇◇◇◇◇◇◇◇◇◇◇◇◇◇

We can expect Millennial leaders to base their decisions on personal values.

◇◇◇◇◇◇◇◇◇◇◇◇◇◇◇◇◇◇

Millennials seek employers with similar values to their own—reinforced by the finding that, globally, 56 percent have "ruled out ever working for a particular organization because of its values or standard of conduct."[16] For example, if anti-smoking, they would never work for a tobacco company, or if pro-LGBT, they would steer clear of companies with a poor track record of diversity and inclusion. But even when values align, most Millennials have no problem standing their ground when asked to do something that conflicts with their values—almost half have chosen not to undertake a task at work because it went against their personal values or ethics.

This emphasis on personal values continues into the boardroom where the rank order of priorities does not change for senior Millennials. As such, we can expect Millennial leaders to base their decisions as much on personal values as on the achievement of specific targets or goals. This is an important factor for women, which could significantly impact the leadership gender gap. Millennials who enter the boardroom and those in senior positions have a desire to rebalance business priorities by putting people before profit. Let's take a closer look at how these values and priorities apply to women and leadership.

Millennials and Women Leaders

Millennials appear to be steered by strong values at all stages of their careers; it's apparent in the employers they choose, the assignments they're willing to accept, and the decisions they make as they take on more senior-level roles. The Deloitte study showed that even though there are small gender differences in the consideration for senior roles, the reality is that Millennial men (21 percent) are significantly more likely to say they lead a department or are members of the senior management team than women (16 percent)—indicating continued gender bias and barriers, even for our youngest workers.

The generation we are born into has a tremendous influence on the depth and breadth of biases we hold—toward gender, race, ethnicity, sexual orientation, family, lifestyle, and even our views of leadership. As discussed in chapter five, the Implicit Association Tests through Harvard assess personal biases. Most people worldwide strongly associate males with career and females with home, and associate males with science and females with liberal arts. Millennials are generally *better* at these gender associations than previous generations, meaning that they associate men and women more equally and seem to have less biases—positive implications for future women leaders.

The Global Leadership Forecast study gathered data from more than thirteen thousand leaders and HR executives across two thousand organizations in forty-eight countries. It showed that a business that has women and Millennials in leadership roles will be more successful than companies that have less women and Millennials.[17] In other words, they found that companies outperforming their peers financially had more diversity in their leadership ranks—both in gender and in generation. The reason is that including varied perspectives helps decision making and problem solving, which improves business success. One of the study authors, Evan Sinar, said, "We focused on women and Millennials in particular because those are groups in which companies have specific initiatives directed toward the encouragement and identification of leaders. Approximately a third of companies have initiated programs focused on female leaders, and a third of companies have programs focused on Millennial-generation leaders."[18]

◇◇◇◇◇◇◇◇◇◇◇◇◇◇◇◇◇◇

Millennials are generally better at gender associations and seem to have less biases than previous generations.

◇◇◇◇◇◇◇◇◇◇◇◇◇◇◇◇◇◇

The findings indicate that of the participating organizations, those in the top 20 percent of financial performance have 37 percent female leadership, and organizations in the bottom 20 percent count only 19 percent of their leaders as women. The study found that gender had the *strongest* link to an organization's financial success. Effective management of gender diversity generally accompanies doing many other things right. For example, these companies take subjectivity and stereotyping out of their talent management practices. They tend to be very visible and transparent about how they develop, manage, and identify their leaders. Companies which do a better job identifying and promoting female leaders see many positive outcomes.

Having Millennials in leadership roles impact an organization's growth. Companies with aggressive growth had a higher proportion of Millennials in leadership positions and were also more financially successful compared to low growth companies. Need proof? Just look at Google and Facebook. The tech industry (with many Internet companies and start-ups) shows dramatic growth and hires lots of Millennials—they bring unique skills and perspectives to work, such as how to adapt to and use new technologies, and using social and mobile methods to learn how to be better leaders.

Having higher percentages of both gender and generational diversity stem from well-planned leadership development practices that are rigorous and transparent. These practices promote diversity and drive organizational success more broadly. The Global Leadership Forecast study looked at how companies who participated in their research three years ago, were performing today. Companies that had high-quality leadership development programs in place back then were more likely to have high-quality leadership and be financially successful today—which shows the sustained impact of these programs over time.

Millennials and EQ

I've noticed a subtle movement transpiring over the past several years. The Millennials, and likely Gen Z behind them, possess more feminine characteristics than previous generations—which means that our global organizations in the future will become more feminine. In the workplace, the dynamics of this new reality are colliding with the old establishment like tectonic plates. We are in the early stages of it now, but if it continues and characteristics and values hold steady, then we are heading for a major organizational tipping point.

In their book, *The Athena Doctrine*, John Gerzema and Michael D'Antonio surveyed sixty-four thousand people in thirteen nations from the Americas and Europe to Asia. Their data point to widespread dissatisfaction with typically male ways of doing business and a growing appreciation for the traits, skills and competencies that are perceived as more feminine. Two-thirds of survey respondents felt that "The world would be a better place if men thought more like women."[19] This data includes majorities of *men* who equate masculine incumbency with income disparity, high levels of unemployment, and political gridlock—issues that are front-and-center in today's world.

Their data show that 57 percent of people were dissatisfied with the conduct of men in their country, including 79 percent of Japanese and South Koreans, and more than two-thirds of people in Indonesia, Mexico, U.K., and the U.S. This sentiment is amplified among Millennials of whom nearly 80 percent are dissatisfied. This marks a global trend away from the winner-takes-all, masculine approach to getting things done.

◇◇◇◇◇◇◇◇◇◇◇◇◇◇◇◇◇

Millennials possess more feminine characteristics than previous generations.

◇◇◇◇◇◇◇◇◇◇◇◇◇◇◇◇◇

Curious as to how leaders could "think more like women", they asked half their sample—thirty-two thousand people around the world—to classify 125 different human characteristics as either masculine, feminine or neither, while the other half rated the same words (without gendering) on their importance to leadership, success, morality, and happiness. Their statistics revealed strong consensus that what people felt was "feminine" they also deemed essential to leading in an increasingly social, interdependent and transparent world.[20] Below are the top ten competencies desired for modern leaders.

1. Expressive (feminine)
2. Plans for future (feminine)
3. Decisive (masculine)
4. Reasonable (feminine)
5. Loyal (feminine)
6. Flexible (feminine)

7. Patient (feminine)
8. Resilient (masculine)
9. Intuitive (feminine)
10. Collaborative (feminine)

As you can see, eight out of the ten characteristics deemed essential for today's leaders are feminine. This is consistent with the discussion in chapter two about the transformational leadership style, as well as other leadership styles, that are inherent in women. Millennials naturally possess or value many of these traits as well.

Many of the positive perceptions listed in the table above are also feminine traits, more than masculine. For example, both women and Millennials seek meaning in their work, value work-life integration and flexibility, value collaboration and teamwork, prefer flat structures (not hierarchies), are at ease with diversity (and pro-equality in general), have a proactive communication style, value real-time feedback and recognition, and are socially responsible. In addition, Millennials have a greater global perspective consistent with women's divergent style of thinking and problem solving.

Recall that from an emotional intelligence perspective, men tend to score higher than women in areas of self-confidence, assertiveness, and stress tolerance, and women outperform men in areas of empathy, social responsibility, and interpersonal relationships. Since Millennials overall demonstrate more feminine traits, they would likely score higher in female-specific EQ attributes.

◇◇◇◇◇◇◇◇◇◇◇◇◇◇◇◇

When HR practices adapt to meet Millennial expectations, the organization itself becomes more feminine.

◇◇◇◇◇◇◇◇◇◇◇◇◇◇◇◇

Because of their shared characteristics, women and Millennials tend to be drawn to spiritual organizations. These organizations have several cultural characteristics:

- Benevolence—Spiritual organizations value showing kindness toward others and promoting the happiness of employees and other organizational stakeholders.
- Strong sense of purpose—Spiritual organizations build their cultures around a meaningful purpose. Although profits may be important, they're not the primary value of the organization.
- Trust and respect—Spiritual organizations are characterized by mutual trust, honesty, and openness. Employees are treated with esteem and value, consistent with the dignity of each individual.
- Open-mindedness—Spiritual organizations value flexible thinking and creativity among employees.

There are many reasons for the growing interest in spirituality. First, it can counterbalance the pressures and stress of a turbulent pace of life. Contemporary lifestyles, such as single-parent families, the temporary nature of jobs, and new technologies that create distance between people, underscore the lack of community many people feel and the increased need for involvement and connection. Second, formalized religion hasn't worked for many people, and they continue to look for anchors to replace lack of faith and to fill a growing feeling of emptiness. Third, job demands have made the workplace dominant in many people's lives, yet they continue to question the meaning of work. Fourth, people want to integrate personal life values with their professional lives. And, fifth, an increasing number of people are finding that the pursuit of more material acquisitions leaves them unfulfilled.[21]

Many organizations have grown interested in spirituality, but have had difficulty putting its principles into practice. Several types of practices can facilitate a spiritual workplace, such as support of work-life balance; leaders demonstrating values that trigger intrinsic motivation and a sense of calling through work; and encouraging employees to consider how their work provides a sense of purpose through community building. These practices are consistent with female-specific EQ traits, transformational leadership style, and corporate social responsibility. Given the characteristics of spiritual organizations, and the values held by women, Millennials (and likely Gen Z), I believe we will see more of these types of organizations in the future.

Millennials show less gender bias, and have more favorable perceptions of women as leaders than older generations. Because they have high expectations for themselves and others, are driven by strong values (trust, honesty, ethics, integrity), and are not afraid to challenge the status quo—I am very encouraged for the future of women in leadership.

Older workers have complained about young people for generations. The Veterans grumbled about the Baby Boomers, the Boomers griped about Gen X, and Gen X lamented about Millennials. In that regard, Millennials aren't any different than others. But what is different is that Millennials' unique expectations (like those for emotional support, feedback, and mentoring relationships) are deeply, yet subtly, gendered. So, when HR practices adapt to meet those expectations, the organization itself becomes more feminine. Some of the frustrations and negative perceptions of Millennials could be encompassing frustrations about the way feminine organizing practices are challenging traditionally masculine workplaces. This tension between generations points to a shift away from masculine organizations which causes generational growing pains.

However, true leadership effectiveness requires a blend of masculine and feminine traits. Today's global workplaces are steeped in masculine cultures, and drenched in the myth of *The Hero's Journey*. Joseph Campbell wrote about this epic myth that one man can save the world. Nearly all of the action-packed blockbuster movies have this theme—think *Iron Man* (and all superheroes), *Star Wars, Star Trek, Mission Impossible, James Bond, Independence Day, Gladiator, Bourne Identity*, and the list goes on and on and on. In his article, "Why Women Must Change Work," leadership expert Will Marré said, "Men love these myths because they are so grandly narcissistic."[22]

◇◇◇◇◇◇◇◇◇◇◇◇◇◇◇◇◇◇

The hero's journey is mostly linear—work, achieve, gain status, and peer respect.

◇◇◇◇◇◇◇◇◇◇◇◇◇◇◇◇◇◇

In the history of the world, very few people have had a "change the world" impact, which leaves virtually all of us to be heroes of our own lives. By now, it should not be surprising that the way men and women pursue their best lives is very different because their sources of self-worth and barriers they face are different. For most men, their personal hero's journey is pretty simple. As we've learned, the male culture is built around competition and hierarchy. This causes men to focus on achievement, status, money, "desirable" women, and fathering capable offspring. In the male journey, overcoming personal tests and achieving their destiny takes precedence over family and friends. Male lives are mostly linear—work, achieve, gain status, and peer respect. These are the ideals that dominate work cultures, and they are distinctly heroic and masculine.

The heroine's journey is very different—and much more complicated. Female lives are driven by competing commitments and values that make a work-centered life stressful. And, it is not only women who are questioning the hero's paradigm. As Millennial men flood the workplace they are also questioning the value of living work-centered lives. These masculine cultures, such as the tech industry, are driven by status-building commitments to overwork, 24/7 availability, and exclusionary environments that promulgate bias.

In Greek mythology, there are strong goddesses like Athena—achievers and warriors that are leaders, goal-focused, invulnerable, address conflict head on, and are confident and assertive. However, they can feel emotionally isolated and overworked, and are candidates for burnout. On the other end of the spectrum are warm goddesses like Hera—nurturers, caregivers, and helpers who are collaborative, supportive, creative, and intuitive. However, this behavior can leave women vulnerable to being exploited, overlooked, and passed over (such as our earlier discussions about office housework). Finding the balance between these two yin and yang type forces is the challenge of the heroine's journey. Sound familiar? It's the same delicate balance women must strike between opposing gender stereotypes and expectations.

◇◇◇◇◇◇◇◇◇◇◇◇◇◇◇

Female lives are driven by competing commitments and values that make a work-centered life stressful.

◇◇◇◇◇◇◇◇◇◇◇◇◇◇◇

"Male leaders continue to sustain work cultures where they expect women to serve as warm goddesses helping to implement the goals and priorities of the mostly male heroes at the top. As for women who see their path to promotion as becoming an Athena, they will likely experience disillusionment with the hero's journey because it denies the richness of their full feminine values," says Marré.[23] In an age in which both the information and relationships needed to succeed are widely dispersed and diverse, we need cultures that are both warm and strong. We need men and women working together in a new synergy of respect and collaboration.

While men may look at today's power structure and see it (perhaps reassuringly) dominated by their own gender, they must look around their classrooms, their homes, their communities, and their businesses, and see the reality shifting before their eyes. Women have shown that humans can flex across the whole spectrum of traditionally male and female roles. Can we allow men this freedom? Can men allow each other this freedom?

Men and women alike are recognizing significant value in traits commonly associated with women, such as nurturing, cooperation, collaboration, listening, communication, and sharing—and *The Athena Doctrine* shows why femininity is the operating system of twenty-first century prosperity. The times are indeed changing, and organizations need to adapt or risk being left behind. Today's work requires a new leadership paradigm. The good news is that anyone—whether you're a man or woman—can lead with a more feminine ethos.

Millennial Strategies

By 2025, 75 percent of the global workforce will be comprised of Millennials.[24] The need to attract, retain, and help them maximize their performance at work will continue to be a challenge for global businesses. As stated earlier, Millennials will be the ones in charge in ten years, so it might be wise for companies to start tailoring their rules, regulations and policies to their desires and expectations.

Many people reading this book will be Millennials themselves, or parents and coworkers of Millennials, and have experienced firsthand the shift needed to communicate effectively across generations. As we've seen in this chapter, the unique preferences, attitudes, and practices of Millennials present both change and opportunity for the future of work. This bodes well for a global workplace that continues to grow more diverse every day. Below are strategies and advice for Millennials, older generations, and organizations— to help maximize our interactions together.

First off, coaching and mentoring across age groups makes sense. There is surely much each can learn from the other. We typically imagine that the young can help the old understand technology and the old can impart general wisdom, but it goes further than that. Baby Boomers and Gen Xers can help younger workers control their work (schedules, time management, workload, and prioritizing). They can also help them control their impulses and show restraint when needed, how to navigate and address conflict, and how to be more empathetic.

◇◇◇◇◇◇◇◇◇◇◇◇◇◇◇◇◇◇

Millennial preferences, attitudes and practices present both change and opportunity for the future of work.

◇◇◇◇◇◇◇◇◇◇◇◇◇◇◇◇◇◇

For example, empathy—the ability to read and understand other's emotions, needs, and thoughts—is one of the core competencies of emotional intelligence and a critical leadership skill. It is what allows us to influence, inspire, and help people achieve their dreams and goals. Empathy enables us to connect with others in a real and meaningful way, which in turn makes us happier and more effective at work. Here are a few simple things you can do:

1. Observe, listen, and ask questions. Pay attention to people's body language rather than thinking about what you're going to say next.

Ask yourself—are you truly listening or are you waiting to speak? This can be harder than it sounds, because you must let go of the notion that you know what's best or have the right answer. You also need to stop assuming that you know what people are thinking and feeling—you probably don't. And even if you are right, or partly right, there's always more to learn if you're quiet and curious.

2. Avoid distractions and try to be fully present when you are with people. This too is difficult for the simple reason that our organizations are insanely distracting. There's always a deadline looming, a crisis to deal with, or an annoyance to put to rest. All of this takes us out of the moment and puts us into a "sky is falling" mentality. When we are in this state of mind, our bodies are poised for fight or flight—just the opposite of what we need to build good relationships. Staying present and being mindful of our thoughts and actions can help in this effort.

3. Stop multi-tasking. It's essentially doing more than one thing with less than your whole brain, or giving partial attention to multiple things. This is fine when you are walking and chewing gum, but it's not okay when it comes to dealing with people or complex cognitive tasks. If you are writing an email to one person while talking with another, neither one is getting the best of you—and at least one of them knows it.

By doing these things, you set yourself up to learn and practice the deeper behaviors required for empathy—to ask people for feedback rather than assuming you know; to talk about how people feel rather than dismissing people's emotions as unimportant; and to make them believe that you care (and hopefully you do). People want to feel valued and appreciated at work—and if you're not giving them that, you're failing as a leader.

I'd also advise older generations to keep an open mind about Millennials and don't automatically assume the negative perceptions outlined above. Give your younger colleagues a chance before dismissing their contributions. Make sure you proactively communicate with each other to address any misperceptions or differences in opinion, attitude, expectations, or beliefs.

Be sure to provide regular feedback, especially if you are in a leadership position. Millennials prefer to receive feedback once a month, if not more. Try to understand their values, which is a key element in job retention—recall that over half of Millennials have ruled out ever working for a company that clashed with their personal values. Finally, be a role model. Given your years of experience, accumulated knowledge and skills, you are in the best position to show your young colleagues what success can look like.

◇◇◇◇◇◇◇◇◇◇◇◇◇◇◇◇◇◇◇

Keep an open mind about Millennials and don't automatically assume negative perceptions.

◇◇◇◇◇◇◇◇◇◇◇◇◇◇◇◇◇◇◇

Millennials can help Boomers and Xers in many ways too. Other than the obvious technology lessons that younger workers can impart, they can also help older workers to build diverse relationships and networks. In general, those over the age of fifty simply maintain their current networks and fail to build new networks. Thus, their networks become increasingly homogenous, static, and comfortable. This homogeneity will not serve them well when they want or need to transform.

When people start their careers, it's second nature to reach out—to meet new people, build diverse networks, and actively find coaches and mentors. Millennials can help coach their older colleagues in how to create and maintain diverse networks (most likely using technology). As our work life expands, everyone goes through changes and transitions. Having the skills and transformational assets to support this change tends to be strongest in the young—and as people live longer, they need to display these skills throughout their lives. Millennials could be instrumental in offering advice and insights in this area.

I'd also advise Millennials to respect the wisdom and knowledge of older workers and be willing to learn from them. Previous generations have already been down the road you are on, and can help you navigate the paths much easier. Keep an open mind and don't make assumptions that older workers can't learn new things or are inept with technology. Just as with older generations, proactively communicate with each other to address any misperceptions or differences in opinion, attitude, or expectations. Try to understand older worker's values and where they stem from. Remember that values are shaped and influenced by the formative events that occur in each generation—and each grew up with very different economic, political, social, and cultural circumstances.

◇◇◇◇◇◇◇◇◇◇◇◇◇◇◇

Respect the wisdom and knowledge of older workers and be willing to learn from them.

◇◇◇◇◇◇◇◇◇◇◇◇◇◇◇

One caution I'd suggest for Millennials is to be aware of how technology can impact your interpersonal relationships. Even though there are more ways to connect to each other than ever, it does *not* mean we are better communicators. Technology, such as social media and texting, has replaced many of our face-to-face interactions. Because of this, we communicate in short bursts of information and there is less emphasis on process, problem solving and building relationships. Since we spend less time on these things, we don't develop adequate skills for addressing conflict, listening, asking questions, or conveying our emotions. After all, we can't effectively communicate frustration, confusion, mistrust, concern, or empathy with an emoticon!

In today's world, if there is one second of free or idle time, what do we do? We go to our smartphones. Technology has made the world smaller because it connects us in ways like never before. However, less interactions with each other makes the world bigger because it puts us in silos where we don't truly dialogue with one another. My advice is to be mindful about how you use technology—and how it not only impacts you, but how it impacts your relationships. If you have the opportunity, meet in-person so you can look each other in the eye, read body language, assess facial expressions, gauge emotions, and have a real conversation.

Knowing what we know about Millennials, there are many things that organizations can do to attract, motivate, connect with, listen to, engage, develop, and retain their young talent. One of the biggest and best things a company can do is to create a more inclusive culture that acknowledges and develops leaders at all levels. Recall that nearly half of all Millennials said they would leave their employers in the next two years, if given the choice. The top reasons cited were the perceived lack of leadership skill development and feelings of being overlooked. If organizations shift from a structured hierarchy to a more collaborative and team-centric dynamic, there will be a growing demand for leaders.

To remain competitive, companies must identify potential leaders much earlier in their careers to create a robust pipeline of new and innovative thinkers. Leadership should no longer be viewed as top-down management. Building teams with multigenerational male and female leaders can promote more diverse perspectives while leveraging the insight of both younger and older employees. This multigenerational think tank can maximize knowledge and give leadership experience to less seasoned employees.

◇◇◇◇◇◇◇◇◇◇◇◇◇◇◇◇

One of the best things a company can do is create an inclusive culture that acknowledges and develops leaders at all levels.

◇◇◇◇◇◇◇◇◇◇◇◇◇◇◇◇

We learned that work-life integration and the desire for flexibility rank very highly among Millennials. Recall that nearly 90 percent wish they could have greater opportunity to start and finish work at the times they choose. Meanwhile, a majority wish to have greater mobile connectivity, such as via tablets and smartphones. But, the greatest gap between current supply and demand surrounds the issue of remote working—three-quarters would like to start to, or more frequently, work from home or other locations where they feel more productive. This is nearly double the number that currently do so.[25] As stated in chapter seven, because Boomers occupy more management positions and hold more traditional values, they are probably less inclined to favor telecommuting. Nonetheless, these areas deserve serious consideration if businesses desire to compete.

Finally, all organizations should encourage coaching and mentoring. Coaching brings everything together. It converts learning into performance, builds continuity into a person's job, and shows how it is relevant to the organization's success. Among Millennials, over 80 percent are satisfied with this aspect of their working lives. Those intending to stay with their organization for more than five years are twice as likely to have a mentor than not. In the Millennials' ideal workweek, there would be significantly more time devoted to coaching and mentoring, to the discussion of new ideas and ways of working, and on the development of their leadership skills.

Managers today are faced with expanding diversity in their work force, and one of the biggest challenges is the widening age range of their employees who, despite their differences, must come together to form a cohesive and viable corporate culture. In the hectic work environments of the global economy, it is easy to fall into a standard set of management practices, yet the reality of diversity requires a significantly different course of action. Managers must exercise leadership flexibility and sophistication. Their supervisory style must be situation- and strength-based, being thoughtful about matching individuals to assignments and leadership roles. By navigating these changes, managers can build an effective organizational culture out of increasing diversity.

All the major factors that define the future workplace are already in play. Gen Z are now in their high school years, the technologies that will define work are in design stages today, globalization and large-scale economies are emerging as major forces, and the introduction of new ways of working, thinking, and interacting are changing as we speak due to Millennial influence.

The landscape is exciting and dynamic, and it promises to redefine much of the conventional wisdom about work, organizational success, personal accomplishment, and so much more. As we scan the workplace of the future, we see that everything we know about work—where we work, how we work, what skills we need to stay employable, what technologies we use to connect with colleagues and customers—is changing.

As the quote at the beginning of the chapter reads, "If you want something you've never had, you must be willing to do something you've never done." If we truly desire a more open, inclusive and diverse workforce that's reflective of our global society, then we must be willing to make organizational changes and adapt to the needs and expectations of incoming talent.

Summary Points

- By the year 2020, there will be five generations working side-by-side.
- As of April 2016, Millennials surpassed Baby Boomers as the nation's largest living generation.
- Millennial couples split household chores more evenly than previous generations, even though women under thirty still do most of the child care.
- Forty-four percent of Millennials would like to leave their current employers in the next two years.
- Millennials who enter the boardroom have a desire to rebalance business priorities by putting people before profit.
- Millennial men are significantly more likely to report that they lead a department or are members of the senior management team than Millennial women.
- Millennials are generally better at gender associations and seem to have less biases than previous generations.
- Companies outperforming their peers financially had more diversity in their leadership ranks—both in gender and in generation.
- Millennials possess more feminine characteristics than previous generations—which means that future global organizations will become more feminine.
- There are several strategies to help Millennials, older generations, and organizations work more effectively together.

Reflection Questions

- ✓ What generation do you belong to? Do you identify with the descriptors and characteristics of your generation?

✓ What key events have shaped your attitude, behavior, and preferences about work?

✓ Do you have experience working with Millennials? Are you a Millennial yourself? What has been your experience?

✓ What are your perceptions of Millennials (positive or negative)? Which perceptions have you found to be true? Which ones are inaccurate? How has this affected your work?

✓ What are your top five job satisfaction motivators?

✓ If given the choice, when would you leave your current employer? How often would you be comfortable changing jobs?

✓ What key values do you seek in an employer (e.g., flexibility, fair treatment, trust, integrity, quality products, customer satisfaction, innovation, corporate social responsibility)? Do your values align with your current company? What values would you not compromise on?

✓ Does your current company have leadership development practices in place? Do they focus specifically on women and Millennials? Are they effective?

✓ Are the general characteristics in your organization masculine or feminine? What are the general characteristics of leaders in your organization? Have you noticed a shift or change?

✓ Do you identify more with the Greek goddess Athena or the goddess Hera? How have you applied this to your work? What has been the outcomes?

TWELVE

Conclusion:

Implications for Men, Women and the World

How wonderful it is that nobody need wait a single moment
before starting to improve the world.
Anne Frank

W e've covered much ground in this book. The Introduction laid the
foundation, and in Part I, we explored leadership and emotional
intelligence. We reviewed the startling statistics, talked about
leadership styles and characteristics, discussed emotional intelligence as it
pertains to gender and leadership, and examined my research on these topics.
In Part II, we reviewed the multitude of barriers and perceptions that keep
women from fully contributing—from bias and structural barriers, to work-
life balance and limiting ourselves, to the many gender culture differences

and how they show up every day around the world at work and home. In Part III, we discussed the changes and opportunities that both global diversity and our youngest generations are bringing to the workplace. In this last chapter, we'll address strategies for both individuals and organizations, and how we can keep the awareness, dialogue, action, and momentum moving forward to fully leverage talent and achieve gender parity. Finally, we'll evaluate the implications for men, women, and the world, and close with concluding thoughts.

As stated in the Introduction, women have historically been viewed as less important than men socially, economically, politically, and culturally, and have a smaller gender footprint than men—which equates to less power. Women have been disempowered for centuries, and as we all know, there are still extreme inequities in some countries, such as the Middle East and North Africa. Women have made significant strides in education, employment, and in their communities. Despite these efforts, men outpace women in leadership roles across *every* sector in the world—corporate, not-for-profit, government, education, medicine, military, and religion. And, women are still significantly underrepresented at *every* corporate and pipeline level—from entry-level up to the CEO. Because of this, men still rule the world because men are in decision-making positions of power.

The leadership gender gap, pay wage gap, and other inequities have been widely reported since early 2000s. Like many others, I am concerned about the slow progress and paltry statistics I've outlined in this book. Women offer so much to our world, yet they are among the poorest, most disenfranchised, and most disempowered segment of our society. As mentioned earlier, when women have more power—a larger and stronger gender footprint—families, communities, and societies at large benefit.

◇◇◇◇◇◇◇◇◇◇◇◇◇◇◇

Perception is reality—and it's powerful.

◇◇◇◇◇◇◇◇◇◇◇◇◇◇◇

When I conducted my research on the topics of leadership, emotional intelligence and gender, and examined the research of many others, it became clear that the reasons we don't see more women leading our global businesses have nothing to do with women's skills and competencies. It has everything to do with our *perceptions* of women as leaders, as workers, as mothers, and as wives. This perception has had, and is continuing to have, a significant impact on promotion for many women. Perception is reality—and it's powerful.

Moreover, it is clear that men and women are wired and socialized differently. We live in two different worlds both biologically *and* culturally, and our differences are due to both nature (science) *and* nurture (socialization). The differences themselves are not the issue, and many of our differences are complementary. What is problematic is that as a global society, women's vision, values, strengths, and contributions are simply not *valued* as much as men's. If we want our global societies and businesses to be competitive, sustainable, and prosperous, this must change. There are two documentaries on the topic of socialization and gendered stereotypes that I'd highly recommend—*Miss Representation* addresses girls and women, and *The Mask You Live In* addresses boys and men.[1]

To achieve change, we need both men and women working together in partnership. When I speak to audiences, I often get asked by both genders about who created these barriers, and who's to blame. My answer is neither and both. Some of the barriers—such as bias, stereotypes, and role congruity beliefs—have been passed down from generation to generation, and reinforced through social and cultural systems. Some of the barriers men contribute more to—such as restricting women's access to informal networks or not sponsoring women. Other barriers women contribute more to—such as limiting themselves by not taking risks or self-selecting out of the workforce. The bottom line is that both men and women contribute to the leadership gender gap, and we need both men and women working together to close the gap and tackle the barriers that women face in organizations. To help with this, let's examine some individual and organizational strategies.

Individual Strategies

At the end of each chapter in this book, I've provided practical strategies, summary points, and reflection questions to help individuals. Think of these strategies as actionable intelligence that you can use right away. As you know, any major change starts with baby steps or small interventions that encourage people to behave in slightly different ways at critical moments—such as hiring and promotion decisions, selecting project leaders, or assigning developmental opportunities. We need to be aware of our beliefs and biases and be willing to talk about them. Talking can transform minds, which can transform behaviors, which can transform organizations—and eventually transform the world. Every precious drop of change has a ripple effect on the ocean.

MEN. You are critically important partners—and we can't effect any change or break from the status quo without you. Since most leaders and managers are men, we need you to feel comfortable dialoging and addressing issues directly with female employees. For example, when a woman gets interrupted or ignored in a meeting, you need to stop the meeting to point it out. Similarly, if a woman has plans to have children, talk candidly with her about it, and continue to support her career ambitions before and after the birth. Or, if a woman is excluded from an informal group, help her identify the reasons for it and find ways to create equal opportunities for inclusion.

I have found that many men care about gender inequality, and most men are simply unaware of the barriers that women face. For most men, their lack of awareness and exclusionary behavior (such as the old boy's network or favoritism toward other men) is unintentional. Remember, men and women are raised in different gender cultures, and men are simply acting in accordance to the lessons they've been taught their entire lives. We need you to peer outside of your culture and think broadly about talent development and diversity. We need you to be aware of your biases and behaviors, and the impact they might have on women. We need you to be willing to try a new approach. One suggestion is to consider whether your team has sufficient diversity of thought and experience to avoid groupthink and develop innovative solutions. Another idea is to critically consider where unconscious bias impacts your decisions about who to hire, who to work with, and who to develop. The workplace was created by men for men, and it's going to take a willful shift in attitude, beliefs, expectations, and values to make our workplaces more inclusive and welcoming for everyone.

◇◇◇◇◇◇◇◇◇◇◇◇◇

Most men are simply unaware of the barriers that women face.

◇◇◇◇◇◇◇◇◇◇◇◇◇

Men—we need your help. You have wives, sisters, and daughters who will likely face many of the barriers and misperceptions addressed in this book. They, like all other women, need the same opportunities as your sons. We need you to actively *hire* women, *mentor* women, *sponsor* women, *include* women, *support* women, *develop* women, and finally, *promote* women. Senior leader support and sponsorship of women is the most critical factor to drive women's advancement. We need you to commit to changing the leadership ratios. Women can only succeed if they get the opportunities to succeed—this means getting the chance to develop their skills, gain valuable experience, and become more comfortable as leaders. It should be a badge of honor for a great male leader to mentor, sponsor, and support women.

When it comes to mentoring, some men shy away from helping women for fear of office gossip about their relationship. As adults in a professional environment, we need to trust men and women to be alone with each other without the veil of a sexual relationship. When senior men avoid these relationships, junior women pay the price—denied access to power-holders and potential career mentors, these women are excluded and marginalized. The net outcome is unsatisfactory for women and for the organizations that hire them.

The issues relate back to our discussions about gender and the brain, socialization, and emotional intelligence. As we learned, there are differences in how we process and express our emotions. Men should appreciate women's neurological tendencies to absorb and retain more emotional information, be verbally expressive in connecting memories to current events, and be more analytical of relational feelings. Men can be more effective mentors for women if they practice listening skills with the goal of showing empathy versus trying to quickly fix the problem for her. In the process of listening, male mentors might find they develop and appreciate enhanced interpersonal skills, access to larger networks, and insider knowledge of their organization that makes them more effective leaders.

In a recent *Harvard Business Review* piece, researchers interviewed male mentors who stated that they often learned more from their female mentee than she did from him. They state that men must take it in stride if a female mentee cries. Men who mentor must appreciate that passion and conviction may be intertwined with tears for some women—not a sign of weakness or distress. Rather than run for the exit at the first teardrop, confident mentors stock up on Kleenex, appreciate the differences, and get on with the business of championing promising women.[2]

Men can also be effective mentors by realizing that sometimes women just need a boost of confidence. Recall that we talk about our successes and failures very differently, with women often taking the blame for failures and not taking credit for their successes. Women also underestimate their ability and downplay their achievements. Excellent mentors for women persistently affirm that they belong (particularly in male-centric organizations) and coach them to take full ownership of their accomplishments and their contributions to team projects.

◇◇◇◇◇◇◇◇◇◇◇◇◇◇◇◇◇

Men can be effective mentors by realizing that sometimes women just need a boost of confidence.

◇◇◇◇◇◇◇◇◇◇◇◇◇◇◇◇◇

A healthy understanding of cross-gender relationships is vital in fostering an inclusive workplace in which talent management is foundational. Self-aware and thoughtful male mentors who intentionally and conscientiously mentor both women and men will find their mentees enjoy more promotions and higher salaries, more job satisfaction and commitment to the organization, and ultimately more self-worth and career success. Similarly, their organizations are better positioned for future success, enjoy more creativity, and find their bottom-line outperforming the competition. If that's not convincing enough, productive cross-gender mentorships help men to be more effective leaders and valued rainmakers in their industry. And in the end, more self-awareness and a wider range of interpersonal skills may make them better husbands, fathers, and men—and what man doesn't aspire to that?

WOMEN. Be authentically female. You offer tremendous assets to organizations. These skills are highly relevant to businesses today, and are distinctly different from what men bring to the workplace. Believe in your vision and communicate its strength upward. Understand the power of what you notice and have faith in it. Women see broad-spectrum and pick up on nuanced interactions, such as non-verbal communication. For example, suppose that you're in a group and observe two leaders talking with each other. Because of their body language, you conclude that they hate each other. You may not say anything to other people in the group because you assume that they observed what you did. But, in many cases, people come away with very different conclusions. Don't assume that others are observing what you are and that they get it. This perceptual capability is one of women's greatest gifts, so don't lose confidence in the value of what you see. Trust your gut, your intuition, and your instincts.

Your strengths and ability to build relationships has increasing marketplace value. Changes in technology and globalization have made relationships—within and outside of organizations—a far more vital resource than in years past. Relationships are no longer the fluffy stuff. They are essential to innovation, teamwork, customer satisfaction, engagement, and talent retention. Recall that women excel in the EQ skills of interpersonal relationships and empathy. Use these to your advantage in collaborating, motivating and leading others. Refer to chapter three for strategies to improve other EQ competencies, such as problem solving, stress-tolerance, impulse control, confidence, or assertiveness.

◇◇◇◇◇◇◇◇◇◇◇◇◇◇

Perceptual capability is one of women's greatest gifts.

◇◇◇◇◇◇◇◇◇◇◇◇◇◇

Make your aspirations and needs clear—whether it's the desire to advance, pay inequity concerns, the need for more work-life balance, or simply feeling less valued. Negotiate your value—if you don't ask you don't get. Women negotiate strongly on behalf of others and you can do this for yourself too. If needed, mold work around your needs—come in early, work remotely, or break up your vacation days. Let your boss and others know what you're working on. You don't have to be overly self-promoting to do this. It can be subtle, such as sending your boss an email every two weeks with lists of people you've been in touch with, or a list of tasks you've accomplished, or progress you've made on a project. Also, be sure to leverage your networks. Let them know what you're doing, how they can help you, and how you may be able to help them. Be visible, valuable, and vocal at all times.

As discussed in chapter eight, change your language to make you more credible and sound more confident and decisive—you don't need to disclose all your vulnerabilities and fears. If you don't know how to do something, be confident in your ability to figure it out. Take risks and try new things—everything is a learning opportunity and it's the only way you're going to grow. Think about a time when you stepped out of your comfort zone and succeeded and how good it felt—and think about how much you learned when you didn't succeed. Take charge of your own career and leadership development—if you aren't getting it, ask for it or find it outside of your organization.

Don't believe the negative thoughts you tell yourself—such as, "I'm a fraud", "I can't do that", "I won't be a good leader", or "Conflict is bad". Remember, women are much harder on themselves than men are, and we need to let go of this negative self-talk. An acronym that may help is QTIP (Quit Taking It Personally). Don't waste time on things you can't control. Learn to let go and leave if you hit a wall—not all battles can be won and sometimes you just need to move on.

Treat your boss like a coach and seek advice and input. Get mentors and sponsors (especially male sponsors). If you don't have a mentor or sponsor, get help in finding one (your network will be helpful here). Stick up for one another. Within organizations, there are more women's groups and initiatives than ever before, and HR departments are scrambling to try and develop more female-friendly policies. Outside of organizations, there are more networks, associations and conferences than ever before to help empower, inspire, and bring women together. The more that women participate, share, support, and lean on each other, the better. The more that women help each other, the more we help ourselves.

Societal biases about leaders and women have created opposing gender expectations. It makes it difficult for a woman to lead because she's expected to act like a woman (feminine characteristics), but she's also expected to act like a leader (masculine characteristics). The only way we're going to change these long-held beliefs is through awareness, education, dialog, and getting more women into these roles so they are no longer the exception. If leadership is your goal, start thinking about it today. Understand what it takes and what you are willing to sacrifice to achieve it. Know what your priorities are and stick to them, even if it means saying no when you need to.

◇◇◇◇◇◇◇◇◇◇◇◇◇◇◇◇

*The more that women help each other,
the more we help ourselves.*

◇◇◇◇◇◇◇◇◇◇◇◇◇◇◇◇

Women naturally possess transformational leadership traits, and possess characteristics that favor democratic, affiliative, authentic, ethical and servant leadership styles. As opposed to dominant or coercive styles more commonly seen with men, these styles are suited to women because they focus on relationships, leverage empathy and interpersonal skills, and can even be used without formal authority. These styles are effective in empowering people and fostering innovation because they are less directive and more supportive—they also help women with the likeability issue (dominant styles aren't liked very much). You have several innate skills and abilities that companies today need, and you should be encouraged to lead. And, as a leader, make sure you tune in to your organization and acquire the business, strategic and financial acumen necessary to be effective.

A recent Gallup study in over 300,000 adults examined women in America.[3] One of the aspects of the study looked at individual strengths that people use every day to do their work, achieve their goals and interact with others (CliftonStrengths and StrengthsFinder assessments are trademarks of the Gallup Organization). Gallup has been studying the science of strengths for five decades, and have accumulated data from more than fourteen million individuals worldwide who have completed the assessment. Understanding the general similarities and differences between women's and men's strengths has important implications for the workplace. The results show that women and men lead with similar strengths, but women rank higher than men in certain Relationship Building themes (Developer, Includer and Empathy). Conversely, men rank higher in certain Strategic Thinking themes (Context, Analytical, Ideation and Strategic).

Of thirty-four possible themes, both genders share four out of five top strengths (Responsibility, Learner, Input, and Relator), but women lead with Empathy and men lead with Achievement. Looking at this combination of themes, we can say that generally, women take psychological ownership for what they do and commit to completing projects and tasks (Responsibility). They have a strong desire to expand their knowledge (Learner) and seek out new information (Input). They also enjoy close relationships (Relator) and naturally understand other people's feelings and perspectives (Empathy). These variances in strengths ranking are consistent with all the other data I've presented in this book that help explain differences in men's and women's behavior and their approach to work and life.

◇◇◇◇◇◇◇◇◇◇◇◇◇◇◇

Women lead with empathy, and men lead with achievement.

◇◇◇◇◇◇◇◇◇◇◇◇◇◇◇

It is important to note that these discoveries apply to men and women in *general* and do not apply to individual men and women. Differences are much greater within genders than between genders. The best organizations give all employees the tools to understand and develop their strengths. Focusing on what people do right rather than on what they do wrong is not difficult. Focusing on strengths also gives managers a powerful method for understanding, developing and celebrating their individual employees. When managers know what their team members do best, they can better match employees with projects that are a fit for their strengths, incorporate strengths into performance reviews and conversations, and reward and recognize employees for what they do well.[4] Some managers tend to reward and recognize employees for accomplishments that can be easily documented, such as meeting a sales goal or completing a big project. What's important for women is that a focus on strengths ensures that people who are stronger in Relationship Building themes also get praise and recognition for their accomplishments, whether they're leading a team or taking time to invest in the development of a new employee.

Finally, most people would agree that gender bias exists…in others. We judge our ourselves by our intentions, and others by their actions. We are overconfident in our ability to be objective which can make bias worse by creating a bias blind spot. Because of the blind spot, we fail to correct for bias. As presented in chapter five, we are all biased in one way or another, and our brains are wired toward bias. We all have opinions that are not based on facts or direct experience, but rather emotional thinking shortcuts. You see, thinking takes a lot of energy and discipline, but our brains are built for efficiency, so it's always designing shortcuts. The name of these mental shortcuts is stereotypes.

Although we reflexively have automatic preferences toward people who look like us, act like us, and seem to believe what we believe, this thinking is proving the be one of the most destructive challenges of our time. Consider this, given the global diversity trends—never in history have human beings been exposed to so many other human beings who are *not* like us. The variety of beliefs and cultures is astonishing. This requires a new way of thinking.

It requires open minds rather than defensive ones. Collaboration rather than competition. Innovation rather than stagnation. Inclusion rather than exclusion.

◇◇◇◇◇◇◇◇◇◇◇◇◇◇◇◇◇◇◇◇

Diversity challenges our biases that traditional leaders are unlikely to value.

◇◇◇◇◇◇◇◇◇◇◇◇◇◇◇◇◇◇◇◇

The bottom line is that we live in a complex, diverse world that our brains and emotions seek to simplify by separating people into groups of those like us and not like us. Diversity challenges our biases that traditional leaders are unlikely to value. Women have gender brain and social strengths that make them better suited to harvest the value of cognitive diversity through practical innovations. However, the bias against women advancing to leadership in organizations inhibits women from using their strengths. Leaders can dramatically increase the group intelligence of their senior leadership and organizational performance by making sure qualified women make up at least 30 percent of their C-level and senior level leaders. Note—one woman on a board won't suffice. We need several women or several men and women who are pushing for change.

Organizational Strategies

Global talent and customers are more diverse than ever before, which makes gender balance a big business opportunity with huge economic implications. It boosts bottom-line results, drives growth with new customer insights, and enhances productivity with better talent acquisition and retention. The *case* for the bottom-line benefits of gender balance keeps getting made, and the *will* to get there keeps growing. Does your company really understand this twenty-first-century shift? Here are strategies for organizations that CEOs, HR and senior leaders can take to reach gender parity within a generation (twenty years) rather than a century (one hundred years).

CEO. As a CEO, do you personally understand why gender balance is such an important issue for your workforce and for your customers? Do you believe the financial data that's been presented about women in leadership? Do you believe diversity will improve innovation and help you to be more competitive? If not, are you willing to invest some time for you and your team to learn?

If you're not personally convinced, your team won't be either. When it comes to gender balance, a lot of people don't get it, don't like it, or, frankly, resist it. That's why you as the CEO need to be well-versed at explaining why you think gender balance in your organization is so important—and getting your team to understand this is your first hurdle.

◇◇◇◇◇◇◇◇◇◇◇◇◇◇◇◇◇

Gender balance is a big business opportunity with huge economic implications.

◇◇◇◇◇◇◇◇◇◇◇◇◇◇◇◇◇

First, know your numbers. How imbalanced is your company? Do you have a recruitment, retention, or promotion issue? Is it all three? Do you even know? Are men and women split by level, role, or function? What's the gender split of your customers? What's the gender split of your suppliers, regulators, or government contracts? Make sure your team accurately identifies your own company's issues before you start trying to solve them. Too many companies are wasting time and money recruiting more women when the real issue is that they aren't retaining or promoting them.

Avivah Wittenberg-Cox, CEO of the gender consulting firm 20-first, explains that often companies get lost in mounds of Excel data and miss the real problem: recruitment, retention, or promotion.[5] Each issue requires different responses, and solving one will not solve the others. Do you know where your problem actually lies? Good graphs usually tell the story. Let's look at a few examples.

If you have a gap right from the start, but the lines showing men and women at each level stay roughly parallel after that, you have a *recruitment* issue.

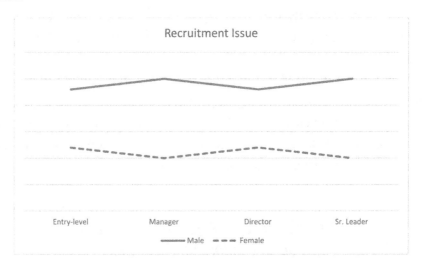

If the lines widen precipitously at each level, going in opposite directions for men and women, you have an early-promotion issue that will likely cause a turnover gap or *retention* issue.

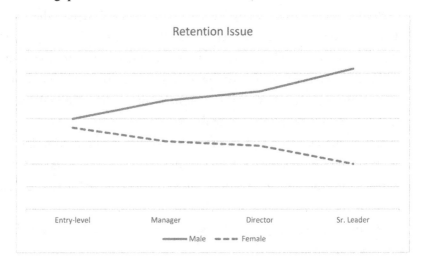

If your lines stay relatively close together, but then open wide at the most senior levels, you have a glass ceiling or *senior-promotion* issue.

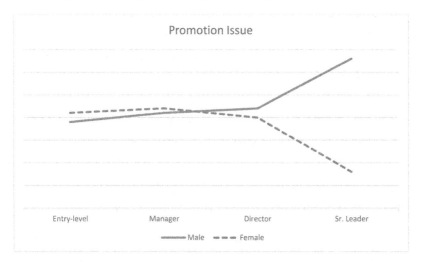

If you have a recruitment issue: Figure out what ratio of men and women you'd consider balanced. It may be fifty-fifty, or it may reflect the gender makeup of graduate programs that feed new hires into your industry. For instance, remember that tech firms have 80 percent Caucasian and Asian males, so the recruitment of these groups would likely be high. If you have an imbalance, reevaluate the schools and programs you recruit from, and assess your brand image, culture, and recruitment efforts. Do they skew masculine or feminine?

If you have a retention issue: If one gender is leaving your company in disproportionate numbers (e.g., if you are recruiting 40 percent women and 60 percent men, but your turnover is 60 percent women and 40 percent men), you have a retention gap. If this is the case, there's little point in thinking that more recruitment will stem the flow. You will simply be throwing good money after bad. Here, you will want to address deeper issues and systems. Law firms are a great example of this problem. Despite recruiting more women, they see massive losses of female lawyers after about two years. By the time you get to the senior partner level, 80 percent of the lawyers are male.[6]

If you have a promotion issue: Many companies think they have a glass ceiling when the reality is more complicated. They are suffering from a situation in which gender ratios shift in favor of one gender from the very first promotions and then just keep getting more imbalanced. To solve this, you need a major management and cultural shift that involves most of your employees. Get them involved in management development programs to understand what they are doing and why. As we've discussed throughout this book, it's likely not overt sexism, but rather unconscious biases and prejudices that are driving it. If you really have an issue only at the most senior levels, then you need a session with your executive team to help build awareness of their behavior and beliefs and to get them to establish key performance indicators that will hold them accountable for promotion results.

◇◇◇◇◇◇◇◇◇◇◇◇◇◇◇

The issue for most companies is managing the middle and addressing retention and promotion issues there.

◇◇◇◇◇◇◇◇◇◇◇◇◇◇◇

In my experience, most large companies today don't have a recruitment issue. Aside from a handful of sectors, most are gender-balanced at entry-level—or imbalanced in favor of women. Also, relatively few companies have a real glass ceiling issue just at the senior leader level. The bigger problem is the pipeline into senior leadership trickles to a drought much earlier, especially in core functions or line roles (not staff roles). The crux of the issue for most companies now is managing the middle and addressing retention and promotion issues there. The key is to get clear about the cause of the imbalance, and understand management's role (as individuals) in creating these systematic and self-perpetuating cultures and systems that reinforce recurring models of leadership.

Second, be attuned to gender culture differences. As detailed in chapter nine, men and women approach virtually every aspect of business differently. Learn how to distinguish between real differences and stereotypes. If you want to effectively engage both men and women, you will need to find the words and the messages that resonate with 100 percent of your talent and 100 percent of your customers. Be careful not to overuse sports metaphors—*step up to bat, swing for the fence, don't drop the ball, hit it out of the park, take the offensive, lose or strike out, slam dunk, par for the course, play to win*—and the most offensive, *play like a girl.*[7]

Although sports metaphors are ready-made inspirational catch-phrases and can sometimes be effective for team building, there are many negative aspects. Using pervasive sports language is not only alienating to those men and women who didn't play sports, but the winners-and-losers dichotomy can be harmful to business. If you really look at companies that are sustained and successful over time, their focus is very different. It's on building a good organization and making the pieces fit together, making sure everybody is aligned and motivated, and ensuring an inclusive workplace. A singular focus on beating the competition can backfire because it promotes the idea that more resources and greater effort produce better results. However, this is misguided. Sometimes an organization simply needs more time, or better innovation, or more collaboration—and working harder to achieve the win will not address the issue.

In addition, the use of sports metaphors reflects cultural values—namely masculine values. An international study of the use of metaphors in offices around the world showed that countries with more individualistic attitudes (such as the U.S.) favor sports metaphors.[8] The focus is on who's up and who's down, who's winning, and what's the final score. If you're a woman, or from a non-American collectivist culture, or even a Millennial, this type of language can be exclusionary.

◇◇◇◇◇◇◇◇◇◇◇◇◇◇◇◇

Be careful not to overuse sports metaphors.

◇◇◇◇◇◇◇◇◇◇◇◇◇◇◇◇

Third, make sure that your actions are consistent with your desired outcomes. Your commitment to a gender-balanced organization—or your indifference—predicts your organization's success at being truly balanced.

Are you explaining and leading the company's efforts? Who is accountable for the change? If it isn't you and your executive team, you're wasting your time. You all need to be personally invested and actively role model the desired mindsets and behaviors to build a more open and accepting culture. When a CEO is the chief advocate and storyteller, more people believe that gender diversity matters. You need to be measuring and comparing your executive team's success in balancing their functions as a routine part of your staff meetings. And, you don't need a million different initiatives. You just need a new strategic lens through which you can look at the talent and customers you already have—or want to get.[9]

But, beware of the easy defaults: Recruiting the first woman to join your board of directors; or selecting one woman from a support function to join your team and then asking her to lead a gender initiative is doomed to fail. Recognize that the people you will most need to convince are today's dominant majority. It's better to have any efforts be visibly led by one of them. Appoint well-respected managers across a variety of functions to shine the spotlight on diversity issues and help drive continual vigilance. For example, diversity leaders can guide the organization in the process making explicit the hidden mindsets that emerge in talent-management discussions.

Fourth, make gender balance a strategic lever to achieving business goals. Period. It's a business issue, not a personnel issue. Where, when, and with whom you discuss gender issues defines their relevance to your business. Put gender balance on your agenda as one of your top goals. A CEO who is not committed may fold women into diversity and diversity into talent which diffuses focus. Point out the strategic link to your future business goals— people often don't see the link, so you will need to explain it regularly and repeatedly.[10] Talk about it in key management meetings. Talk about it outside of your company if you want business leaders to take it seriously. Don't delegate to HR or think a woman is better able to address the issue. Speak to your dominant group, and visibly reward managers who build balanced teams. Teach your teams how to gender balance as part of your leadership development programs. And finally, groom your successor to support gender balance too, because it takes more than one CEO to get change into the corporate DNA.

◇◇◇◇◇◇◇◇◇◇◇◇◇◇◇◇

When a CEO is chief advocate and storyteller, more people believe that gender diversity matters.

◇◇◇◇◇◇◇◇◇◇◇◇◇◇◇◇

Fifth, implement key initiatives that support gender equality. These include increased and more inclusive networking opportunities, skill-building and career development programs (like mentoring, EQ and unconscious bias training), and leadership development (such as coaching and sponsorship programs). These should be formal programs to identify potential female leaders, and the CEO and diversity leader should be personally accountable for the programs. As noted earlier, successful female leaders need to make a conscious effort to be mentors for other women, and we need more male leaders to step up and sponsor women. Affinity groups (or ERGs) are also powerful ways for women and other diverse groups to share ideas, build skills, access resources, get visibility, and network with others across the organization both locally and globally.

Sixth, set targets and measure them. Establish concrete targets regarding gender parity, and then measure the progress toward these targets by using clear metrics to count the numbers of women at all levels and in all areas of your business. Who is getting promoted most often? Who is leaving the company and at what point? What types of roles do men and women hold? Create graphs, like those shown above, to help paint a picture. Establish and track metrics for other measures of diversity as well, including race/ethnicity, age, disability, and LGBT employees.

Seventh, create family-friendly policies so your employees can be good workers *and* parents—and help women feel empowered to progress. Even if employees do not have children, they still desire flexible programs and policies to help them better integrate their work and lives. The simple fact is that it's hard for women to be leaders if their time is fractured. We need to do a better job of respecting women's contributions by making it easier for them to hold jobs, gain new skills, and rise in the workplace—while still being there for their families. We also need to encourage men to take paternity leave, not only as good fathers, but to set an example for other men about taking time off.

Eighth, create a robust talent management program. Companies that excel at promoting women adapt existing recruiting, promotion, and succession-planning processes to call out performance regarding gender diversity. For example, behind closed doors, HR should be having candid conversations about why there are so few women in leadership roles at their company, or why women fall off precipitously at each level, or why women receive lower performance evaluations. Detailed data should be shared broadly so that everyone has the facts, and discussions scheduled regularly. Create competency-based performance and succession plans to promote the best qualified employees based on merits. Even better, create intentional talent succession plans focused on gender balance that generate a stronger female leadership pipeline—and are part of overall corporate strategy. Competency-based plans also serve another function—they help take bias out of organizational decision-making processes.

◇◇◇◇◇◇◇◇◇◇◇◇◇◇

Create family-friendly policies so your employees can be good workers and parents.

◇◇◇◇◇◇◇◇◇◇◇◇◇◇

Ninth, assess employee motivation, engagement and commitment through ongoing conversations with management, individual development plans, and regular surveys. Create plans to improve engagement and stick to them. Employees know whether leadership is serious about change based on how they respond—or whether it's just lip service. Do everything you can to keep the talented people you have. It's much easier and more cost-effective to retain, develop, and promote the talent you have, rather than constantly recruiting. To identify and address hidden bias, give an employee an experience survey that serves to help leadership understand what employees' experiences are in their respective jobs. Your surveys could also assess employee's feelings and experiences with your policies and programs, to determine what's working well and what's not.

As you would imagine, organizations vary widely in the policies, programs, and benefits they offer. They also differ significantly in the types of cultures they sustain and in what traits they value. An organization's priorities can be understood by looking at the way it spends its time and money. Often, organizations will say they value their employees—that the workforce is critical to their success, or that without their talented workers, they would be nowhere. However, there's often a considerable disconnect between these words and organizational actions. It's difficult to believe a company truly values its employees if it spends very little time training them and invests very little money developing them.

Every year, the Association for Talent Development provides a definitive review of talent development trends. Per the 2016 State of the Industry report, organizations spent $1,252 per employee (or 4 percent of payroll) on training, and the average number of hours spent annually in training sessions was thirty-four hours per employee.[11] Most employers provide their employees with eighty hours of sick time, which is more than double the amount of time they use to train them. Additionally, not all training programs are created equal. Most of those thirty-four hours are spent on mandatory, compliance, process, procedure, and business practice trainings rather than leadership training and professional development. If companies really value their employees, they should spend more time and resources on them. Employees in companies rated as "Best Companies to Work For" had substantially higher amounts of training, averaging forty-three hours per employee per year.

Every organization needs to ask, "What type of organization do we want to build?" By the way, if you don't know how your company compares to this data you have identified your first problem. I worked in pharmaceutical learning and development roles for more than ten years. Often, my colleagues and I would tell our organizations that they would benefit greatly from more employee training. Inevitably, the responses were, "What happens if I spend all this money to train them and they leave?" I responded with, "What happens if you save the money and they stay?" The irony is that managers will put up with poor employees who cost the company tens of thousands of dollars per year, but won't spend a fraction of that to help employees reach their full potential. So, how do you spend your time and money? Are you striving to be a top-notch organization that invests in employee development because you realize it will pay enormous dividends? Or, is your strategy, "We are going to save our way to success"?

Global Implications

Over the past four decades, women have been increasingly transforming society through their growing contributions to the world economy. They represent half of the world's population and their participation rate in the labor force today equals men. The U.S. Council of Economic Advisors calculates that the U.S. economy today is 14 percent larger—by an additional $2.0 trillion in Gross Domestic Product (GDP)—due to women's increased participation in the workforce since 1970.[12]

Globally, women are also earning higher educational credentials at a growing rate—female college graduates now match or exceed men both in college attendance and graduation rates. Like the U.S., in Europe, women represent 60 percent of university graduates.[13] And, women are just as likely as men to have advanced degrees—accounting for half of all JD and MD degrees conferred today in the U.S.[14] What's interesting, is that even though the number of women enrolling in MBA programs has grown substantially over the years, it's not as high as enrollment in law and medical schools.

This is where the role of graduate business schools becomes increasingly important since they are a primary talent pipeline for future business leaders. MBA degrees conferred to women in 2013 were 31 percent in Latin America, 36 percent in the U.S., 38 percent in Asia, and 40 percent in Europe. So, roughly one-third of women obtain an MBA compared to two-thirds of men globally. Closing the gender gap in MBA enrollment would go a long way to expanding the pipeline of women prepared to step into leadership roles in business. An MBA is not a prerequisite for access to the upper reaches of corporate governance, but qualifications matter in an increasingly competitive global economy, and an MBA degree is a highly-valued credential—the "gold standard"— for organizations seeking to hire top business talent to fill their ranks. More than 40 percent of CEOs of both genders in the top one hundred companies have MBAs.[15] So, for women especially, an MBA is a natural pathway to the ranks of corporate leadership.

◇◇◇◇◇◇◇◇◇◇◇◇◇◇◇

The earnings gap is directly tied to the leadership gap.

◇◇◇◇◇◇◇◇◇◇◇◇◇◇◇

Despite the huge economic and educational gains women have made, there remains a persistent gap in women's earnings globally compared with men, and a lack of females in top leadership roles that cuts across industries and job levels. This is all indicative of the work that still needs to be done to address the biases, barriers, and misperceptions that make it harder for women to advance and accrue the same financial rewards as men. The earnings gap is directly tied to the leadership gap because women are not advancing to the higher levels (and higher paying jobs) that their educational credentials and job tenure would seem to warrant.

In addition, emerging markets comprise two-thirds of future growth with total GDP projections of $151 trillion by 2050. Sixty-eight percent of this will be driven by Brazil, Russia, India, China, South Africa, Hong Kong, Singapore, and Turkey. The remaining 32 percent will come from mature markets, such as the U.S., U.K., and Japan.[16] So, in a little over thirty years, the world's growth will be driven by multiracial, multiethnic, and multicultural individuals—and increasingly more women.

Thus, companies will need policies that reflect the local market. For example, a Western company's family leave provision might not be acceptable in India, where women tend to stay home longer after the birth of a child. Or, a standardized dress code in Europe will mean something different in Saudi Arabia, where women must wear black head scarves. Companies should adapt their expectations of employee performance as well. Time with family is highly valued in emerging market countries, so companies should establish boundaries limiting weekend email and travel. Savvy companies keen to tap the new candidate pool of women need to be ready to recruit, but they must foresee the challenges of developing and retaining these uniquely equipped individuals.

◇◇◇◇◇◇◇◇◇◇◇◇◇◇

If women do not achieve their full economic potential, the global economy will suffer.

◇◇◇◇◇◇◇◇◇◇◇◇◇◇

A McKinsey Global Institute report finds that $12 trillion could be added to global GDP by 2025 by advancing women's equality. This is equivalent in size to the current GDP of Germany, Japan, and the United Kingdom combined. Gender inequality is not only a pressing moral and social issue, but also a critical economic challenge. If women—who account for half the world's working-age population—do not achieve their full economic potential, the global economy will suffer.[17]

Globalization is heating up the competition for innovative and talented workers with the skills needed for tomorrow's workplace. Women, by virtue of higher educational attainment, are becoming the most skilled workers in the job market. And, as discussed throughout this book, women offer unique skills, strengths, vision, and values that are aligned with the needs of contemporary organizations. These demographic trends provide a roadmap—and companies would be remiss not to develop this high-potential talent pool as their next generation of leaders.

Concluding Thoughts

I believe that one of the biggest reasons that companies have struggled to put their commitment to gender diversity into practice, is that many CEOs and employees do not view it as a priority. Despite a growing consensus among top executives that gender diversity is both an ethical and a business imperative, there's a disconnect between what the CEO says about gender diversity and what employees believe. There's also a disconnect between men and women about what women experience and the perceived impact of gender at work. Women are less likely than men to see practices intended to promote gender diversity, and less likely to think their company is doing what it takes. Simply put, men and women have different perceptions of the issues, different perceptions of each other, and different perceptions of themselves.

These disconnects are similar to unconscious bias. There are mounds of data that show the benefits of being unbiased at work, yet people don't change their daily behavior because they are unclear about what to look for and what to do. Change must come from the top and it must be believed in the middle. It must be incentivized and people must see that diversity drives the bottom line from their own experience. Diversity takes work, it takes listening, it takes time. Organizations need to get crystal clear about gender diversity—where they're at, what are the issues, what are the goals, what are the strategies, who's accountable for it, how to measure it, and how to communicate it throughout the organization. Although there's no one size fits all solution, there are many steps companies can take to advance their gender diversity efforts and create a fairer, more inclusive work environment.

Creating a more inclusive workplace is important for women and men—and men would also benefit from a broader definition of leadership. According to McKinsey, only about half of men say their companies embrace diverse leadership styles. Men cite similar reasons as women for not wanting a top executive spot—it's not consistent with who they are as a person, they wouldn't be able to balance family and work commitments, or they don't think they'd be successful because they lack "the typical style of a top executive"[18] Men will benefit too when we can all be our true selves and realize the benefits of all talents.

Home is an area of conflict for men, and work is an area of conflict for women. Men are largely unaware of the issues that women face at the office because men simply go there and hang out—they're completely and unconsciously themselves. The same can be said of women with childcare or domestic duties. This must change—we need to replace our outdated attitudes, biases and beliefs about men's and women's roles. If we want more women to be leaders, we need to encourage more men to be fathers. Put another way—the more parity there is at home, the more parity there will be at work. Both work and home are vital parts of our lives, and we need to be comfortable in both.

◇◇◇◇◇◇◇◇◇◇◇◇◇◇◇

Home is an area of conflict for men, and work is an area of conflict for women.

◇◇◇◇◇◇◇◇◇◇◇◇◇◇◇

For women, their accomplishments in the entire education system—from grade school to college—exceed men's. When women enter the workforce, these accomplishments come to a screeching halt. Why? Because women go from an environment that rewards focus and discipline, to an environment that rewards political networking. It shifts from an egalitarian to a masculine environment, which is often hostile to women—and this is when the barriers become reality. Women start their careers hungry to attain a powerful job, but lose their appetite as they age. Even for women without children, and those who are breadwinners, power loses its luster for the thirty-five to fifty age group. Many women do not aspire for powerful positions because they perceive the burdens of leadership outweighing the benefits.

Given the barriers discussed throughout this book, it is not surprising that women have not achieved parity with men at the upper echelons of leadership. What is surprising is that women are not further along than they are—after forty years in the workforce, only 4 percent run our largest companies. It's a fact that women are often confronted with barriers that men do not have to face. Thus, many women have opted for the private sector, nonprofit, or start-up companies. At these companies, a significant number of women are owners, leaders, and make up a large percentage of the workforce. Therefore, some of the barriers women face in large public companies are minimized—such as less gender bias and stereotyping, more role models and mentors, and more leadership support to help women advance their careers.

The leadership gap is a global phenomenon whereby women are disproportionately concentrated in lower-level and lower-authority leadership positions than men. The gap has obvious implications for all of us at work. It represents how we develop our talent, what type of culture we work in, how we make decisions, how we engage our employees, how we connect with our customers, how we plan for the future, and how we value diversity and inclusion. There are several important reasons for removing these barriers to advancement. First, doing so will fulfill the promise of equal opportunity by allowing everyone the possibility of taking on leadership roles. Second, by increasing the pool of potential candidates, a company will have a greater chance of finding talented human resources. Third, promoting a richly diverse group of women into leadership roles will help make societal institutions, businesses, and governments more representative of society. Fourth, diversity is associated with greater group productivity and innovation. And, finally, research has shown a strong connection between gender diversity and organizational performance—as the number of women at the top increases, so does financial success.

Today, many women have found windows in the glass ceiling through which they are climbing, and have more opportunities, options, and power than ever before. But, it's still not a level playing field. Regardless of where you are in the corporate structure and what industry you work in, if you find yourself in a leadership position, you must behave differently than a man. You face many unique challenges—you may have to consider how you present and carry yourself, what you say, what you wear, which battles to choose, how to manage friendships with former co-workers, and how you're going to lead and motivate your team.[19] If you're going to be successful, you need support from your female and male counterparts, as well as those below you. You will need to exhibit behaviors effective in both gender cultures, such as a goal-focused approach to getting things done, and a process-focused approach to cultivating your team.

◇◇◇◇◇◇◇◇◇◇◇◇◇◇◇

When you're one of the pieces, it doesn't feel like a game.

◇◇◇◇◇◇◇◇◇◇◇◇◇◇◇

When boys and girls grow up, they play business in much the same way they play as children—men continue to see business as a team sport, while women perceive business as a series of separate personal encounters. Many popular women's books focus on how women need to change. They also imply that business is a game, and provide strategies on how to play the game and survive in a man's world. Some of these books include *Hardball for Women, Nice Girls Don't Get the Corner Office*, and *Play Like a Man, Win Like a Woman*. Even men agree. Mark Cuban, the billionaire entrepreneur and investor, has written two books on the subject, *How to Win at the Sport of Business* and *Wisdom: 105 Rules on How to Play the Game and Win*. I acknowledge that the general approach to business is a game, and it's essential for women to know the unspoken rules and play the game to the best of their ability. However, when you are one of the pieces, it doesn't feel like a game.

Since women value and cultivate relationships at work, this does not accord with the attitude in sports, in which bonding primarily serves the purpose of the game. Games are strictly bounded; work is not. Games have clear rules; work is subject to ceaseless reinterpretation. Games are played in the short-term; work can play out over several decades. Games have clear winners and losers; work is about attaining personal goals and fulfillment (which is different for everyone). What happens in one game has no impact on what happens in the next game; what happens in work has consequences on other aspects of work. And finally, the history and future of an ongoing relationship between players is irrelevant in sports; in work the quality of our ongoing relationships are key. By setting business transactions in a win-or-lose frame, it undervalues the larger context and the need for building relationships. Focusing too much on a winning outcome can result in a competitor (or colleague) feeling burned, which may have a negative impact on future interactions. We are a new and diverse generation, and we need a new approach.

It's a fact that the twenty-first century demands business strategy that is fundamentally different than the twentieth century models most are used to following.[20] Just look at the shift in workplace expectations from the past to the present:

- My Paycheck shifts to My Purpose
- My Satisfaction shifts to My Development
- My Boss shifts to My Coach
- My Annual Performance Review shifts to Ongoing Conversations
- My Weaknesses shifts to My Strengths
- My Job shifts to My Life

Women and Millennials are driving these changes. It's a shift in mindset from convergent to divergent thinking with a more holistic approach. The forces behind the shift include a global economy, new technologies, the power and intelligence of the consumer, a focus on knowledge instead of industrial production, and the changing face and demands of a new workforce. We now live in a global, competitive, and dynamic business world, and these forces are causing organizations to alter their beliefs about leadership, structure, culture, and strategy. They are moving towards a flatter, more collaborative, and more nuanced way of doing business that can better connect with the marketplace and operate more efficiently in a global environment. Organizations that do not recognize these changes, or are unwilling to make these changes, will be at a competitive disadvantage—and will be left behind.

◇◇◇◇◇◇◇◇◇◇◇◇◇◇◇◇

We are not yet at a gender tipping point, but I believe we are heading toward one.

◇◇◇◇◇◇◇◇◇◇◇◇◇◇◇◇

Organizational change can seem like a monumental task, but you do not have to complete the job tomorrow...only to start a dialogue. Bringing awareness and teaching people the language of gender differences, barriers, biases, and emotional intelligence is the first step. People internalize it, then go share it with other people in the organization, and that marks the beginning of change. It takes what is invisible, and turns it into an entity that can be actively managed. We all experience inequities. Men and women working together is the path past them into a world where every person is encouraged to bring their best selves to the table.

We are not yet at a gender tipping point, but I believe we are heading toward one. Based on research reports from women who have reached the uppermost ranks in their companies, there is a tipping point that makes the difference in a company's culture. For some, this occurs when 20 percent of the people who report to the CEO are women—and we know that organizations are more successful when at least 30 percent of women are in senior leadership. Other women have described the "rule of three"—that is, once there are three women at the executive management level, the culture of the organization begins to shift. People begin to feel that they can behave in ways that are natural to them rather than needing to adjust to ways of the opposite gender.[21] Here's the key—you've got to keep women in the game until they can get up to those levels and make a difference.

When there are enough women in the room so that everyone stops counting, women become free to act like women. It's then that we can eliminate double standards, stereotypes, and other biases, and accept that men and women are different—and that they bring a different range of experiences, skills, and strengths to business. It's then that we can start to value women as much as men and retool our institutions to fit the broad range of needs of a diverse global society. It's then that we can expand our definition of leadership, and the language we use to describe it.[22] It's then that we'll have more representative government, business, religion, military, medicine, and education. Gender is the most powerful determinant of how we see the world and everything in it. It's more significant than age, income, ethnicity, or geography. As noted earlier, since there are many different types of diverse groups in the workplace, the easiest place to start with is gender. Hence, gender diversity accelerates all diversity.

◇◇◇◇◇◇◇◇◇◇◇◇◇◇◇

Gender diversity accelerates all diversity.

◇◇◇◇◇◇◇◇◇◇◇◇◇◇◇

Election Day, Nov 8, 2016. Women leaders are confronted with cross-pressures that men do not face, and the 2016 U.S. presidential election was the grandest display of that. Hillary Clinton's campaign worked hard to find the right balance between agentic and communal traits, and to counter the stereotypes that women aren't tough enough and are less prepared to be commander in chief. Ultimately, Clinton was unable to find a good equilibrium in her bid to become the first woman president. Or, could it be that we didn't appreciate her achievements because she's good at politics in a way we haven't learned to appreciate—taking a more feminine approach to fighting for the highest office—an approach not yet recognized as valid?

Some believe that diversity lost that day; some believe that women lost. I was particularly touched by a short TV news segment that showed long lines of men, women, and children in a Rochester, New York cemetery waiting to put their "I voted" stickers on Susan B. Anthony's tombstone—believing they were a part of history (prior to the ultimate results that evening). Although Clinton didn't break through the highest and hardest glass ceiling for president, she broke barriers and opened the door, making it easier for other women and young girls to pursue their dreams and make decisions that suit their own lives. In Clinton's concession speech, she said this, "To all little girls, never doubt that you are valuable and powerful and deserving of every chance and opportunity in the world to pursue and achieve your dreams." I couldn't agree more.

In June 1992, the cover of *LIFE* magazine read, "If Women Ran America: How Things Would be Different in Washington, in the Cities, at Work and at Home."[23] The magazine conducted an exclusive poll of a cross-section of 1,222 Americans. Back then there were only two women in the U.S. Senate, just three states had female governors, only one female Supreme Court Justice, and one female CEO of a *Fortune* 500 company. The authors imagined the opposite of what has become the natural order—a Madame President, ninety-eight female Senators, eight female Supreme Court Justices, countless female college presidents, Army generals, and labor leaders, more men stay home raising children, the old-girl network, and yes—499 female *Fortune* 500 CEOs!

Even though the magazine is laden with gender stereotypes, sexual innuendos, and off-color jokes (and lots of cigarette ads), it asked the same questions we are asking today. If women ran America, would child care be more affordable and maternity leave guaranteed? Would government be more attentive to the needy? Would there be stricter gun control and less crime and violence? Would there be greater equality for working women? Would there be greater tolerance for diversity? And, the biggest question—Would America be better with a woman president?

The results show that more women than men favor government and employer support of programs that help working parents; believe the problem of poverty and homelessness (and fighting crime and violence) should be an "extremely important" government priority; favor making gun control, drug dealing, rape/sexual assault, domestic abuse, and drunk driving laws tougher; would vote for a gay or lesbian candidate; and consider unequal pay for the same work to be a "very serious problem" for women in the workplace.[24] It's not that men don't care about these issues. It's simply that women care more.

◇◇◇◇◇◇◇◇◇◇◇◇◇◇

You don't need a majority to make things change.

◇◇◇◇◇◇◇◇◇◇◇◇◇◇

The article states that, "The ultimate looking glass would have us electing a female president". However, while 61 percent of Americans hoped to see a woman as president in their lifetime, when asked to identify the person they'd like to have as president, only eleven of those polled named a woman—and of those eleven women, Georgia O'Keefe and Mother Teresa were dead.[25] These responses speak to societal bias in favor of men as leaders, and twenty-five years later, we're still talking about it.

So, how do we get more women into positions of power? One doesn't need miracles to create miracles. Critical mass is the smallest amount of material required to create a chain reaction. A lone woman in a room of ten men speaks differently than she does in a room of ten women. But, add more women to the mix, and soon it is the men who start changing the way they talk. In other words, you don't need a majority to make things change. There is a certain consciousness as a subgroup, a higher feeling of support and clout. When you stand behind a barrier, it looks very forbidding; it can look indestructible. But, you find so often that once you jump that hurdle, the next hurdle and the rest of them don't seem as forbidding. And, in fact, the magic is that they can kind of disappear.

In 2020, the U.S. will celebrate the 100th anniversary of the 19th Amendment, which allowed women the right to vote. Over the course of nearly a century, women have traveled a winding path, pushing to define and redefine their roles inside and outside the home. I am optimistic about the opportunities that Gen Z, and generations after them, will face as they undoubtedly define their own roles in society.

In my research, and in this book, I've set out to explain the reasons behind the significant leadership gender gap—and why men still lead women in every single industry across the world. Unfortunately, there is no silver bullet, no quick fix, and no single reason for the gap. It is a myriad of different reasons— to varying degrees—which is why it is so hard for companies to pinpoint, measure, and solve. I hope that the insights, examples, stories, and strategies I've provided in this book are valuable for women, men, and organizations to press forward, and ultimately achieve gender balanced leadership. Equality is not a zero-sum game. The more women that advance, the better it will be for men and their organizations. We should not have to wait more than one hundred years for gender parity. Per Anne Frank, "How wonderful it is that nobody need wait a single moment before starting to improve the world." The good news is we don't have to.

Summary Points
- We don't see more women leading because of the perceptions of women as leaders, as workers, as mothers, and as wives.

- As a global society, women's vision, values, strengths, and contributions are simply not valued as much as men's.
- The bottom line is that both men and women contribute to the leadership gender gap, and we need both men and women working together to close the gap and tackle the barriers that women face in organizations.
- Organizations are more successful when at least 30 percent of senior leaders are female.
- Closing the gender gap in MBA enrollment, would go a long way to expanding the pipeline of women prepared to step into leadership roles in business.
- Twelve trillion dollars could be added to global GDP by 2025 by advancing women's equality.
- Most men in our organizations are simply unaware of the barriers that women face.
- Women and Millennials are driving a fundamental shift in the workplace.
- There are several individual strategies to guide men in supporting women's careers.
- There are several individual strategies to guide women in advancing their careers.
- There are several strategies to guide CEOs and their organizations toward gender balance.

Reflection Questions

✓ What are other's perceptions of you as a worker, leader, mother, or wife? Do you agree with them? If you don't agree, what do you think gives them this perception? How can you change these perceptions?

✓ Do you feel that your contributions (your vision, strengths, and skills) at work are valued? If not, what can you do to show others your value? How can you bring more value to your organization?

✓ What type of support do you have from men in your organization (e.g., as mentors, sponsors, bosses, coaches, or advisors)? How can you leverage more men to support you? Who do you need to support you?

✓ What is the quality of your relationships at work? Can you use your interpersonal skills and empathy to improve these relationships? Are you effective at collaborating, motivating, or leading others? If not, how can you enhance these skills?

✓ Do you let your boss and others know what you're working on? If not, why not? What methods are you most comfortable with (e.g., having regular face-to-face meetings, sending periodic emails, creating monthly reports)?

✓ Have you taken risks and tried new things in your career? What are some examples? If not, what has held you back?

✓ Are you getting career or leadership development in your position? If not, what can you do to ensure that you are developing your skills and remaining relevant in your industry?

✓ Have you ever taken a strengths-based assessment? If so, what are your top five strengths? How do you use these in your life and in your job? Have you shared these with your boss or in interviews? If not, how can you leverage them?

✓ Have you received any type of bias training? Was it helpful for you and your organization? What can you do to correct for personal biases you may have?

✓ Has your CEO expressed that gender diversity or diversity and inclusion are priorities for your company? What initiatives have they taken? Are the policies and programs effective?

ABOUT THE AUTHOR

Shawn Andrews is a professional speaker and organizational consultant. She speaks and consults to a diverse range of clients, including SABMiller Brewing Company, Broadcom, Johnson and Johnson, Biogen, Edwards Life Sciences, and the Healthcare Businesswomen's Association. She also leads workshop sessions at a variety of conferences, including the Association for Talent Development and the Society of Human Resource Management.

She is a frequent contributor to the publications of the Association for Talent Development, Life Sciences Trainers & Educators Network, and Training Industry. She is also the Diversity & Inclusion columnist for *Training Industry* magazine.

Andrews, who has over two decades of experience in the biopharmaceutical industry, has helped thousands of leaders improve and develop using presentations, workshops, coaching, and psychological instruments. She is an accredited practitioner for EQ-i 2.0 and EQ 360 Model, Insights Discovery Colors, and Blanchard's Situational Leadership.

She serves as adjunct professor at Pepperdine University's Graziadio School of Business and Management, and teaches courses on Organizational Behavior, Leadership and Ethics, and Diversity in Organizations. Her specific areas of focus include Organizational Leadership, Learning & Development, Talent Management, and Diversity & Inclusion.

She holds an Ed.D. degree in Organizational Leadership from Pepperdine University, an M.B.A. degree from Pepperdine University, and a B.A. degree in Psychology from University of California, Irvine.

She serves on advisory and editorial Boards of Directors, and is founder and CEO of Andrews Research International.

You can access information on her website, *www.drshawnandrews.com*, and follow her on Twitter @drshawnandrews.

ACKNOWLEDGEMENTS

I want to acknowledge and thank the women who participated in my dissertation research, and the women who allowed me to interview them for this book. I am grateful for your time, insights, and your willingness to help others. Your stories of perseverance and success, the roadblocks you have faced along the way, and your courage and advice have inspired me, and I know will inspire other women who seek to advance in their careers.

I would also like to acknowledge the many MBA students I have taught over the years. Thank you for showing me your courage, your vulnerabilities, your hopes, and your fears. Your actions have given me inspiration and insights that were invaluable for this book.

I want to thank David Hancock and everyone at Morgan James Publishing for giving me the opportunity to write and share my research and stories on these very important topics. I appreciate your faith in me, and especially your patience, as I toiled through the process.

I'd also like to thank my editor, Anna Floit of The Peacock Quill, for her unwavering support and commitment to this project. I sincerely appreciate your guidance and grammatical prowess throughout the process.

To my family, friends, business and academic colleagues, thank you for your support, encouragement, and words of wisdom throughout this journey. I'm deeply thankful to Janet Bamper for your unwavering support, understanding, and patience for reaching each milestone and climbing each mountain. Thank you for serving as my unofficial editor and critic when I needed it most. And, to Sammy and Sebastian, the world's best cats and editors.

Classroom or Book Club Discussion Questions

Discussing the broad topics of leadership, emotional intelligence and gender with other people is the best way to start a meaningful dialogue about these important subjects. Use these questions to build your group's awareness and understanding of the barriers that impact women's advancement. You can also refer to the *Reflection Questions* at the end of every chapter to gain a deeper understanding of how each of the issues affect you personally.

1. Consider the following findings and discuss them as a group:
    a. Women represent 57 percent of the workforce and 60 percent of bachelor degrees, yet they hold only 4 percent of CEO positions at *Fortune* 500 companies
    b. A woman earns seventy-nine cents for every dollar a man earns for the same work

    c.   The top three female occupations for women are administrative assistant, teacher, and nurse, which are all staff roles

2. How many members of the group were familiar with the concept of emotional intelligence before reading this book? What's the most important thing you discovered after reading this book?

3. Were you surprised to learn about gender-specific EQ competencies? What are your top EQ skills? What EQ skills could you improve on? How are these perceived at work?

4. What leadership styles do you most commonly see at your work? What leadership style do you use the most? What style do you respond best to?

5. Which barriers or obstacles outlined in this book have you faced the most? How have you dealt with them? How have they impacted your career?

6. Learn from other people in the group about how they:
   a. Address bias, stereotypes, and prejudice
   b. Access informal networks, mentors, and sponsors
   c. Integrate their work and lives
   d. May limit themselves (e.g. behaviors, language, executive presence, lack of confidence, not taking risks, etc.)

7. What gender lessons did you learn as a child/adult? How has this impacted your behavior at work? How do others perceive you? How do you navigate these differences at home and work?

8. Discuss the global demographic trends. How do you think it will change the future workplace?

9. What are your perceptions of Millennials? Do you think they will change how we work?

10. Do you think we will achieve gender parity in leadership positions in less than one hundred years? Why or why not? How long do you think it will take?

11. What was your biggest a-ha moment or takeaway from this book?

12. What will you do to facilitate change that will help make the workplace more diverse and inclusive for the next generation of workers?

13. What are the top three strategies you will use to enhance your career and your life?

BIBLIOGRAPHY

Adato, Allison, and Melissa Stanton. 1992. "If Women Ran America: An Exclusive Poll: How Things Would Be Different." *Life Magazine* 36-46.

Amanatullah, E., and M. Morris. 2010. "Negotiating Gender Roles: Gender Differences in Assertive Negotiating are Mediated by Women's Fear of Backlash and Attenuated when Negotiating on Behalf of Others." *Journal of Personality and Social Psychology* 98 (2): 256-267.

Amazon. 2016. *Diversity at Amazon.* Accessed December 20, 2016. https://www.amazon.com/b?node=10080092011.

Anderson, Cameron, and Gavin Kilduff. 2009. "Why Do Dominant Personalities Attain Influence in Face-to-face Groups? The Competence Signaling Effects of Trait Dominance." *Journal of Personality and Social Psychology* 96 (2): 491-503. doi:10.1037/a0014201.

Andrews, Shawn D. 2013. *Emotional Intelligence Implications on the Career Advancement of Women in a Fortune 500 Pharmaceutical Company.* Dissertation, Ann Arbor: ProQuest, LLC.

Annis, Barbara, and John Gray. 2013. *Work with Me: The 8 Blind Spots Between Men and Women in Business.* New York: Palgrave Macmillan.

Annis, Barbara, and Keith Merron. 2014. *Gender Intelligence.* New York: HarperCollins Publishers.

Association for Talent Development. 2016. "The 2016 State of the Industry Report." *Association for Talent Development.* Accessed December 5, 2016. https://www.td.org/Publications/Research-Reports/2013/~/link.aspx?_id=AAB5B551916342BCAC0FCE7DBE5D4EF6&_z=z&_ga=1.258847498.1250209447.1470270334.

Avery, D., P. McKay, S. Tonidandel, S Volpone, and M. Morris. 2012. "Is There a Method to the Madness? Examining how Racioethinic Matching Influences Retail Store Productivity." *Personnel Psychology* 65.

Barnett, Chance. 2015. "Trends Show Crowdfunding to Surpass VC in 2016." *Forbes.*

Barsh, J., and L. Yee. 2012. "Unlocking the Full Potential of Women at Work." *McKinsey & Company.* April 1. Accessed August 10, 2017. http://www.mckinsey.com/business-functions/organization/our-insights/unlocking-the-full-potential-of-women-at-work.

Bass, B. 1990. "From Transactional to Transformational Leadership: Learning to Share the Vision." *Organizational Dynamics* 18: 19-31. doi:10.1016/0090-2616(90)90061-S.

Boatwright, K., and L. Forrest. 2000. "Leadership Preferences: The Influence of Gender and Needs for Connection on Worker's Ideal Preferences for Leadership Behaviors." *Journal of Leadship and Organizational Studies* 7 (2): 18-34. doi:10.1177/107179190000700202.

Bradberry, T., and J. Greaves. 2009. *Emotional Intelligence 2.0.* San Diego: TalentSmart.

Brody, E., and L. Bradley. 2008. "Generational Differences in Virtual Teams." In *The Handbook of High-Performing Virtual Teams,* by J. Nemiro, M. Beyerlein, L. Bradley and S. Beyerlein, 263-271. San Francisco: Jossey-Bass.

Brown, Brene. 2010. "The Power of Vulnerability." *TEDxHouston.* June 1. Accessed June 30, 2016. https://www.ted.com/talks/brene_brown_on_vulnerability?language=en.

Brown, S., R. Neese, A. Vinokur, and D. Smith. 2003. "Providing Social Support May be More Beneficial than Receiving it: Results from a Prospective Study of Mortality." *Psychology Science* 20-35. http:// pss.sagepub.com/content/14/4/320.short.

Bruggeman, Paula, and Hillary Chan. 2016. "Minding the Gap: Tapping the Potential of Women to Transform Business." *Graduate Management Admission Council.* March 28. Accessed December 5, 2016. http:// www.gmac.com/~/media/Files/gmac/Research/diversity-enrollment/ rr-16-01-tapping-potential-of-women-final-for-web.pdf.

Brummelhuis, L. 2012. "A Resource Perspective on the Work-Home Interface." *American Psychologist* 545-556.

Burns, Crosby. 2012. *Center for American Progress.* March 10. Accessed March 20, 2017. https://www.americanprogress.org/wp-content/ uploads/issues/2012/03/pdf/lgbt_biz_discrimination.pdf.

Burns, J. 1978. *Leadership.* New York: Harper and Row.

Butts, M., W. Caster, and T. Yang. 2013. "How Important are Work-Family Support Policies? A Meta-analytic Investigation of their Efforts on Employee Outcomes." *Journal of Applied Psychology* 98: 1-25.

Carter, A. 2006. "Lighting a Fire Under Campbell." *Business Week* 96-101.

Catalyst. 2015. *Still Too Few: Women of Color on Boards.* March 17. Accessed September 1, 2016. http://www.catalyst.org/knowledge/still-too-few-women-color-boards.

Catalyst. 2007. "The Bottom Line: Corporate Performance and Women's Representation on Boards." *Catalyst.* October 1. Accessed January 10, 2017. http://www.catalyst.org/knowledge/bottom-line-corporate-performance-and-womens-representation-boards.

Catalyst. 2016. "Women CEOs of the S&P 500." *Catalyst.* December 1. Accessed December 31, 2016. http://www.catalyst.org/knowledge/ women-ceos-sp-500.

Catalyst. 2014. "Women's Share of Board Seats at Asia-Pacific Stock Index Companies." *Catalyst.* October 1. Accessed November 5, 2016. http://www.catalyst.org/knowledge/2014-catalyst-census-women-board-directors.

Center for Creative Leadership. 2003. *Leadership Skills and Emotional Intelligence.* June 15. Accessed January 10, 2017. https://myccl.ccl. org/leadership/pdf/assessments/skills_intelligence.pdf.

Coltrane, Scott. 2004. "2004." *Journal of Marriage and Family* 62 (4): 1208-1233. doi:10.1111/j.1741-3737.2000.01208.x/abstract.

Conable, Barber B. 1991. "The Conable Years at the World Bank: Major Policy Addresses of Barber B. Conable, 1986-91." *The World Bank.* July 10. Accessed December 15, 2016. http://documents.worldbank. org/curated/en/241661468762576834/The-Conable-years-at-the-World-Bank-major-policy-addresses-of-Barber-B-Conable-1986-91.

Corporate Executive Board. 2013. "Creating Competitive Advantage Through Workforce Diversity." *Corporate Executive Board.* June 1. Accessed January 5, 2017. www.executiveboard.com.

Crenshaw, Kimberle. 2016. "Why Intersectionality Can't Wait." *The Washington Post.* https://www.washingtonpost.com/news/in-theory/wp/2015/09/24/why-intersectionality-cant-wait/?utm_term=.19b06ca7712c.

Croft, A., T. Schmader, K. Block, and A. Baron. 2014. "The Second Shift Reflected in the Second Generation: Do Parent's Gender Roles at Home Predict Children's Aspirations?" *Psychological Science* 1-15. http://www.ncbi.nlm.nih.gov/pubmed/24890499.

Davis, S. 2009. "President's First Law: Obama Signs Lilly Ledbetter Wage Bill." *Wall Street Journal.*

Deloitte. 2016. "The 2016 Deloitte Millennial Survey: Winning Over the Next Generation of Leaders." *Deloitte.* Accessed November 17, 2016. www.deloitte.com/MillennialSurvey.

Desilver, Drew. 2016. "More Older Americans are Working, and Working More, Than They Used to." *Pew Research Center.* June 20. Accessed October 10, 2016. http://www.pewresearch.org/fact-tank/2016/06/20/more-older-americans-are-working-and-working-more-than-they-used-to/.

Desvaux, G., S. Devillard-Hoellinger, and M. Meaney. 2008. "A Business Case for Women." *The McKinsey Quarterly* 10-32. Accessed October

8, 2016. http://www.rctaylor.com/images/A_Business_Case_for_
Women.pdf.

Development Dimensions International; The Conference Board. 2015.
"Ready-now Leaders: 25 Findings to Meet Tomorrow's Business
Challenges." *Development Dimensions International.* Accessed
October 3, 2016. http://www.ddiworld.com/DDI/media/trend-
research/global-leadership-forecast-2014-2015_tr_ddi.pdf?ext=.pdf.

Dezso, Cristian, and David Gaddis Ross. 2012. "Does Female Representation
in top Management Improve Firm Performance? A Panel Data
Investigation." *Strategic Management Journal* 33 (9).

Dimaratino, Mediha. 2016. "Why Advantage Solution's Boss Chose to Lean
In." *Orange County Business Journal* 18-25. www.ocbj.com.

Drory, A., and T. Romm. 1990. "The Definition of Organizational Politics: A
Review." *Human Relations* 1133-1154.

Duckworth, Angela. 2016. *Grit: The Power of Passion and Perseverance.*
New York: Simon & Schuster.

Eagly, A., and L. Carli. 2003. "The Female Leadership Advantage: An
Evaluation of the Evidence." *The Leadership Quarterly* 14 (6): 807-
834. doi:10.1016/j.leaqua.2003.09.004.

Eagly, A. and L. Carli. 2007. *Through the Labyrinth: The Truth About How
Women Become Leaders.* Boston: Harvard Business School Press.

Eagly, A., S. Karau, and M. Makhijani. 1995. "Gender and the Effectiveness
of Leaders: A Meta-analysis." *Psychological Bulletin* 117: 125-145.
doi:10.1037/0033-2909.117.1.125.

Ephron, Nora. 1996. "1996 Commencement Address." *Wellesley College.*
June 15. Accessed January 1, 2017. http://new.wellesley.edu/events/
commencementarchives/1996commencement.

Ernst & Young. 2015. "Global Generations: A Global Study on Work-
life Challenges Across Generations." *Ernst & Young.* Accessed
September 28, 2016. http://www.ey.com/Publication/vwLUAssets/
EY-global-generations-a-global-study-on-work-life-challenges-
across-generations/$FILE/EY-global-generations-a-global-study-on-
work-life-challenges-across-generations.pdf.

European Commission. 2014. "Tackling the Gender Pay Gap in the European Union." *European Commission.* Accessed October 4, 2016. http://ec.europa.eu/justice/gender-equality/files/gender_pay_gap/140319_gpg_en.pdf.

Fields, R. Douglas. 2008. "White Matter Matters." *Scientific American* 298 (3): 54-61.

Fisher, Helen. 2000. *The First Sex: The Natural Talents of Women and How They are Changing the World.* New York: Ballantine Books.

Foley, Meghan. 2015. *This is What the Recession Did to Millennials: The Cheat Sheet.* May 13. Accessed December 1, 2016. http://www.cheatsheet.com/politics/this-is-what-the-recession-did-to-Millennials.html/?a=viewall.

Frankel, Lois. 2014. *Nice Girls Still Don't Get the Corner Office: Unconscious Mistakes Women Make that Sabotage their Careers.* New York: Hachette Book Group.

Friedman, Thomas. 2007. *The World is Flat: A Brief History of the Twenty-first Century.* New York: Picador.

Fry, Richard. 2016. "Millennials Overtake Baby Boomers as America's Largest Generation." *Pew Research Center.* April 25. Accessed January 8, 2017. http://www.pewresearch.org/fact-tank/2016/04/25/Millennials-overtake-baby-Boomers/.

Gallup. 2016. "Women in America: Work and Life Well-Lived." *Gallup.* Accessed December 20, 2016. http://www.gallup.com/reports/195359/women-america-work-life-lived-insights-business-leaders.aspx.

Geiger, Abigail, and Lauren Kent. 2017. *Number of Women Leaders Around the World has Grown, but They're Still a Small Group.* March 8. Accessed March 15, 2017. http://www.pewresearch.org/fact-tank/2017/03/08/women-leaders-around-the-world/.

Gemba Marketing. 2016. *The Millennial Shift: Work-Life Balance vs. Work-Life Integration.* March 1. Accessed December 20, 2016. http://gembamarketing.com/the-millennial-shift-work-life-balance-vs-work-life-integration/.

Gerzema, John, and Michael D'Antonio. 2013. *The Athena Doctrine: How Women (and the Men Who Think Like Them) Will Rule the Future.* San Francisco: Jossey-Bass: A Wiley Imprint.

Gibson, Cristina, and Mary Zellmer-Bruhn. 2001. "Metaphors and Meaning: An Intercultural Analysis of the Concept of Teamwork." *Administrative Science Quarterly* 46 (2): 274-303. doi:10.2307/2667088.

Global Footprints. 2017. *Gender Footprints.* January 1. Accessed March 22, 2017. http://www.globalfootprints.org/women.

Goleman, Daniel. 2000. "Leadership that Gets Results." *Harvard Business Review* 1-15.

Goleman, Daniel. 1998. *Working with Emotional Intelligence.* New York: Bantam Dell.

Google. 2016. *Google Diversity.* Accessed December 20, 2016. https://www.google.com/diversity/index.html.

Gottman, John, and Nan Silver. 1994. *Why Marriages Succeed or Fail.* New York: Fireside.

Greenstein, F. 2001. *The Presidential Difference: Leadership Style from FDR to Clinton.* Princeton: Princeton University Press.

Greenwald, T., M. Banaji, and B. Nosek. 2007. *Project Implicit.* January 1. Accessed January 31, 2017. https://implicit.harvard.edu/implicit/aboutus.html.

Gurian, Michael. 2004. *What Could He Be Thinking? A Guide to the Mysteries of a Man's Mind.* New York: St. Martin's Griffin.

Healthcare Businesswomen's Association. 2016. "Addressing Gender Parity: Male Leaders on the Topic of Women in Leadership Positions." *HBA Advantage Magazine.*

Heim, P., and S. Golant. 2005. *Hardball for Women: Winning at the Game of Business.* New York: Plume: Penguin Group.

Heim, P., S. Murphy, and S. Golant. 2001. *In the Company of Women.* New York: Penguin Putnam, Inc.

Helgesen, Sally. 2010. *The Female Vision: Women's Real Power at Work.* San Francisco: Berrett-Koehler Publishers.

Helgesen, Sally. 2005. *The Web of Inclusion: Architecture for Building Great Organizations*. Washington D.C.: Beard Books.

Hewlett, Sylvia Ann. 2013. "Executive Presence." *Center of Talent Innovation.* August 1. Accessed January 15, 2017. http://www.talentinnovation. org/assets/ExecutivePresence-KeyFindings-CTI.pdf.

Hewlett, Sylvia Ann. 2016. "Unlocking the Value of Talent in the Global Workforce." *Hewlett Consulting.* Accessed December 7, 2016. http:// www.hewlettconsultingpartners.com/HCP_who-we-are.pdf.

Hewlett, Sylvia Ann. 2014. "What's Holding Women Back in Science and Technology Industries." *Harvard Business Review* 1-15.

Hewlett, Sylvia Ann, Melinda Marshall, Laura Sherbin, and Tara Gonsalves. 2013. "Innovation, Diversity and Market Growth." *Center for Talent Innovation.* September 15. Accessed November 2, 2016. www. talentinnovation.org.

Higgs, M., U. Plewnia, and J. Ploch. 2005. "Influence of Team Composition and Task Complexity on Team Performance." *Team Performance Management* 11 (7).

Hirst, Peter. 2016. "How a Flex-time Program at MIT Improved Productivity, Resilience, and Trust." *Harvard Business Review* 1-15. https:// hbr.org/2016/06/how-a-flex-time-program-at-mit-improved- productivity-resilience-and-trust?referral=00563&cm_mmc=email- _-newsletter-_-daily_alert-_-alert_date&utm_source=newsletter_ daily_alert&utm_medium=email&utm_campaign=alert_date.

Hofstede, Geert. 1991. *Cultures and Organizations: Software of the Mind.* London: McGraw-Hill.

Hopkins, M., and D. Bilimoria. 2008. "Social and Emotional Competencies Predicting Success for Male and Female Executives." *Journal of Management Development* 27 (1): 13-35. doi:10.1108/02621710810840749 .

Human Rights Campaign. 2017. "Corporate Equality Index 2017: Rating Workplaces on Lesbian, Gay, Bisexual and Transgender Equality." *Human Rights Campaign.* January 1. Accessed March 25, 2017.

http://assets.hrc.org//files/assets/resources/CEI-2017-FinalReport. pdf?_ga=1.214675217.746753115.1490401864.

Human Rights Campaign. 2016. *The Need for Full Federal LGBT Equality.* June 15. Accessed March 10, 2017. http://hrc.org/fullfederalequality/.

Ibarra, H., N. Carter, and C. Silva. 2010. "Why Men Still Get More Promotions than Women." *Harvard Business Review* 1-15. https://hbr.org/2010/09/why-men-still-get-more-promotions-than-women/ar/1?referral=00134.

Intel. 2016. *2016 Diversity Mid-year Progress Report.* June 1. Accessed December 20, 2016. http://www.intel.com/content/www/us/en/diversity/diversity-in-technology-report.html.

International Labour Organization. 2012. *ILO Global Estimates of forced Labour, Results and Methodology.* January 1. Accessed February 5, 2017. http://www.ilo.org/wcmsp5/groups/public/---ed_norm/---declaration/documents/publication/wcms_182004.pdf.

Inter-Parliamentary Union. 2017. *Women in National Parliaments.* March 1. Accessed March 15, 2017. http://www.ipu.org/wmn-e/world.htm.

Jogulu, U., and G. Wood. 2006. "The Role of Leadership Theory in Raising the Profile of Women in Management." *Equal Opportunities International* 25 (4): 236-250. doi:10.1108/02610150610706230.

Kacmar, K., D. Bachrach, K. Harris, and S. Zivnuska. 2011. "Fostering Good Citizenship through Ethical Leadership: Exploring the Moderating Role of Gender and Organizational Politics." *Journal of Applied Psychology* 96: 633-642.

Lamb, Michael. 2010. *The Role of the Father in Child Development.* Hoboken: John Wiley & Sons.

Lapierre, L., and T. Allen. 2012. "Control at Work, Control at Home and Planning Behavior: Implications for Work-Family Conflict." *Journal of Management* 1500-1516.

Lendrem, Ben, Dennis Lendrem, Andy Gray, and John Isaacs. 2014. *The Darwin Awards: Sex Differences in Idiotic Behavior.* December 11. Accessed December 2, 2016. http://www.bmj.com/content/349/bmj. g7094.

Lind, Scott. 2002. "Competency-based Student Self-assessment on a Surgery Rotation." *Journal of Surgical Research* 105 (1): 31-34.

Lollis, Helene. 2016. "Making it Personal: The Four Pillars of High-Impact Mentoring." *Training Industry Magazine* 20-28.

Mandell, B., and S. Perwani. 2003. "Relationship Between Emotional Intelligence and TL Style: A Gender Comparison." *Journal of Business and Psychology* 17 (3): 387-404.

Marre, Will. 2016. *Why Women Must Change Work*. March 16. Accessed October 14, 2016. http://willmarre.com/why-women-must-change-work/.

McKinsey & Company. 2015. *Gender Equality: Taking Stock of Where We Are*. September 1. Accessed November 5, 2016. http://www. mckinsey.com/insights/organization/gender_equality_taking_stock_ of_where_we_are.

McKinsey & Company; Leanin.org. 2016. "Women in the Workplace 2016." *McKinsey & Company*. September 1. Accessed October 1, 2016. http://www.mckinsey.com/business-functions/organization/our-insights/women-in-the-workplace-2016.

Microsoft. 2016. *Global Diversity and Inclusion*. Accessed December 20, 2016. https://www.microsoft.com/en-us/diversity/inside-microsoft/ default.aspx#epgDivFocusArea.

Mor Barak, Michalle. 2014. *Managing Diversity: Toward a Globally Inclusive Workplace, 3rd Edition*. Thousand Oaks: Sage.

Multi-Health Systems. 2012. "EQ-i 2.0 FAQ." *Multi-Health Systems*. Accessed October 25, 2016. http://ei.mhs.com/EQi20FAQ.aspx.

Murry, B. 1998. "Does Emotional Intelligence Matter in the Workplace." *APA Monitor* 29 (7): 156.

Myers, Dee Dee. 2008. *Why Women Should Rule the World*. New York: HarperCollins.

National Center for Education Statistics. 2015. *Bachelor's, Master's and Doctor's Degrees Conferred by Post-Secondary Institutions, by sex of student and discipline division: 2013-2014*. June 1. Accessed

March 1, 2017. https://nces.ed.gov/programs/digest/d15/tables/ dt15_318.30.asp?current=yes.

Northouse, Peter G. 2010. *Leadership: Theory and Practice, 5th Edition.* Thousand Oaks: Sage Publications.

Northrup, Christiane. 1998. *Women's Bodies, Women's Wisdom: Creating Physical and Emotional Health and Healing.* New York: Bantam Books.

Parrotta, P., D. Pozzoli, and M. Pytlikova. 2012. "The Nexus Between Labor Diversity and Firm's Innovation: Discussion Paper Series." *Forschunginstitut zur Zukunft der Arbeit* 6972.

Paustian-Underdahl, S., L. Walker, and D. Woehr. 2014. "Gender and Perceptions of Leadership Effectiveness." *Applied Psychology* 99 (6): 1129-1145. doi:10.1037/a0036751.

Peterson, S., F. Galvin, and D. Lange. 2012. "CEO Servant Leadership: Exploring Executive Characteristics and Firm Performance." *Personnel Psychology* 65: 565-596.

Pink, Daniel. 2006. *A Whole New Mind: Why Right-Brainers Will Rule the Future.* New York: Riverhead Books: The Penguin Group.

Platt, L., and J. Polavieja. 2014. "Nurse or Mechanic? The Role of Parental Socialization and Children's Personality in the Formation of Sex-Typed Occupational Aspirations." *Oxford Journals* 21-32. http:// sf.oxfordjournals.org/content/early/2014/05/12/sf.sou051.abstract.

Polach, J. 2006. *Working with Veterans, Boomers, Xers, Ys: It's About Their Age, Not When They Were Born.* St. Louis: Leadership Solutions.

Pucino, Janet. 2012. *Not in the Club: An Executive Woman's Journey through the Biased World of Business.* Beverly Hills: Deep Canyon Media, LLC.

Radcliffe Public Policy Center. 2000. *Life's Work: Generational Attitudes Toward Work and Life Integration.* Cambridge: Radcliffe Public Policy Center.

Representation Project. 2017. "Films." *The Representation Project.* Accessed March 28, 2017. http://therepresentationproject.org/film/miss-representation/.

Ritter, B., and J. Yoder. 2004. "Gender Differences in Leader Emergence Persist Even for Dominant Women." *Psychology of Women Quarterly* 28: 187-193. doi:10.1111/j.1471-6402.2004.00135.x.

Robbins, S, and T. Judge. 2014. *Organizational Behavior, 16th Edition.* Upper Saddle River: Pearson Education, Inc.

Roberts, Tomi-Ann, and Susan Nolan-Hoeksema. 1989. "Sex Differences in Reactions to Evaluative Feedback." *Sex Roles* 725-747.

Rutgers Eagleton Institute. 2017. "Current Numbers." *Center for American Women and Politics.* July 1. Accessed February 2, 2017. http://www.cawp.rutgers.edu/current-numbers.

Salovey, P., and J. Mayer. 1990. "Emotional Intelligence: Imagination, Cognition and Personality." *Sage Journals* 9 (3): 185-211. doi:10.2190/DUGG-P24E-52WK-6CDG.

Sandberg, Sheryl, and Adam Grant. 2015. "How Men Can Succeed in the Boardroom and Bedroom." *New York Times* 1-15. http://www.nytimes.com/2015/03/08/opinion/sunday/sheryl-sandberg-adam-grant-how-men-can-succeed-in-the-boardroom-and-the-bedroom.html?_r=0.

Sandberg, Sheryl, and Adam Grant. 2015. "Madame CEO, Get Me a Coffee." *New York Times* 1-15. http://www.nytimes.com/2015/02/08/opinion/sunday/sheryl-sandberg-and-adam-grant-on-women-doing-office-housework.html?_r=0 .

Smialek, Jeanna, and Gregory Giroux. 2015. "The Majority of American Babies are now Minority." *Bloomberg.*

Smith, David, and W. Brad Johnson. 2016. "Men Can Improve How They Mentor Women: Here's How." *Harvard Business Review.* https://hbr.org/2016/12/men-can-improve-how-they-mentor-women-heres-how?referral=00563&cm_mmc=email-_-newsletter-_-daily_alert-_-alert_date&utm_source=newsletter_daily_alert&utm_medium=email&utm_campaign=alert_date&spMailingID=16053421&spUserID=MTMyNzYzNj.

Society for Human Resource Management. 2014. *2014 Workplace Flexibilty Survey: Overview of Flexible Work Arrangements.* March 1. Accessed

November 15, 2016. https://www.shrm.org/research/surveyfindings/ articles/pages/2014-workplace-flexibility-survey.aspx.

Spencer, L., D. McClelland, and S. Kelner. 1997. *Competency Assessment Methods: History and State of the Art.* Boston: Hay/McBer.

Stein, S., and H. Book. 2011. *The EQ Edge: Emotional Intelligence and Your Success.* Mississauga: Jossey-Bass: John Wiley and Sons Canada, Ltd.

Stoller, Robert. 1964. "A Contribution to the Study of Gender Identity." *International Journal of Psychoanalysis* 45: 220-226.

Suddath, C. 2012. "The Art of Haggling." *Bloomberg Businessweek* 98.

Taylor, S., L. Cousino-Klein, and B. Lewis. 2000. "Bio-behavioral Responses to Stress in Females: Tend and Befriend, not Fight-or-Flight." *Psychological Review* 107 (3): 20.

Think Progress. 2015. *Companies in this Country Now Have to Have at Least 30 Percent Women on their Boards.* March 1. Accessed January 5, 2017. http://thinkprogress.org/economy/2015/03/09/3631312/ germany-board-quota/.

Thomas, R. 1996. *Diversity in Organizations: New Perspectives for a Changing Workplace.* Thousand Oaks: Sage.

U.S. Bureau of Labor Statistics. 2016. "Employed Persons by Detailed Industry, Sex, Race, and Hispanic or Latino Ethnicity." *U.S. Bureau of Labor Statistics.* January. Accessed December 10, 2016. https:// www.bls.gov/cps/cpsaat18.pdf.

U.S. Bureau of Labor Statistics. 2015. "Women in the Labor Force: A Databook." *U.S. Bureau of Labor Statistics.* January 1. Accessed March 20, 2017. https://www.bls.gov/opub/reports/womens-databook/archive/women-in-the-labor-force-a-databook-2015.pdf.

U.S. Department of Labor. 2014. *25 Most Common Occupations for Employed Women, 2014 Annual Averages.* January 1. Accessed January 10, 2017. http://www.dol.gov/wb/stats/most_common_occupations_for_ women.htm.

U.S. Department of Labor. 2016. "Data and Statistics: Women in the Labor Force." *U.S. Department of Labor.* June 1. Accessed February 10, 2017. https://www.dol.gov/wb/stats/stats_data.htm.

U.S. Department of Labor. 2014. "Median Annual Earnings by Sex, 1960-2014." *U.S. Department of Labor.* January 1. Accessed March 20, 2017. http://www.dol.gov/wb/stats/earnings_2014.htm.

U.S. Department of Labor. 2014. "Women's to Men's Earnings Ratio and Wage Gap." *U.S. Department of Labor.* July 1. Accessed February 5, 2017. http://www.dol.gov/wb/stats/earnings_2014.htm.

United Nations. 2011. *World Population Prospects.* April 10. Accessed March 20, 2017. http://esa.un.org/unpd/wpp/excel-data/population.htm.

Williamson, Marianne. 1992. *A Return to Love: Reflections on the Principles of a Course in Miracles.* New York: HarperCollins. http://marianne.com/a-return-to-love/ .

Willyerd, K., and J. Meister. 2010. *The 2020 Workforce: How Innovative Companies Attract, Develop, and Keep Tomorrow's Employees Today.* New York: HarperCollins.

Wittenberg-Cox, Avivah. 2016. "How CEOs Can Put Gender Balance on the Agenda at their Companies." *Harvard Business Review.* https://hbr.org/2016/11/how-ceos-can-put-gender-balance-on-the-agenda-at-their-companies?referral=00563&cm_mmc=email-_-newsletter-_-daily_alert-_-alert_date&utm_source=newsletter_daily_alert&utm_medium=email&utm_campaign=alert_date&spMailingID=16018998&sp.

Wittenberg-Cox, Avivah. 2016. "To Understand Your Company's Gender Imbalance, Make a Graph." *Harvard Business Review* https://hbr.org/2016/03/to-understand-your-companys-gender-imbalance-make-a-graph.

Woetzel, Jonathon. 2015. "How Advancing Women's Equality Can Add $12 Trillion to Global Growth." *McKinsey & Company.* September. Accessed December 10, 2016. http://www.mckinsey.com/global-themes/employment-and-growth/how-advancing-womens-equality-can-add-12-trillion-to-global-growth.

Woolley, Frances. 2003. *Marriage and the Economy: Theory and Evidence from Advanced Industrial Societies.* Cambridge: Cambridge University Press.

World Bank. 2001. *Engendering Development.* New York: Oxford University Press.

World Bank. 2016. "Women, Business and the Law: Getting to Equal." *World Bank.* January 1. Accessed 1 2017, January. http://wbl.worldbank. org/.

World Economic Forum. 2016. *The Global Gender Gap Report.* June 1. Accessed January 1, 2017. http://www3.weforum.org/docs/GGGR16/ WEF_Global_Gender_Gap_Report_2016.pdf.

World Health Organization. 2015. *World Report on Ageing and Health.* Accessed November 1, 2016. http://apps.who.int/iris/ bitstream/10665/186463/1/9789240694811_eng.pdf?ua=1.

Yammarino, F., A. Dubinsky, L. Comer, and M. Jolson. 1997. "Women and Transformational and Contingent Reward Leadership: A Multiple Levels of Analysis Perspective." *Academy of Management Journal* 40: 205-222. doi:10.2307/257027.

Young, Ernst &. 2015. *Global Generations: A Global Study on Work-Life Challenges Across Generations.* May 1. Accessed Janaury 10, 2017. http://www.ey.com/Publication/vwLUAssets/EY-global-generations- a-global-study-on-work-life-challenges-across-generations/$FILE/ EY-global-generations-a-global-study-on-work-life-challenges- across-generations.pdf.

Zaidi, Zeenat. 2010. "Gender Differences in the Human Brain: A Review." *Open Anatomy Journal* 2: 37-55.

NOTES

Introduction – The Missing Gender

1. Conable, Barber B. 1991. "The Conable Years at the World Bank: Major Policy Addresses of Barber B. Conable, 1986-91." *The World Bank.* July 10. Accessed December 15, 2016. http://documents.worldbank.org/curated/en/241661468762576834/The-Conable-years-at-the-World-Bank-major-policy-addresses-of-Barber-B-Conable-1986-91.

2. Global Footprints. 2017. *Gender Footprints.* January 1. Accessed March 22, 2017. http://www.globalfootprints.org/women.

Chapter 1 – Startling Statistics

1. Geiger, Abigail, and Lauren Kent. 2017. *Number of Women Leaders Around the World Has Grown, but They're Still a Small Group.* March 8. Accessed March 15, 2017. http://www.pewresearch.org/fact-tank/2017/03/08/women-leaders-around-the-world/.

2. Inter-Parliamentary Union. 2017. *Women in National Parliaments.* March 1. Accessed March 15, 2017. http://www.ipu.org/wmn-e/world.htm.

3. World Bank. 2016. "Women, Business and the Law: Getting to Equal." *World Bank.* January 1. Accessed 1 2017, January. http://wbl.worldbank.org/.

4. Global Footprints. 2017. *Gender Footprints.* January 1. Accessed March 22, 2017. http://www.globalfootprints.org/women.

311

5.   International Labour Organization. 2012. *ILO Global Estimates of forced Labour, Results and Methodology.* January 1. Accessed February 5, 2017. http://www.ilo.org/wcmsp5/groups/public/---ed_norm/---declaration/documents/publication/wcms_182004.pdf.

6.   Global Footprints. 2017. *Gender Footprints.* January 1. Accessed March 22, 2017. http://www.globalfootprints.org/women.

7.   U.S. Bureau of Labor Statistics. 2015. "Women in the Labor Force: A Databook." *U.S. Bureau of Labor Statistics.* January 1. Accessed March 20, 2017. https://www.bls.gov/opub/reports/womens-databook/archive/women-in-the-labor-force-a-databook-2015.pdf.

8.   National Center for Education Statistics. 2015. *Bachelor's, Master's and Doctor's Degrees Conferred by Post-Secondary Institutions, by sex of student and discipline division: 2013-2014.* June 1. Accessed March 1, 2017. https://nces.ed.gov/programs/digest/d15/tables/dt15_318.30.asp?current=yes.

9.   Rutgers Eagleton Institute. 2017. "Current Numbers." *Center for American Women and Politics.* July 1. Accessed February 2, 2017. http://www.cawp.rutgers.edu/current-numbers.

10. U.S. Department of Labor. 2014. *25 Most Common Occupations for Employed Women, 2014 Annual Averages.* January 1. Accessed January 10, 2017. http://www.dol.gov/wb/stats/most_common_occupations_for_women.htm.

11. U.S. Department of Labor. 2014. *25 Most Common Occupations for Employed Women, 2014 Annual Averages.* January 1. Accessed January 10, 2017. http://www.dol.gov/wb/stats/most_common_occupations_for_women.htm.

12. U.S. Department of Labor. 2014. "Median Annual Earnings by Sex, 1960-2014." *U.S. Department of Labor.* January 1. Accessed March 20, 2017. http://www.dol.gov/wb/stats/earnings_2014.htm.

13. U.S. Department of Labor. 2014. "Women's to Men's Earnings Ratio and Wage Gap." *U.S. Department of Labor.* July 1. Accessed February 5, 2017. http://www.dol.gov/wb/stats/earnings_2014.htm.

14. U.S. Bureau of Labor Statistics. 2016. "Employed Persons by Detailed Industry, Sex, Race, and Hispanic or Latino Ethnicity." *U.S. Bureau of Labor Statistics.* January. Accessed December 10, 2016. https://www.bls.gov/cps/cpsaat18.pdf.

15. U.S. Bureau of Labor Statistics. 2015. "Women in the Labor Force: A Databook." *U.S. Bureau of Labor Statistics.* January 1. Accessed March 20, 2017. https://www.bls.gov/opub/reports/womens-databook/archive/women-in-the-labor-force-a-databook-2015.pdf.

16. Catalyst. 2016. "Women CEOs of the S&P 500." *Catalyst.* December 1. Accessed December 31, 2016. http://www.catalyst.org/knowledge/women-ceos-sp-500.

17. Catalyst. 2015. *Still Too Few: Women of Color on Boards.* March 17. Accessed September 1, 2016. http://www.catalyst.org/knowledge/still-too-few-women-color-boards.

18. Pucino, Janet. 2012. *Not in the Club: An Executive Woman's Journey through the Biased World of Business.* Beverly Hills: Deep Canyon Media, LLC.

19. Catalyst. 2014. "Women's Share of Board Seats at Asia-Pacific Stock Index Companies." *Catalyst.* October 1. Accessed November 5, 2016. http://www.catalyst.org/knowledge/2014-catalyst-census-women-board-directors.

20. Think Progress. 2015. *Companies in this Country Now Have to Have at Least 30 Percent Women on their Boards.* March 1. Accessed January 5, 2017. http://thinkprogress.org/economy/2015/03/09/3631312/germany-board-quota/.

21. Catalyst. 2007. "The Bottom Line: Corporate Performance and Women's Representation on Boards." *Catalyst.* October 1. Accessed January 10, 2017. http://www.catalyst.org/knowledge/bottom-line-corporate-performance-and-womens-representation-boards.

22. McKinsey & Company; Leanin.org. 2016. "Women in the Workplace 2016." *McKinsey & Company.* September 1. Accessed October 1, 2016. http://www.mckinsey.com/business-functions/organization/our-insights/women-in-the-workplace-2016.

23. World Economic Forum. 2016. *The Global Gender Gap Report.* June 1. Accessed January 1, 2017. http://www3.weforum.org/docs/GGGR16/WEF_Global_Gender_Gap_Report_2016.pdf.

24. World Economic Forum. 2016. *The Global Gender Gap Report.* June 1. Accessed January 1, 2017. http://www3.weforum.org/docs/GGGR16/WEF_Global_Gender_Gap_Report_2016.pdf.

25. World Economic Forum. 2016. *The Global Gender Gap Report.* June 1. Accessed January 1, 2017. http://www3.weforum.org/docs/GGGR16/WEF_Global_ Gender_Gap_Report_2016.pdf.

26. World Economic Forum. 2016. *The Global Gender Gap Report.* June 1. Accessed January 1, 2017. http://www3.weforum.org/docs/GGGR16/WEF_Global_ Gender_Gap_Report_2016.pdf.

27. McKinsey & Company; Leanin.org. 2016. "Women in the Workplace 2016." *McKinsey & Company.* September 1. Accessed October 1, 2016. http://www.mckinsey. com/business-functions/organization/our-insights/women-in-the-workplace-2016.

Chapter 2 – Leadership is Leadership, or is It?

1. Northouse, Peter G. 2010. *Leadership: Theory and Practice, 5th Edition.* Thousand Oaks: Sage Publications.

2. Burns, J. 1978. *Leadership.* New York: Harper and Row.

3. Bass, B. 1990. "From Transactional to Transformational Leadership: Learning to Share the Vision." *Organizational Dynamics* 18: 19-31. doi:10.1016/0090-2616(90)90061-S.

4. Jogulu, U., and G. Wood. 2006. "The Role of Leadership Theory in Raising the Profile of Women in Management." *Equal Opportunities International* 25 (4): 236-250. doi:10.1108/02610150610706230.

5. Yammarino, F., A. Dubinsky, L. Comer, and M. Jolson. 1997. "Women and Transformational and Contingent Reward Leadership: A Multiple Levels of Analysis Perspective." *Academy of Management Journal* 40: 205-222. doi:10.2307/257027.

6. Mandell, B., and S. Perwani. 2003. "Relationship Between Emotional Intelligence and TL Style: A Gender Comparison." *Journal of Business and Psychology* 17 (3): 387-404.

7. Eagly, A., and L. Carli. 2003. "The Female Leadership Advantage: An Evaluation of the Evidence." *The Leadership Quarterly* 14 (6): 807-834. doi:10.1016/j. leaqua.2003.09.004.

8. Helgesen, Sally. 2005. *The Web of Inclusion: Architecture for Building Great Organizations.* Washington D.C.: Beard Books.

9. Boatwright, K., and L. Forrest. 2000. "Leadership Preferences: The Influence of Gender and Needs for Connection on Worker's Ideal Preferences for

Leadership Behaviors." *Journal of Leadership and Organizational Studies* 7 (2): 18-34. doi:10.1177/107179190000700202.

10. Northouse, Peter G. 2010. *Leadership: Theory and Practice, 5th Edition.* Thousand Oaks: Sage Publications.

11. Eagly, A., S. Karau, and M. Makhijani. 1995. "Gender and the Effectiveness of Leaders: A Meta-analysis." *Psychological Bulletin* 117: 125-145. doi:10.1037/0033-2909.117.1.125.

12. Northouse, Peter G. 2010. *Leadership: Theory and Practice, 5th Edition.* Thousand Oaks: Sage Publications.

13. Paustian-Underdahl, S., L. Walker, and D. Woehr. 2014. "Gender and Perceptions of Leadership Effectiveness." *Applied Psychology* 99 (6): 1129-1145. doi:10.1037/a0036751.

14. Robbins, S, and T. Judge. 2014. *Organizational Behavior, 16th Edition.* Upper Saddle River: Pearson Education, Inc.

15. Carter, A. 2006. "Lighting a Fire Under Campbell." *Business Week* 96-101.

16. Peterson, S., F. Galvin, and D. Lange. 2012. "CEO Servant Leadership: Exploring Executive Characteristics and Firm Performance." *Personnel Psychology* 65: 565-596.

Chapter 3 – Why You Should Care About EQ

1. Greenstein, F. 2001. *The Presidential Difference: Leadership Style from FDR to Clinton.* Princeton: Princeton University Press.

2. Salovey, P., and J. Mayer. 1990. "Emotional Intelligence: Imagination, Cognition and Personality." *Sage Journals* 9 (3): 185-211. doi:10.2190/DUGG-P24E-52WK-6CDG.

3. Andrews, Shawn D. 2013. *Emotional Intelligence Implications on the Career Advancement of Women in a Fortune 500 Pharmaceutical Company.* Dissertation, Ann Arbor: ProQuest, LLC.

4. Robbins, S, and T. Judge. 2014. *Organizational Behavior, 16th Edition.* Upper Saddle River: Pearson Education, Inc.

5. Murry, B. 1998. "Does Emotional Intelligence Matter in the Workplace." *APA Monitor* 29 (7): 156.

6. Stein, S., and H. Book. 2011. *The EQ Edge: Emotional Intelligence and Your Success.* Mississauga: Jossey-Bass: John Wiley and Sons Canada, Ltd.

7. Helgesen, Sally. 2010. *The Female Vision: Women's Real Power at Work.* San Francisco: Berrett-Koehler Publishers.

8. Hopkins, M., and D. Bilimoria. 2008. "Social and Emotional Competencies Predicting Success for Male and Female Executives." *Journal of Management Development* 27 (1): 13-35. doi:10.1108/02621710810840749 .

9. Bradberry, T., and J. Greaves. 2009. *Emotional Intelligence 2.0.* San Diego: TalentSmart.

10. Spencer, L., D. McClelland, and S. Kelner. 1997. *Competency Assessment Methods: History and State of the Art.* Boston: Hay/McBer.

11. Center for Creative Leadership. 2003. *Leadership Skills and Emotional Intelligence.* June 15. Accessed January 10, 2017. https://myccl.ccl.org/leadership/pdf/assessments/skills_intelligence.pdf.

12. Goleman, Daniel. 2000. "Leadership that Gets Results." *Harvard Business Review* 1-15.

13. Goleman, Daniel. 2000. "Leadership that Gets Results." *Harvard Business Review* 1-15.

14. Stein, S., and H. Book. 2011. *The EQ Edge: Emotional Intelligence and Your Success.* Mississauga: Jossey-Bass: John Wiley and Sons Canada, Ltd.

15. Stein, S., and H. Book. 2011. *The EQ Edge: Emotional Intelligence and Your Success.* Mississauga: Jossey-Bass: John Wiley and Sons Canada, Ltd.

16. Bradberry, T., and J. Greaves. 2009. *Emotional Intelligence 2.0.* San Diego: TalentSmart.

17. Stein, S., and H. Book. 2011. *The EQ Edge: Emotional Intelligence and Your Success.* Mississauga: Jossey-Bass: John Wiley and Sons Canada, Ltd.

18. Stein, S., and H. Book. 2011. *The EQ Edge: Emotional Intelligence and Your Success.* Mississauga: Jossey-Bass: John Wiley and Sons Canada, Ltd.

19. Bradberry, T., and J. Greaves. 2009. *Emotional Intelligence 2.0.* San Diego: TalentSmart.

Chapter 4 – A Bit of Research Goes a Long Way

1. Eagly, A., and L. Carli. 2003. "The Female Leadership Advantage: An Evaluation of the Evidence." *The Leadership Quarterly* 14 (6): 807-834. doi:10.1016/j. leaqua.2003.09.004.

2. Goleman, Daniel. 1998. *Working with Emotional Intelligence.* New York: Bantam Dell.

3. Multi-Health Systems. 2012. "EQ-i 2.0 FAQ." *Multi-Health Systems.* Accessed October 25, 2016. http://ei.mhs.com/EQi20FAQ.aspx.

4. Bradberry, T., and J. Greaves. 2009. *Emotional Intelligence 2.0.* San Diego: TalentSmart.

5. Goleman, Daniel. 1998. *Working with Emotional Intelligence.* New York: Bantam Dell.

Chapter 5 – The Power of Bias

1. Eagly, A. and L. Carli. 2007. *Through the Labyrinth: The Truth About How Women Become Leaders.* Boston: Harvard Business School Press.

2. Hewlett, Sylvia Ann. 2014. "What's Holding Women Back in Science and Technology Industries." *Harvard Business Review* 1-15.

3. Ritter, B., and J. Yoder. 2004. "Gender Differences in Leader Emergence Persist Even for Dominant Women." *Psychology of Women Quarterly* 28: 187-193. doi:10.1111/j.1471-6402.2004.00135.x.

4. Suddath, C. 2012. "The Art of Haggling." *Bloomberg Businessweek* 98.

5. Hofstede, Geert. 1991. *Cultures and Organizations: Software of the Mind.* London: McGraw-Hill.

6. Greenwald, T., M. Banaji, and B. Nosek. 2007. *Project Implicit.* January 1. Accessed January 31, 2017. https://implicit.harvard.edu/implicit/aboutus.html.

7. Eagly, A. and L. Carli. 2007. *Through the Labyrinth: The Truth About How Women Become Leaders.* Boston: Harvard Business School Press.

8. Barsh, J., and L. Yee. 2012. "Unlocking the Full Potential of Women at Work." *McKinsey & Company.* April 1. Accessed August 10, 2017. http://www.mckinsey.com/business-functions/organization/our-insights/unlocking-the-full-potential-of-women-at-work.

9. Robbins, S, and T. Judge. 2014. *Organizational Behavior, 16th Edition.* Upper Saddle River: Pearson Education, Inc.

Chapter 6 – The Glass Golf Club

1. Pucino, Janet. 2012. *Not in the Club: An Executive Woman's Journey through the Biased World of Business.* Beverly Hills: Deep Canyon Media, LLC.

2. Eagly, A. and L. Carli. 2007. *Through the Labyrinth: The Truth About How Women Become Leaders.* Boston: Harvard Business School Press.

3. Robbins, S, and T. Judge. 2014. *Organizational Behavior, 16th Edition.* Upper Saddle River: Pearson Education, Inc.

4. Heim, P., S. Murphy, and S. Golant. 2001. *In the Company of Women.* New York: Penguin Putnam, Inc.

5. Heim, P., S. Murphy, and S. Golant. 2001. *In the Company of Women.* New York: Penguin Putnam, Inc.

6. McKinsey & Company; Leanin.org. 2016. "Women in the Workplace 2016." *McKinsey & Company.* September 1. Accessed October 1, 2016. http://www.mckinsey.com/business-functions/organization/our-insights/women-in-the-workplace-2016.

7. Ibarra, H., N. Carter, and C. Silva. 2010. "Why Men Still Get More Promotions than Women." *Harvard Business Review* 1-15. https://hbr.org/2010/09/why-men-still-get-more-promotions-than-women/ar/1?referral=00134.

8. Lollis, Helene. 2016. "Making it Personal: The Four Pillars of High-Impact Mentoring." *Training Industry Magazine* 20-28.

Chapter 7 – Lead the Meeting, Change the Diaper

1. Ernst & Young. 2015. "Global Generations: A Global Study on Work-life Challenges Across Generations." *Ernst & Young.* Accessed September 28, 2016. http://www.ey.com/Publication/vwLUAssets/EY-global-generations-a-global-study-on-work-life-challenges-across-generations/$FILE/EY-global-generations-a-global-study-on-work-life-challenges-across-generations.pdf.

2. Ernst & Young. 2015. "Global Generations: A Global Study on Work-life Challenges Across Generations." *Ernst & Young.* Accessed September 28, 2016. http://www.ey.com/Publication/vwLUAssets/EY-global-generations-a-global-study-on-work-life-challenges-across-generations/$FILE/EY-global-generations-a-global-study-on-work-life-challenges-across-generations.pdf.

3. Gemba Marketing. 2016. *The Millennial Shift: Work-Life Balance vs. Work-Life Integration.* March 1. Accessed December 20, 2016. http://gembamarketing. com/the-millennial-shift-work-life-balance-vs-work-life-integration/.

4. Ernst & Young. 2015. "Global Generations: A Global Study on Work-life Challenges Across Generations." *Ernst & Young.* Accessed September 28, 2016. http://www.ey.com/Publication/vwLUAssets/EY-global-generations-a-global-study-on-work-life-challenges-across-generations/$FILE/EY-global-generations-a-global-study-on-work-life-challenges-across-generations.pdf.

5. McKinsey & Company; Leanin.org. 2016. "Women in the Workplace 2016." *McKinsey & Company.* September 1. Accessed October 1, 2016. http://www.mckinsey. com/business-functions/organization/our-insights/women-in-the-workplace-2016.

6. Duckworth, Angela. 2016. *Grit: The Power of Passion and Perseverance.* New York: Simon & Schuster.

7. U.S. Department of Labor. 2016. "Data and Statistics: Women in the Labor Force." *U.S. Department of Labor.* June 1. Accessed February 10, 2017. https://www. dol.gov/wb/stats/stats_data.htm.

8. McKinsey & Company; Leanin.org. 2016. "Women in the Workplace 2016." *McKinsey & Company.* September 1. Accessed October 1, 2016. http://www.mckinsey. com/business-functions/organization/our-insights/women-in-the-workplace-2016.

9. Lapierre, L., and T. Allen. 2012. "Control at Work, Control at Home and Planning Behavior: Implications for Work-Family Conflict." *Journal of Management* 1500-1516.

10. Brummelhuis, L. 2012. "A Resource Perspective on the Work-Home Interface." *American Psychologist* 545-556.

11. Butts, M., W. Caster, and T. Yang. 2013. "How Important are Work-Family Support Policies? A Meta-Analytic Investigation of their Efforts on Employee Outcomes." *Journal of Applied Psychology* 98: 1-25.

12. McKinsey & Company; Leanin.org. 2016. "Women in the Workplace 2016." *McKinsey & Company.* September 1. Accessed October 1, 2016. http://www.mckinsey. com/business-functions/organization/our-insights/women-in-the-workplace-2016.

13. Ernst & Young. 2015. "Global Generations: A Global Study on Work-life Challenges Across Generations." *Ernst & Young.* Accessed September 28, 2016. http://www.ey.com/Publication/vwLUAssets/EY-global-generations-a-global-study-

on-work-life-challenges-across-generations/$FILE/EY-global-generations-a-global-study-on-work-life-challenges-across-generations.pdf.

14. Hirst, Peter. 2016. "How a Flex-time Program at MIT Improved Productivity, Resilence, and Trust." *Harvard Business Review* 1-15. https://hbr.org/2016/06/how-a-flex-time-program-at-mit-improved-productivity-resilience-and-trust?referral=00563&cm_mmc=email-_-newsletter-_-daily_alert-_-alert_date&utm_source=newsletter_daily_alert&utm_medium=email&utm_campaign=alert_date.

15. Society for Human Resource Management. 2014. *2014 Workplace Flexibilty Survey: Overview of Flexible Work Arrangements.* March 1. Accessed November 15, 2016. https://www.shrm.org/research/surveyfindings/articles/pages/2014-workplace-flexibility-survey.aspx.

16. Hirst, Peter. 2016. "How a Flex-time Program at MIT Improved Productivity, Resilience, and Trust." *Harvard Business Review* 1-15. https://hbr.org/2016/06/how-a-flex-time-program-at-mit-improved-productivity-resilience-and-trust?referral=00563&cm_mmc=email-_-newsletter-_-daily_alert-_-alert_date&utm_source=newsletter_daily_alert&utm_medium=email&utm_campaign=alert_date.

17. Coltrane, Scott. 2004. "2004." *Journal of Marriage and Family* 62 (4): 1208-1233. doi:10.1111/j.1741-3737.2000.01208.x/abstract.

18. Brown, S., R. Neese, A. Vinokur, and D. Smith. 2003. "Providing Social Support May be More Beneficial than Receiving it: Results from a Prospective Study of Mortality." *Psychology Science* 20-35. http://pss.sagepub.com/content/14/4/320.short.

19. Croft, A., T. Schmader, K. Block, and A. Baron. 2014. "The Second Shift Reflected in the Second Generation: Do Parent's Gender Roles at Home Predict Children's Aspirations?" *Psychological Science* 1-15. http://www.ncbi.nlm.nih.gov/pubmed/24890499.

20. Lamb, Michael. 2010. *The Role of the Father in Child Development.* Hoboken: John Wiley & Sons.

21. Woolley, Frances. 2003. *Marriage and the Economy: Theory and Evidence from Advanced Industrial Societies.* Cambridge: Cambridge University Press.

22. Radcliffe Public Policy Center. 2000. *Life's Work: Generational Attitudes Toward Work and Life Integration.* Cambridge: Radcliffe Public Policy Center.

23. Sandberg, Sheryl, and Adam Grant. 2015. "How Men Can Succeed in the Boardroom and Bedroom." *New York Times* 1-15. http://www.nytimes.com/2015/03/08/opinion/sunday/sheryl-sandberg-adam-grant-how-men-can-succeed-in-the-boardroom-and-the-bedroom.html?_r=0.

24. Brown, Brene. 2010. "The Power of Vulnerability." *TEDxHouston.* June 1. Accessed June 30, 2016. https://www.ted.com/talks/brene_brown_on_vulnerability?language=en.

25. Ephron, Nora. 1996. "1996 Commencement Address." *Wellesley College.* June 15. Accessed January 1, 2017. http://new.wellesley.edu/events/commencementarchives/1996commencement.

Chapter 8 – Are We Limiting Ourselves?

1. Platt, L., and J. Polavieja. 2014. "Nurse or Mechanic? The Role of Parental Socialization and Children's Personality in the Formation of Sex-Typed Occupational Aspirations." *Oxford Journals* 21-32. http://sf.oxfordjournals.org/content/early/2014/05/12/sf.sou051.abstract.

2. Barsh, J., and L. Yee. 2012. "Unlocking the Full Potential of Women at Work." *McKinsey & Company.* April 1. Accessed August 10, 2017. http://www.mckinsey.com/business-functions/organization/our-insights/unlocking-the-full-potential-of-women-at-work.

3. Barsh, J., and L. Yee. 2012. "Unlocking the Full Potential of Women at Work." *McKinsey & Company.* April 1. Accessed August 10, 2017. http://www.mckinsey.com/business-functions/organization/our-insights/unlocking-the-full-potential-of-women-at-work.

4. Dimaratino, Mediha. 2016. "Why Advantage Solution's Boss Chose to Lean In." *Orange County Business Journal* 18-25. www.ocbj.com.

5. Desvaux, G., S. Devillard-Hoellinger, and M. Meaney. 2008. "A Business Case for Women." *The McKinsey Quarterly* 10-32. Accessed October 8, 2016. http://www.rctaylor.com/images/A_Business_Case_for_Women.pdf.

6. Dimaratino, Mediha. 2016. "Why Advantage Solution's Boss Chose to Lean In." *Orange County Business Journal* 18-25. www.ocbj.com.

7. Sandberg, Sheryl, and Adam Grant. 2015. "Madame CEO, Get Me a Coffee." *New York Times* 1-15. http://www.nytimes.com/2015/02/08/opinion/sunday/sheryl-sandberg-and-adam-grant-on-women-doing-office-housework.html?_r=0 .

8. Heim, P., and S. Golant. 2005. *Hardball for Women: Winning at the Game of Business*. New York: Plume: Penguin Group.

9. Roberts, Tomi-Ann, and Susan Nolan-Hoeksema. 1989. "Sex Differences in Reactions to Evaluative Feedback." *Sex Roles* 725-747.

10. Anderson, Cameron, and Gavin Kilduff. 2009. "Why Do Dominant Personalities Attain Influence in Face-to-face Groups? The Competence Signaling Effects of Trait Dominance." *Journal of Personality and Social Psychology* 96 (2): 491-503. doi:10.1037/a0014201.

11. Lind, Scott. 2002. "Competency-based Student Self-assessment on a Surgery Rotation." *Journal of Surgical Research* 105 (1): 31-34.

12. Heim, P., S. Murphy, and S. Golant. 2001. *In the Company of Women*. New York: Penguin Putnam, Inc.

13. Heim, P., and S. Golant. 2005. *Hardball for Women: Winning at the Game of Business*. New York: Plume: Penguin Group.

14. Heim, P., S. Murphy, and S. Golant. 2001. *In the Company of Women*. New York: Penguin Putnam, Inc.

15. Heim, P., S. Murphy, and S. Golant. 2001. *In the Company of Women*. New York: Penguin Putnam, Inc.

16. Drory, A., and T. Romm. 1990. "The Definition of Organizational Politics: A Review." *Human Relations* 1133-1154.

17. Frankel, Lois. 2014. *Nice Girls Still Don't Get the Corner Office: Unconscious Mistakes Women Make that Sabotage their Careers*. New York: Hachette Book Group.

18. Kacmar, K., D. Bachrach, K. Harris, and S. Zivnuska. 2011. "Fostering Good Citizenship through Ethical Leadership: Exploring the Moderating Role of Gender and Organizational Politics." *Journal of Applied Psychology* 96: 633-642.

19. Hewlett, Sylvia Ann. 2013. "Executive Presence." *Center of Talent Innovation*. August 1. Accessed January 15, 2017. http://www.talentinnovation.org/assets/ExecutivePresence-KeyFindings-CTI.pdf.

20. Hewlett, Sylvia Ann. 2013. "Executive Presence." *Center of Talent Innovation.* August 1. Accessed January 15, 2017. http://www.talentinnovation.org/assets/ExecutivePresence-KeyFindings-CTI.pdf.

21. Sandberg, Sheryl, and Adam Grant. 2015. "Madame CEO, Get Me a Coffee." *New York Times* 1-15. http://www.nytimes.com/2015/02/08/opinion/sunday/sheryl-sandberg-and-adam-grant-on-women-doing-office-housework.html?_r=0 .

22. Williamson, Marianne. 1992. *A Return to Love: Reflections on the Principles of a Course in Miracles.* New York: HarperCollins. http://marianne.com/a-return-to-love/ .

Chapter 9 – Why Does S/He Do That?

1. Heim, P., and S. Golant. 2005. *Hardball for Women: Winning at the Game of Business.* New York: Plume: Penguin Group.

2. Stoller, Robert. 1964. "A Contribution to the Study of Gender Identity." *International Journal of Psychoanalysis* 45: 220-226.

3. Heim, P., S. Murphy, and S. Golant. 2001. *In the Company of Women.* New York: Penguin Putnam, Inc.

4. Heim, P., and S. Golant. 2005. *Hardball for Women: Winning at the Game of Business.* New York: Plume: Penguin Group.

5. Heim, P., and S. Golant. 2005. *Hardball for Women: Winning at the Game of Business.* New York: Plume: Penguin Group.

6. Gottman, John, and Nan Silver. 1994. *Why Marriages Succeed or Fail.* New York: Fireside.

7. Gurian, Michael. 2004. *What Could He Be Thinking? A Guide to the Mysteries of a Man's Mind.* New York: St. Martin's Griffin.

8. Heim, P., S. Murphy, and S. Golant. 2001. *In the Company of Women.* New York: Penguin Putnam, Inc.

9. Fisher, Helen. 2000. *The First Sex: The Natural Talents of Women and How They are Changing the World.* New York: Ballantine Books.

10. Helgesen, Sally. 2010. *The Female Vision: Women's Real Power at Work.* San Francisco: Berrett-Koehler Publishers.

11. Pink, Daniel. 2006. *A Whole New Mind: Why Right-Brainers Will Rule the Future.* New York: Riverhead Books: The Penguin Group.

12. Friedman, Thomas. 2007. *The World is Flat: A Brief History of the Twenty-first Century.* New York: Picador.

13. Friedman, Thomas. 2007. *The World is Flat: A Brief History of the Twenty-first Century.* New York: Picador.

14. Zaidi, Zeenat. 2010. "Gender Differences in the Human Brain: A Review." *Open Anatomy Journal* 2: 37-55.

15. Fields, R. Douglas. 2008. "White Matter Matters." *Scientific American* 298 (3): 54-61.

16. Northrup, Christiane. 1998. *Women's Bodies, Women's Wisdom: Creating Physical and Emotional Health and Healing.* New York: Bantam Books.

17. Northrup, Christiane. 1998. *Women's Bodies, Women's Wisdom: Creating Physical and Emotional Health and Healing.* New York: Bantam Books.

18. Taylor, S., L. Cousino-Klein, and B. Lewis. 2000. "Bio-behavioral Responses to Stress in Females: Tend and Befriend, not Fight-or-Flight." *Psychological Review* 107 (3): 20.

19. Heim, P., and S. Golant. 2005. *Hardball for Women: Winning at the Game of Business.* New York: Plume: Penguin Group.

20. Annis, Barbara, and Keith Merron. 2014. *Gender Intelligence.* New York: HarperCollins Publishers.

21. Heim, P., and S. Golant. 2005. *Hardball for Women: Winning at the Game of Business.* New York: Plume: Penguin Group.

22. Heim, P., and S. Golant. 2005. *Hardball for Women: Winning at the Game of Business.* New York: Plume: Penguin Group.

23. Heim, P., and S. Golant. 2005. *Hardball for Women: Winning at the Game of Business.* New York: Plume: Penguin Group.

24. Heim, P., and S. Golant. 2005. *Hardball for Women: Winning at the Game of Business.* New York: Plume: Penguin Group.

25. Heim, P., and S. Golant. 2005. *Hardball for Women: Winning at the Game of Business.* New York: Plume: Penguin Group.

26. Heim, P., and S. Golant. 2005. *Hardball for Women: Winning at the Game of Business.* New York: Plume: Penguin Group.

27. Heim, P., and S. Golant. 2005. *Hardball for Women: Winning at the Game of Business.* New York: Plume: Penguin Group.

28. Heim, P., and S. Golant. 2005. *Hardball for Women: Winning at the Game of Business*. New York: Plume: Penguin Group.

29. Lendrem, Ben, Dennis Lendrem, Andy Gray, and John Isaacs. 2014. *The Darwin Awards: Sex Differences in Idiotic Behavior*. December 11. Accessed December 2, 2016. http://www.bmj.com/content/349/bmj.g7094.

30. Heim, P., and S. Golant. 2005. *Hardball for Women: Winning at the Game of Business*. New York: Plume: Penguin Group.

31. Robbins, S, and T. Judge. 2014. *Organizational Behavior, 16th Edition*. Upper Saddle River: Pearson Education, Inc.

32. Amanatullah, E., and M. Morris. 2010. "Negotiating Gender Roles: Gender Differences in Assertive Negotiating are Mediated by Women's Fear of Backlash and Attenuated when Negotiating on Behalf of Others." *Journal of Personality and Social Psychology* 98 (2): 256-267.

33. Annis, Barbara, and John Gray. 2013. *Work with Me: The 8 Blind Spots Between Men and Women in Business*. New York: Palgrave Macmillan.

34. Heim, P., and S. Golant. 2005. *Hardball for Women: Winning at the Game of Business*. New York: Plume: Penguin Group.

35. Heim, P., and S. Golant. 2005. *Hardball for Women: Winning at the Game of Business*. New York: Plume: Penguin Group.

36. Heim, P., and S. Golant. 2005. *Hardball for Women: Winning at the Game of Business*. New York: Plume: Penguin Group.

37. Heim, P., and S. Golant. 2005. *Hardball for Women: Winning at the Game of Business*. New York: Plume: Penguin Group.

38. Heim, P., and S. Golant. 2005. *Hardball for Women: Winning at the Game of Business*. New York: Plume: Penguin Group.

39. Heim, P., and S. Golant. 2005. *Hardball for Women: Winning at the Game of Business*. New York: Plume: Penguin Group.

Chapter 10 – Diversify or Die

1. Smialek, Jeanna, and Gregory Giroux. 2015. "The Majority of American Babies are now Minority." *Bloomberg*.

2. United Nations. 2011. *World Population Prospects*. April 10. Accessed March 20, 2017. http://esa.un.org/unpd/wpp/excel-data/population.htm.

3. Mor Barak, Michalle. 2014. *Managing Diversity: Toward a Globally Inclusive Workplace, 3rd Edition.* Thousand Oaks: Sage.

4. United Nations. 2011. *World Population Prospects.* April 10. Accessed March 20, 2017. http://esa.un.org/unpd/wpp/excel-data/population.htm.

5. Davis, S. 2009. "President's First Law: Obama Signs Lilly Ledbetter Wage Bill." *Wall Street Journal.*

6. Mor Barak, Michalle. 2014. *Managing Diversity: Toward a Globally Inclusive Workplace, 3rd Edition.* Thousand Oaks: Sage.

7. World Bank. 2001. *Engendering Development.* New York: Oxford University Press.

8. Mor Barak, Michalle. 2014. *Managing Diversity: Toward a Globally Inclusive Workplace, 3rd Edition.* Thousand Oaks: Sage.

9. Catalyst. 2007. "The Bottom Line: Corporate Performance and Women's Representation on Boards." *Catalyst.* October 1. Accessed January 10, 2017. http://www.catalyst.org/knowledge/bottom-line-corporate-performance-and-womens-representation-boards.

10. Dezso, Cristian, and David Gaddis Ross. 2012. "Does Female Representation in top Management Improve Firm Performance? A Panel Data Investigation." *Strategic Management Journal* 33 (9).

11. Higgs, M., U. Plewnia, and J. Ploch. 2005. "Influence of Team Composition and Task Complexity on Team Performance." *Team Performance Management* 11 (7).

12. Parrotta, P., D. Pozzoli, and M. Pytlikova. 2012. "The Nexus Between Labor Diversity and Firm's Innovation: Discussion Paper Series." *Forschunginstitut zur Zukunft der Arbeit* 6972.

13. Avery, D., P. McKay, S. Tonidandel, S Volpone, and M. Morris. 2012. "Is There a Method to the Madness? Examining how Racioethinic Matching Influences Retail Store Productivity." *Personnel Psychology* 65.

14. Hewlett, Sylvia Ann, Melinda Marshall, Laura Sherbin, and Tara Gonsalves. 2013. "Innovation, Diversity and Market Growth." *Center for Talent Innovation.* September 15. Accessed November 2, 2016. www.talentinnovation.org.

15. Corporate Executive Board. 2013. "Creating Competitive Advantage Through Workforce Diversity." *Corporate Executive Board.* June 1. Accessed January 5, 2017. www.executiveboard.com.

16. Healthcare Businesswomen's Association. 2016. "Addressing Gender Parity: Male Leaders on the Topic of Women in Leadership Positions." *HBA Advantage Magazine.*

17. Human Rights Campaign. 2016. *The Need for Full Federal LGBT Equality.* June 15. Accessed March 10, 2017. http://hrc.org/fullfederalequality/.

18. Burns, Crosby. 2012. *Center for American Progress.* March 10. Accessed March 20, 2017. https://www.americanprogress.org/wp-content/uploads/issues/2012/03/pdf/lgbt_biz_discrimination.pdf.

19. Human Rights Campaign. 2017. "Corporate Equality Index 2017: Rating Workplaces on Lesbian, Gay, Bisexual and Transgender Equality." *Human Rights Campaign.* January 1. Accessed March 25, 2017. http://assets.hrc.org//files/assets/resources/CEI-2017-FinalReport.pdf?_ga=1.214675217.746753115.1490401864.

20. Google. 2016. *Google Diversity.* Accessed December 20, 2016. https://www.google.com/diversity/index.html.

21. Amazon. 2016. *Diversity at Amazon.* Accessed December 20, 2016. https://www.amazon.com/b?node=10080092011.

22. Microsoft. 2016. *Global Diversity and Inclusion.* Accessed December 20, 2016. https://www.microsoft.com/en-us/diversity/inside-microsoft/default.aspx#epgDivFocusArea.

23. Intel. 2016. *2016 Diversity Mid-year Progress Report.* June 1. Accessed December 20, 2016. http://www.intel.com/content/www/us/en/diversity/diversity-in-technology-report.html.

24. Corporate Executive Board. 2013. "Creating Competitive Advantage Through Workforce Diversity." *Corporate Executive Board.* June 1. Accessed January 5, 2017. www.executiveboard.com.

25. Thomas, R. 1996. *Diversity in Organizations: New Perspectives for a Changing Workplace.* Thousand Oaks: Sage.

26. Mor Barak, Michalle. 2014. *Managing Diversity: Toward a Globally Inclusive Workplace, 3rd Edition.* Thousand Oaks: Sage.

27. Mor Barak, Michalle. 2014. *Managing Diversity: Toward a Globally Inclusive Workplace, 3rd Edition.* Thousand Oaks: Sage.

28. Mor Barak, Michalle. 2014. *Managing Diversity: Toward a Globally Inclusive Workplace, 3rd Edition.* Thousand Oaks: Sage.

29. Crenshaw, Kimberle. 2016. "Why Intersectionality Can't Wait." *The Washington Post.* https://www.washingtonpost.com/news/in-theory/wp/2015/09/24/why-intersectionality-cant-wait/?utm_term=.19b06ca7712c.

Chapter 11 – Could Millennials Save the Day?

1. World Health Organization. 2015. *World Report on Ageing and Health.* Accessed November 1, 2016. http://apps.who.int/iris/bitstream/10665/186463/1/9789240694811_eng.pdf?ua=1.

2. Desilver, Drew. 2016. "More Older Americans are Working, and Working More, Than They Used to." *Pew Research Center.* June 20. Accessed October 10, 2016. http://www.pewresearch.org/fact-tank/2016/06/20/more-older-americans-are-working-and-working-more-than-they-used-to/.

3. Willyerd, K., and J. Meister. 2010. *The 2020 Workforce: How Innovative Companies Attract, Develop, and Keep Tomorrow's Employees Today.* New York: HarperCollins.

4. Polach, J. 2006. *Working with Veterans, Boomers, Xers, Ys: It's About Their Age, Not When They Were Born.* St. Louis: Leadership Solutions.

5. Fry, Richard. 2016. "Millennials Overtake Baby Boomers as America's Largest Generation." *Pew Research Center.* April 25. Accessed January 8, 2017. http://www.pewresearch.org/fact-tank/2016/04/25/Millennials-overtake-baby-Boomers/.

6. Fry, Richard. 2016. "Millennials Overtake Baby Boomers as America's Largest Generation." *Pew Research Center.* April 25. Accessed January 8, 2017. http://www.pewresearch.org/fact-tank/2016/04/25/Millennials-overtake-baby-Boomers/.

7. Brody, E., and L. Bradley. 2008. "Generational Differences in Virtual Teams." In *The Handbook of High-Performing Virtual Teams*, by J. Nemiro, M. Beyerlein, L. Bradley and S. Beyerlein, 263-271. San Francisco: Jossey-Bass.

8. Fry, Richard. 2016. "Millennials Overtake Baby Boomers as America's Largest Generation." *Pew Research Center.* April 25. Accessed January 8, 2017. http://www.pewresearch.org/fact-tank/2016/04/25/Millennials-overtake-baby-Boomers/.

9. Fry, Richard. 2016. "Millennials Overtake Baby Boomers as America's Largest Generation." *Pew Research Center.* April 25. Accessed January 8, 2017. http://www.pewresearch.org/fact-tank/2016/04/25/Millennials-overtake-baby-Boomers/.

10. Fry, Richard. 2016. "Millennials Overtake Baby Boomers as America's Largest Generation." *Pew Research Center.* April 25. Accessed January 8, 2017. http://www.pewresearch.org/fact-tank/2016/04/25/Millennials-overtake-baby-Boomers/.

11. Fry, Richard. 2016. "Millennials Overtake Baby Boomers as America's Largest Generation." *Pew Research Center.* April 25. Accessed January 8, 2017. http://www.pewresearch.org/fact-tank/2016/04/25/Millennials-overtake-baby-Boomers/.

12. Fry, Richard. 2016. "Millennials Overtake Baby Boomers as America's Largest Generation." *Pew Research Center.* April 25. Accessed January 8, 2017. http://www.pewresearch.org/fact-tank/2016/04/25/Millennials-overtake-baby-Boomers/.

13. Foley, Meghan. 2015. *This is What the Recession Did to Millennials: The Cheat Sheet.* May 13. Accessed December 1, 2016. http://www.cheatsheet.com/politics/this-is-what-the-recession-did-to-Millennials.html/?a=viewall.

14. Barnett, Chance. 2015. "Trends Show Crowdfunding to Surpass VC in 2016." *Forbes.*

15. Deloitte. 2016. "The 2016 Deloitte Millennial Survey: Winning Over the Next Generation of Leaders." *Deloitte.* Accessed November 17, 2016. www.deloitte.com/MillennialSurvey.

16. Deloitte. 2016. "The 2016 Deloitte Millennial Survey: Winning Over the Next Generation of Leaders." *Deloitte.* Accessed November 17, 2016. www.deloitte.com/MillennialSurvey.

17. Development Dimensions International; The Conference Board. 2015. "Ready-now Leaders: 25 Findings to Meet Tomorrow's Business Challenges." *Development Dimensions International.* Accessed October 3, 2016. http://www.ddiworld.com/DDI/media/trend-research/global-leadership-forecast-2014-2015_tr_ddi.pdf?ext=.pdf.

18. Development Dimensions International; The Conference Board. 2015. "Ready-now Leaders: 25 Findings to Meet Tomorrow's Business Challenges." *Development Dimensions International.* Accessed October 3, 2016. http://www.ddiworld.com/DDI/media/trend-research/global-leadership-forecast-2014-2015_tr_ddi.pdf?ext=.pdf.

19. Gerzema, John, and Michael D'Antonio. 2013. *The Athena Doctrine: How Women (and the Men Who Think Like Them) Will Rule the Future.* San Francisco: Jossey-Bass: A Wiley Imprint.

20. Gerzema, John, and Michael D'Antonio. 2013. *The Athena Doctrine: How Women (and the Men Who Think Like Them) Will Rule the Future.* San Francisco: Jossey-Bass: A Wiley Imprint.

21. Robbins, S, and T. Judge. 2014. *Organizational Behavior, 16th Edition.* Upper Saddle River: Pearson Education, Inc.

22. Marre, Will. 2016. *Why Women Must Change Work.* March 16. Accessed October 14, 2016. http://willmarre.com/why-women-must-change-work/.

23. Marre, Will. 2016. *Why Women Must Change Work.* March 16. Accessed October 14, 2016. http://willmarre.com/why-women-must-change-work/.

24. Ernst & Young. 2015. "Global Generations: A Global Study on Work-life Challenges Across Generations." *Ernst & Young.* Accessed September 28, 2016. http://www.ey.com/Publication/vwLUAssets/EY-global-generations-a-global-study-on-work-life-challenges-across-generations/$FILE/EY-global-generations-a-global-study-on-work-life-challenges-across-generations.pdf.

25. Deloitte. 2016. "The 2016 Deloitte Millennial Survey: Winning Over the Next Generation of Leaders." *Deloitte.* Accessed November 17, 2016. www.deloitte.com/MillennialSurvey.

Chapter 12 – Conclusion: Implications for Men, Women, and the World

1. Representation Project. 2017. "Films." *The Representation Project.* Accessed March 28, 2017. http://therepresentationproject.org/film/miss-representation/.

2. Smith, David, and W. Brad Johnson. 2016. "Men Can Improve How They Mentor Women: Here's How." *Harvard Business Review.* https://hbr.org/2016/12/men-can-improve-how-they-mentor-women-heres-how?referral=00563&cm_mmc=email-_-newsletter-_-daily_alert-_-alert_date&utm_source=newsletter_daily_alert&utm_medium=email&utm_campaign=alert_date&spMailingID=16053421&spUserID=MTMyNzYzNj.

3. Gallup. 2016. "Women in America: Work and Life Well-Lived." *Gallup.* Accessed December 20, 2016. http://www.gallup.com/reports/195359/women-america-work-life-lived-insights-business-leaders.aspx.

4. Gallup. 2016. "Women in America: Work and Life Well-Lived." *Gallup.* Accessed December 20, 2016. http://www.gallup.com/reports/195359/women-america-work-life-lived-insights-business-leaders.aspx.

5. Wittenberg-Cox, Avivah. 2016. "To Understand Your Company's Gender Imbalance, Make a Graph." *Harvard Business Review* https://hbr.org/2016/03/to-understand-your-companys-gender-imbalance-make-a-graph.

6. Wittenberg-Cox, Avivah. 2016. "To Understand Your Company's Gender Imbalance, Make a Graph." *Harvard Business Review* https://hbr.org/2016/03/to-understand-your-companys-gender-imbalance-make-a-graph.

7. Heim, P., and S. Golant. 2005. *Hardball for Women: Winning at the Game of Business.* New York: Plume: Penguin Group.

8. Gibson, Cristina, and Mary Zellmer-Bruhn. 2001. "Metaphors and Meaning: An Intercultural Analysis of the Concept of Teamwork." *Administrative Science Quarterly* 46 (2): 274-303. doi:10.2307/2667088.

9. Wittenberg-Cox, Avivah. 2016. "How CEOs Can Put Gender Balance on the Agenda at their Companies." *Harvard Business Review.* https://hbr.org/2016/11/how-ceos-can-put-gender-balance-on-the-agenda-at-their-companies?referral=00563&cm_mmc=email-_-newsletter-_-daily_alert-_-alert_date&utm_source=newsletter_daily_alert&utm_medium=email&utm_campaign=alert_date&spMailingID=16018998&sp.

10. Wittenberg-Cox, Avivah. 2016. "How CEOs Can Put Gender Balance on the Agenda at their Companies." *Harvard Business Review.* https://hbr.org/2016/11/how-ceos-can-put-gender-balance-on-the-agenda-at-their-companies?referral=00563&cm_mmc=email-_-newsletter-_-daily_alert-_-alert_date&utm_source=newsletter_daily_alert&utm_medium=email&utm_campaign=alert_date&spMailingID=16018998&sp.

11. Association for Talent Development. 2016. "The 2016 State of the Industry Report." *Association for Talent Development.* Accessed December 5, 2016. https://www.td.org/Publications/Research-Reports/2013/~/link.aspx?_id=AAB5B551916342BCAC0FCE7DBE5D4EF6&_z=z&_ga=1.258847498.12502 09447.1470270334.

12. Bruggeman, Paula, and Hillary Chan. 2016. "Minding the Gap: Tapping the Potential of Women to Transform Business." *Graduate Management Admission*

Council. March 28. Accessed December 5, 2016. http://www.gmac.com/~/media/ Files/gmac/Research/diversity-enrollment/rr-16-01-tapping-potential-of-women-final-for-web.pdf.

13. European Commission. 2014. "Tackling the Gender Pay Gap in the European Union." *European Commission.* Accessed October 4, 2016. http://ec.europa.eu/ justice/gender-equality/files/gender_pay_gap/140319_gpg_en.pdf.

14. National Center for Education Statistics. 2015. *Bachelor's, Master's and Doctor's Degrees Conferred by Post-Secondary Institutions, by sex of student and discipline division: 2013-2014.* June 1. Accessed March 1, 2017. https://nces.ed.gov/ programs/digest/d15/tables/dt15_318.30.asp?current=yes.

15. Bruggeman, Paula, and Hillary Chan. 2016. "Minding the Gap: Tapping the Potential of Women to Transform Business." *Graduate Management Admission Council.* March 28. Accessed December 5, 2016. http://www.gmac.com/~/media/ Files/gmac/Research/diversity-enrollment/rr-16-01-tapping-potential-of-women-final-for-web.pdf.

16. Hewlett, Sylvia Ann. 2016. "Unlocking the Value of Talent in the Global Workforce." *Hewlett Consulting.* Accessed December 7, 2016. http://www. hewlettconsultingpartners.com/HCP_who-we-are.pdf.

17. Woetzel, Jonathon. 2015. "How Advancing Women's Equality Can Add $12 Trillion to Global Growth." *McKinsey & Company.* September. Accessed December 10, 2016. http://www.mckinsey.com/global-themes/employment-and-growth/how-advancing-womens-equality-can-add-12-trillion-to-global-growth.

18. McKinsey & Company; Leanin.org. 2016. "Women in the Workplace 2016." *McKinsey & Company.* September 1. Accessed October 1, 2016. http://www.mckinsey. com/business-functions/organization/our-insights/women-in-the-workplace-2016.

19. Heim, P., S. Murphy, and S. Golant. 2001. *In the Company of Women.* New York: Penguin Putnam, Inc.

20. Gallup. 2016. "Women in America: Work and Life Well-Lived." *Gallup.* Accessed December 20, 2016. http://www.gallup.com/reports/195359/women-america-work-life-lived-insights-business-leaders.aspx.

21. Heim, P., and S. Golant. 2005. *Hardball for Women: Winning at the Game of Business.* New York: Plume: Penguin Group.

22. Myers, Dee Dee. 2008. *Why Women Should Rule the World.* New York: HarperCollins.

23. Adato, Allison, and Melissa Stanton. 1992. "If Women Ran America: An Exclusive Poll: How Things Would Be Different." *Life Magazine* 36-46.

24. Adato, Allison, and Melissa Stanton. 1992. "If Women Ran America: An Exclusive Poll: How Things Would Be Different." *Life Magazine* 36-46.

25. Adato, Allison, and Melissa Stanton. 1992. "If Women Ran America: An Exclusive Poll: How Things Would Be Different." *Life Magazine* 36-46.

Morgan James
Speakers Group

↗ www.TheMorganJamesSpeakersGroup.com

We connect Morgan James published
authors with live and online events
and audiences who will benefit
from their expertise.

Morgan James makes all of our titles available
through the Library for All Charity Organization.

www.LibraryForAll.org

Printed in the USA
CPSIA information can be obtained
at www.ICGtesting.com
JSHW022206140824
68134JS00018B/899

9 781683 505792